Personal Letters From K

A Legacy of Letters

2006 - 2010

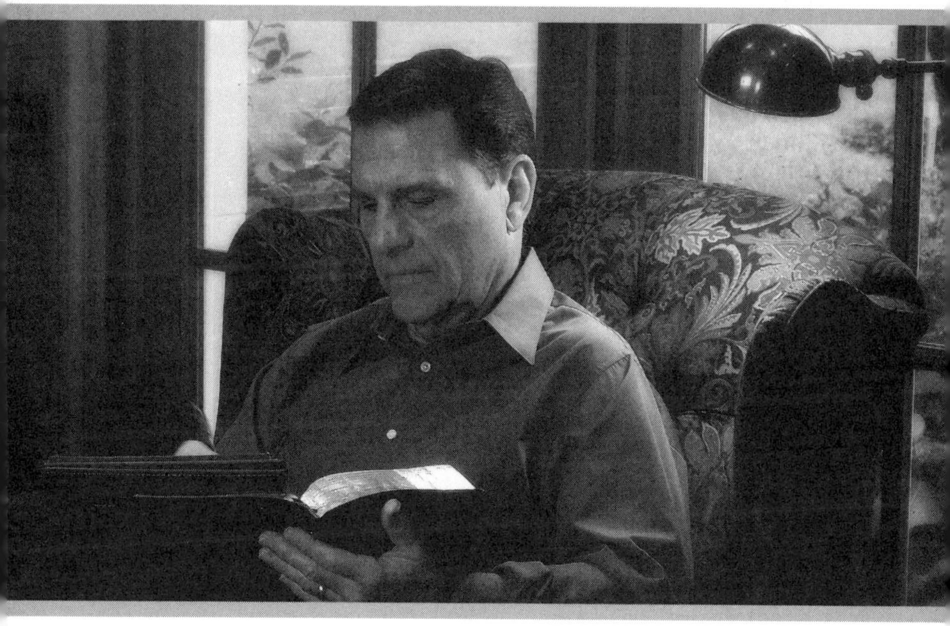

Kenneth Copeland Publications

Unless otherwise noted, all scripture is from the *King James Version* of the Bible.

Scripture quotations marked *The Amplified Bible* are from *The Amplified Bible, Old Testament* © 1965, 1987 by The Zondervan Corporation. *The Amplified New Testament* © 1958, 1987 by The Lockman Foundation. Used by permission.

Scripture quotations marked *New Living Translation* are from the *Holy Bible, New Living Translation* © 1996, 2004 by Tyndale Charitable Trust. Used by permission of Tyndale House Publishers.

A Legacy of Letters, Volume 4
Personal Letters From Kenneth Copeland to His Partners

ISBN 978-1-60463-098-5   10-4001

15 14 13 12 11 10   6 5 4 3 2 1

© 2010 Eagle Mountain International Church Inc. aka Kenneth Copeland Ministries

Kenneth Copeland Publications
Fort Worth, TX 76192-0001

For more information about Kenneth Copeland Ministries, call 800-600-7395 or visit www.kcm.org.

Printed in the United States of America. All rights reserved under International Copyright Law. No part of this book may be reproduced or transmitted in any form or by any means, electronic or mechanical, including photocopying, recording, or by any information storage and retrieval system, without the written permission of the publisher.

Table of Contents

2006

January   11
2006—The Year of the Glory!

February   17
Faith—The Key to Unlimited Treasure!

March   21
Time of the Seed

April   25
JESUS IS ALIVE!

May   29
God's Word Is Kingdom Seed!

June   33
The Blessing!

July   39
The Love Connection

August   45
Hope Deferred Makes the Heart Sick!

September   49
The Lord of the Harvest Is Here Now!

October   53
Ministers of the Harvest

November   57
COMPASSION HAD A PLAN!

December   63
What's the Big Deal?

2007

January   67
The Door Is Open...

February   73
The Blessing's Mission

March   79
Shout the Word,
Then Shut Up and Stand!

April   83
God Wants You Blessed!

May   87
I Am the Seed!

June   91
What Is the Blood-Sworn
Oath of God?

July   95
Who Are You—Really?

August   101
Love—The Key to Life Without Fear

September   105
It's Time to Shout
in the House of Faith!

October   109
In the Beginning God!

November   113
Believe You Receive

December   119
No Word = No faith
Know Word = Know faith

2008

January	123
Faith Activates THE BLESSING	
February	129
The Difference Between Work... and Labor	
March	135
Subdue the Curse and Release the Abundance	
April	141
Persecution and Affliction— THE BLESSING Thieves	
May	145
Sit Down!	
June	151
What Is Rich?	
July	157
Don't Join the Recession— It Doesn't Belong to You!	
August	163
My Heart Is Fixed— Trusting God	
September	169
Why the Commandment of Love?	
October	175
What's the Big Deal?	
November	181
What Are You Going to Do—Now!	
December	187
Keep Your Eyes on Jesus...	

2009

January	193
Have a BLESSED 2009!	
February	199
What Are You Looking At?!	
March	205
Stay on God's Side of Everything!	
April	211
Abounding in Grace	
May	217
Remember! It Is God!	
June	221
The Father Himself Loves Me!	
July	225
From the Top of the World...	
August	231
A Long Way to Go and a Short Time to Get There!	
September	235
The Way of Life Produces Life!	
October	243
THE BLESSING Is THE Place to Be!	
November	249
Flat as a Flitter but Never a Quitter	
December	255
I Believe! I Will! I Take It! I Have Faith! Thank You!	

2010

January   261
Whatever He Says to You, Do It!

February   267
Well Done, Good and Faithful Servant!

March   273
Our Job Is Faith in God!

April   277
Haiti Shall Be Saved!

May   283
Always a Victor Never! a Victim

June   289
Cheer Up! God Has a Plan!

July   293
Jesus Is Our Source

August   297
Hey! Trouble! ...I'm With God!

September   301
Why Do I Do What I Do?

October   307
I'm the Head and Not the Tail!

November   313
Get Yourself Off Your Mind!

December   317
Come to Me—I Will! Give You Rest!

Foreword

When I first came back to Jesus in December 1977, Kenneth Copeland was the man God used to drastically impact my life, and that of my family, as we began our great adventure with God. If I were to try to describe him, I would say he is a mighty man of faith, a heroic giver in every sense of the word, relentlessly true to his calling to teach faith to the world. He visited me in prison, and has stood beside me when many walked away. He is my friend, and taught me with his life what a real friend does.

As I sit here reading this manuscript, I cannot help but reflect on a time when the pain, injustice, loss and hopelessness I felt in my soul had all but taken my life. Even those I loved deeply could not seem to get through the hurt. I felt numb from the inside out; and among other things, I had lost my song.

Now, you must understand, I have been a believer for many years, and in my life the Word of God has been my final authority. I knew the only way I could ever make it through this horrific time was to fill my eyes, my mouth and my heart with what God had to say.

During that time, I had taken Kenneth's first book of letters, *Dear Partner,* with me to prison. I can honestly say that those letters saved my life. I read them every day. They are letters from a man, yes, but they are filled to overflowing with the Word of God, woven into real life by one of the most anointed teachers in the world.

I will never forget my brother Kenneth telling me how Oral Roberts one day had thrown his Bible to him asking, "What is this?" Kenneth looked hesitatingly. "These are letters! This is a book full of letters," Oral said.

Now, as I read the consistent letters of a man who has stayed the course, I think of the countless tens of thousands of lives just like mine who will be encouraged, strengthened, and given hope by the words on these pages. Take the time to open your Bible and read the verses along with Kenneth, and allow the Holy Spirit to guide you. I know He will.

Thank you, Kenneth, for all you have invested in my life and ministry.

Your friend and brother,

Phil Driscoll

Dear Partner

Partnership! It's God's idea and we are thrilled to know Kenneth Copeland Ministries is a living proof in our world today that the plan of God always works!

Every day we hear from hundreds upon hundreds of our Partners and Friends from around the world by way of phone, email, social media and, of course, regular mail! You send your prayer requests for the many circumstances for which you need a partner in faith. And you share your testimonies of how your partnership with us has impacted your life and those whom God has placed in your life. We are always here for you...ready to pray, ready to rejoice and always ready to take up our role in our partnership!

A major part of *my* role in our partnership is to communicate with you monthly in my Partner Letter. Every month throughout the years, the Spirit of the Lord has given me vital messages to share with you. A large part of what I minister on the *Believer's Voice of Victory* TV broadcast and in our meetings began in my spirit as a Partner Letter.

The years 2006 through 2010 have been both challenging and rewarding. Worldwide wars have taken their toll, weather has left its mark, and economies have hung in the balance. And throughout all these, God has been His marvelous, faithful self! Glory to God!

As you read through my Partner Letters from these years in this book, you will see that no matter what may have been going on around the world, God has kept us focused on His Word and all Jesus has done for us. He always makes it clear to us that we are a vital part of His kingdom, where peace and provision prevail!

In 2006, He emphasized the nature of His glory being manifest in the midst of whatever circumstances we encounter. And then He began to focus on THE BLESSING in Christ Jesus...the culmination of His glory! And, from 2006 right through 2010, every month's message from the Lord through the Partner Letters has in some way or another brought us revelation of the many characteristics and expressions of the glory of THE BLESSING. He has broadened our understanding of relationship with Himself, with our own selves in Christ Jesus, and with our fellow man...relationships is what THE BLESSING is all about. These have been marvelous years of letter writing!

Throughout 2010 He let us know that we are equal partners with Jesus, our Source, the relationship that makes all others work. And because we are His partners, we can do whatever He tells us to do!

In all the messages God has ever given me to write to you, they are basically the same message regardless of what's happening in our world. And when it's all said and done, as He has instructed us to do, our declaration according to Mark 11:22-25 will be:

We have faith in God!
We believe what He says. We will do what He says to do.
We receive what we ask for. We take it all.
We thank Him for everything. And we always forgive!

I'm telling you, there is no better way to live than according to His Word! Enjoy these letters! Gloria and I love you!

Ken

January 2006

2006—The Year of the Glory!

Dear Partner,

This ministry is celebrating its 39th birthday this month. And what a 39 years it has been. All of that, and the best is yet to come!

The word of the Lord came to Bishop Keith Butler a few months ago saying, "2006 will be the year of total fulfillment." Those words exploded in my spirit, and I've been saying them in faith and joy ever since. I also heard the Lord say that it is the year of the Glory.

First, let's talk about fulfillment.

For years, every time I studied the Word it seemed as though I was never quite satisfied. It was like getting up from a good meal and thinking, *That was good, but something's missing.*

We've always had good meetings. However, for years we would close one meeting and begin preparing for the next and we'd be the same way. "It was a wonderful meeting, Lord. Thank You, but what's missing?" People were getting saved and set free. The ministry was growing. It wasn't as if something were wrong. There was something <u>out there</u> yet to come, and I didn't know what it was.

In January 1983, I separated myself at our prayer cabin in Arkansas for almost the whole month. During that time I was led to begin a study on the Glory of God and its manifestations. As I did that I heard, *The Glory's coming.* I immediately released my faith for it and preached what the Lord gave me for over a year. Things continued to get better—growing and expanding. But still that dissatisfaction was there. Not disappointment, just that inner knowing that we were not there yet.

Every year was better. Every year was closer. Greater things were happening. The year 2004 was truly a year of fullness for us. And 2005 overflowed. Boy, did it ever!

There was more of everything, especially in our meetings and in our finances. The Citation X was paid for. But even in that, the pattern remained true. We paid for it in '05—OVERFLOW. But we take delivery in March '06—<u>FULFILLMENT.</u>

Each year, at every meeting, that dissatisfaction grew less and less. Every great revelation of Jesus from the Word filled our spiritual bellies a little more. Then as 2005 came to a close, I thought I was going to burst wide open.

<u>The Glory is here!!</u> And I can hardly wait to get into action—meetings, TV, radio and anything else I can get into—and release this glorious thing that is overflowing my inner man. It "blew out" in the healing and miracle service Saturday morning of our Washington, D.C. Victory Campaign in November 2005. I mean, it was like one of those old oil-well gushers, and that was only the beginning.

What a time this is! 2006—The Year of the Glory is here. Get in the meetings. Get in the Word. Do whatever it takes, <u>but get in it!</u>

Let's talk about what we do for a living. "Well, Brother Copeland, I drive a bus for a living," someone might say. Or, "I'm in the car business," or "I'm a lawyer," or "I'm a teacher." My dad would say, "I'm in the sales business." I remember my grandfather saying, "I grow cotton and wheat," when someone asked him what he did.

However, as serious believers and <u>Word-action Christians,</u> that's not our answer. We grow <u>faith</u> for a living. The just shall <u>live</u> by faith! That's not just a saying. It's truth. It's time for that truth to become a reality. Where you work is your seed bin—not your living. The reason you're on that job is because our Father needed you there. If that's not the reason you're there, then begin today seeking Him to find out where He does need you and get there as fast as you can.

What's the first step in growing faith? Of course, we know because of Romans 10:17 that we begin with the Word. But with what word do we begin? <u>Always</u> begin with the command of Jesus. Let's look at this even more carefully today than we ever have before.

First John 3:21-24:

> 21 Beloved, if our heart condemn us not, then have we confidence toward God.
> 22 And whatsoever we ask, we receive of him, because we keep his commandments, and do those things that are pleasing in his sight.
> 23 And this is his commandment, That we should <u>believe on the name</u> of his Son Jesus Christ, and love one another, as he gave us commandment.
> 24 And he that keepeth his commandments dwelleth in him, and he in him. And hereby we know that he abideth in us, by the Spirit which he hath given us.

Notice in verse 23 the command begins with <u>faith.</u> Faith in the Name of <u>His</u> <u>Son</u> <u>Jesus</u> the <u>Anointed.</u> Studying, meditating and building faith in that Name is the first step to mountain-moving, world-overcoming, victorious faith. The next step is to totally commit to becoming a good steward of that command from our Commander in Chief—JESUS.

Remember the healing of the man who could not walk and sat at the Beautiful gate of the temple? Peter and John ministered to him, and he ran shouting and leaping through the temple. It is vitally important to hear what Peter said brought about that miracle of our Father's power.

Acts 3:12-16:

> 12 And when Peter saw it, he answered unto the people, Ye men of Israel, why marvel ye at this? or why look ye so earnestly on us, as though by our own power or holiness we had made this man to walk?
> 13 The God of Abraham, and of Isaac, and of Jacob, the God of our fathers, hath glorified his Son Jesus; whom ye delivered up, and denied him in the presence of Pilate, when he was determined to let him go.
> 14 But ye denied the Holy One and the Just, and

desired a murderer to be granted unto you;
15 And killed the Prince of life, whom God hath raised from the dead; whereof we are witnesses.
16 And his name through faith in his name hath made this man strong, whom ye see and know: yea, the faith which is by him hath given him this perfect soundness in the presence of you all.

It was faith in the Name that released the power. We've been studying for months the Love part of the command of Jesus, but the command is in two parts. These parts—faith and Love—depend on one another. Faith works by Love and Love works by faith. Peter, the man of the Name (Matthew 16:16), and John, the man of Love, working together released this man's miracle.

Philippians 2:9:

9 Wherefore God also hath highly exalted him, and given him a name which is above every name.

<u>Every</u> name must bow its knee to the Name of Jesus.

Cancer is a name. Faith in the name of cancer is to believe in cancer's ability to kill. That's <u>fear.</u> Perfected Love casts out fear (1 John 4:18). Faith in the Name rises up filled with Love power and the cancer <u>must</u> bow its knee and confess, "Jesus is Lord over me!! I must leave! NOW!"

Debt is a name. Faith in the name of debt is to believe it is impossible for you to have anything without it. Having a house depends on it. Having a car depends on it. "These credit card bills are just too big. I'll never get rid of them." All of that is fear! One of Jesus' names is Lord of the Harvest! Perfected Love casts out the fear of debt, and Love-filled faith in the Name of Jesus calls those debts overwhelmed by the harvest return on my <u>faith</u> seed. Debt trembles and bows its knees at the sound of that Name and is washed away forever.

Jesus inherited His Name from the Almighty Creator of all things. He was exalted and given the Name above names. He achieved the greatness of His Name through victory in great combat. He defeated death, hell, satan and all the forces of darkness. His Name has total authority. All of this because God so loved the world—you! Now you have been given His authority to use that Name—it belongs to you (Ephesians 3:15).

Can you see it? Faith filled with Love power! Love filled with faith power! No wonder it's called the VICTORY THAT OVERCOMES THE WORLD.

As you sow your financial seeds this month, meditate on the greatness of the Name of Jesus—the exalted Name of the Son of the Living God. Filled with Love—God is Love. Then speak that Name over your seed and your harvest. That's what you do for a living. You grow faith.

Again, get in the meetings this year! The Glory's here!

Gloria and I and all of the KCM family pray above all things that you prosper and be in wonderful health even as your soul prospers.

We love you and pray for you every day.

Love,

Ken

P.S. Glorious, Happy, faith-filled, Blessed, prosperity overflowing, Healed, Total-ful fill ment New Year Everybody! Jesus is LORD!
KC

"2006 is the year of total fulfillment. I heard Bishop Keith Butler say that by the Spirit a few months ago, and it literally exploded in my heart. It has been ringing in my spiritual ears ever since. Put it in your mouth. Say it, shout it, sing it, tell everybody that 2006 is the year of total fulfillment. I believe it. I receive it." —Kenneth Copeland

February 2006

Faith—The Key to Unlimited Treasure!

Dear Partner

Let's talk about faith.

Every time I arrive at a place where I think I know a little bit about faith, the Holy Spirit opens a whole new insight into the wonders of faith in God.

Faith is the doorway to abundance. It's the key to unlimited treasure. Its laws of operation are sure, steadfast and as unchanging as Jesus Himself. In giving Himself to us, He has given us His faith. Not just a portion of it, but all of it. He did not give us only a portion of Himself. Everything He has and is has been given to us in full measure.

Colossians 2:3 says that all the treasures of wisdom and knowledge are hidden in Him. Well, that's where we are—in Him. Verses 9-10 of that same chapter are shoutin' ground:

> 9 For in him dwelleth all the fulness of the Godhead bodily.
> 10 And ye are complete in him, which is the head of all principality and power.

You have the same right to use the faith of God as Jesus does. After all, He is as much your Father as He is Jesus' Father. You're as much His child as Jesus is. Does the Scripture only say all things are possible with God? No, it also says all things are possible to the believer.

It is up to you and me just how far we go with the faith He has given us. The only limits placed on the growth of our faith are there because of us, not because the Father has limited it in any way. The growth of our faith is in direct proportion to the time spent developing it. It's not like the growth of natural things that have built-in limitations. Faith will continue to grow until it becomes however large it has to be to overcome whatever the storms of life have brought to destroy us.

Satan is limited. Everything, thank God, in this world of sin and death is defeated. Faith is unlimited. Why? Because its source is unlimited.

Faith is born out of the Word Himself—"faith cometh by hearing, and hearing by the word of God" (Romans 10:17). And that is how we are born again. We are born again "not of corruptible seed, but of incorruptible, by the word of God, which liveth and abideth for ever" (1 Peter 1:23). That's why faith is so easy for the person who spends time in the Word. It's as "natural" to the life of the believer as swimming is to a fish. It's what we were born to do—BELIEVE!

The first step to victory <u>every time</u> is confidence in the growth process of the Word. Jesus laid it out in the fourth chapter of Mark's Gospel. Then He summed it all up in verses 26-29:

> 26   And he said, So is the kingdom of God, as if a man should cast seed into the ground;
> 27   And should sleep, and rise night and day, and the seed should spring and grow up, he knoweth not how.
> 28   For the earth bringeth forth fruit of herself; first the blade, then the ear, after that the full corn in the ear.
> 29   But when the fruit is [ripe], immediately he putteth in the sickle, because the harvest is come.

Notice the confidence in the growth process displayed by the man who sowed the seed. Remember, too, we're talking about the seed being the Word of God. It will produce if allowed to run its full course.

Let's look at it like this:

1. The Seed
Find promises that cover your situation and exercise your faith. Believe you receive. Plant that Word in your heart.

2. Rest and Praise
The sower in verse 27 did not lay awake at night worrying about whether or not the seed was growing. Don't allow the devil to talk you out of resting in <u>faith.</u>

3. The Blade
This is the first sign that the miracle is alive. It's doing what it's supposed to do. Stay with it.

4. The Ear
Now it's beginning to look like corn. Remember, there's more going on beneath the soil than on top. Roots. Strength. Stay with the praise and rest.

5. The Full Ear of Corn
It really looks good! Don't pick it green. Let it develop and ripen. Don't try to make something happen, like going into debt, etc. Rest and praise.

6. It's Ripe. Harvest It!
You'll know! The dream in your heart has taken upon itself faith and it will be born.

Once you've sown the seed of the Word in your inner man, don't let it go. Read through Mark 4:14-20 and make note of five things that Jesus said the devil would use to try and stop the process. He has nothing new. He's the same ol' devil, and you can stop him at every turn.

This is the way the 25 percent who won their victories and received 30, 60 and a hundredfold got there. God is no respecter of persons. Neither is His Word. They all had the same opportunity, because it was the Word that brought its own harvest. The Word works when it's put to work. Faith works. The Name of Jesus works.

There is a miracle in you right now crying to be born. All it needs is the seed of life—faith—the law of the Spirit of life in Christ Jesus.

Rise up and take your place in this mighty outpouring of the Father's Glory. It's happening now. Jump in. Get in our meetings. Watch every TV broadcast. Minister to your neighbors. Learn the steps I've outlined in this letter, and share the message of faith with other people in need. Be bold. Greater is He that is in you. You're a winner. Born of a champion—Jesus, Son of the Living God!

As you sow your financial seed this month, apply every step of the faith outline I've shared with you. Put faith to work. We'll receive your offering in faith and immediately put it to work.

We use this process all the time every time. It has produced for Gloria and me for almost 40 years, and it will do the same or better for you. Together we can do everything the Father has assigned us to do. <u>We can do it!</u>

Gloria and I love you and we pray for you every day.

                                      Love,

                                      Ken

March 2006

Time of the Seed

Dear Partner,

Let's continue looking at becoming a grower of faith. Growing faith is heaven's way for the believer to "make a living."

The Word says the just shall <u>live</u> by faith. What the world calls "making a living" is actually the believer's source of seed in this natural world. Second Corinthians 9:9-10 tells us that our Father ministers seed to us. Let's look at it:

9 (As it is written, He hath dispersed abroad; he hath given to the poor: his righteousness remaineth for ever.
10 Now he that ministereth seed to the sower both minister bread for your food, and multiply your seed sown, and increase the fruits of your righteousness.)

As our Father blesses us on the job and as we seek first the kingdom of God and His righteousness, these things—seed, bread and the <u>multiplying of our seed</u>—are added to us. <u>But not apart from faith!</u> You can see now how all this is tied together and brought to full manifestation by the force of faith. That's what we do—we grow faith.

Without faith we, just like the world, are left to live on just the seed or from paycheck to paycheck. That has never been the will of God for His family. We're to live on the harvest that comes from seed multiplied by the power of His riches in glory.

I shared in last month's letter from Luke 17 and Mark 4 the order laid out by Jesus for becoming a grower of faith:

1. The Seed
2. Rest (in faith)
3. Rise Up

4. The Blade (first evidence the seed is growing)
5. The Ear
6. The Full Corn in the Ear (Don't pick it green.)
7. Harvest

Let's talk more about the time of the seed. This is the most vulnerable time. It is the time before there is any natural evidence that the seed is growing. <u>This is when faith is the evidence.</u> Faith <u>cometh</u> by hearing and hearing by the Word of our Father. Faith <u>works</u> by Love. Keep the promise seed that has been sown before your eyes and in your ears. Read it and believe it. Commit it to memory by quoting it aloud over and over and over and over and by saying every time, "I choose to believe that. I'm a believer. I have faith."

Control your mind with the verses you're standing on: "I'm a believer. I choose what to believe and what not to believe, and I believe my Father's Word in Jesus' Name!" Then <u>rest</u> on it in your spirit.

During this time "see" yourself with it. Let your dream machine go to work. Bathe your imagination with the promise seeds. Draw pictures of yourself in the middle of your dream. Let the dream get big.

Somewhere along the way the dream will begin to take upon itself faith. You'll notice yourself beginning to <u>expect</u> it to come to pass. That's when the dream becomes <u>HOPE!</u> Now abides, or <u>lives,</u> faith, <u>HOPE</u> and love—not *wish*. Wish is the world's idea of hope. Bible hope is intense expectation that it's coming to pass <u>now.</u>

Begin acting and talking as though it has already come to pass. <u>In the spirit it has.</u> Faith is transferring what is already done in the spirit world over into the natural world where you need it. Faith is the substance of things hoped for. Stay in Love and stay in faith. Like Jairus in Luke 8, STOP THE FEAR! BELIEVE ONLY! Jesus promised in Mark 4:30-32 that your faith would grow up and become greater. Believe Him. Believe me, it will.

Get out of yourself. This is <u>soooo</u> important. Lose your life and find your future. Jesus has a perfect plan that is glorious and superabundant, and it has your name on it. But the only way to get into it is by faith which <u>works</u> by love.

Begin helping someone else receive. Support their dream. Don't wait until you can start big. Start right where you are. Small beginnings are giant blessings when mixed with faith and love. God's in it. That's big.

Go back over Mark 4:14-32 and Luke 17:1-10. Meditate each verse again and again. Your faith will explode into action.

As you sow your financial seed this month, wrap it in your promise seed. Read the verses of promise you're standing on over your offering. Hold it and just sit there for a while. DREAM. See yourself prosperous and overflowing. Then give your Lord and Savior, Jesus, all the glory and praise Him for paying the price for it all.

Shout with us. This is the month we take delivery of the Citation X. Paid for! The dream became hope. Faith became substance. The substance became ours. This great soul-winning tool has been placed in our hands, and you had so much to do with it coming to pass. We will preach, from the top of the world to the bottom and all the way 'round the middle, this gospel that Jesus saves, Jesus heals, Jesus baptizes with the Holy Ghost, Jesus prospers with life and that abundantly, and Jesus is coming soon. And we will use this marvelous miracle airplane to get it done.

Rejoice with us because you can do the same thing. God is no respecter of persons. To receive the Citation X, Gloria and I did exactly what I have written in this letter. That's the way we have received everything we have. Everything—large and small. Everything!

We love you and pray for you every day.

Love,

Ken

P.S. You can do it. Dream on.—KC

April 2006

JESUS IS ALIVE!

Dear Partner

JESUS IS ALIVE!

I was shouting in my spirit when I wrote the above statement. A few days ago I was preparing to preach in a meeting in Bari, Italy, when suddenly I heard those words come thundering through my being. Every time I have ever heard or read those words over the past 40-plus years it has thrilled me, but never quite like this time. It has lingered in my heart and mind ever since. Think about it. He lives. That means we're alive with the same glorious power that raised Him to immortality.

The morning Jesus came out of the tomb, two men in shining garments spoke to the women who had come to place spices and ointments on His body and said, "Why seek ye the living among the dead? He is not here, but is risen" (Luke 24:5-6). Don't look for Jesus among the dead, lifeless religions of the world. Look for Him where the action is: saving the lost, healing the sick and raising the dead.

If He is alive, then His Word is alive.

Hebrews 4:12:

> 12   For the word of God is quick, and powerful, and sharper than any twoedged sword, piercing even to the dividing asunder of soul and spirit, and of the joints and marrow, and is a discerner of the thoughts and intents of the heart.

The same supernatural power that raised Him from hell and death is in His Word. In fact, the Word of God is what raised Him up. The first chapter of Hebrews is a word-for-word account of what the Father said when He brought Him out. Notice verse 6:

> 6   And again, when he bringeth in the first begotten into the world, he <u>saith,</u> And let all the angels of God worship him.

Hang on to that now and look at 1 Peter 1:23:

> 23   Being born again, not of corruptible seed, but of incorruptible, by the <u>word of God,</u> which liveth and abideth for ever.

You and I were brought forth from death in trespass and sin by the very same Word of His power—the Word of God which <u>lives</u> and <u>abides</u> forever! Look at Ephesians 2:5-6:

> 5   Even when we were dead in sins, hath quickened us together with Christ, (by grace ye are saved;)
> 6   And hath raised us up together, and made us sit together in heavenly places in Christ Jesus:

Can you see that?! We are just as alive as He is. His life is living in us now. Not after we get to heaven—NOW! Maybe now we can begin to see what the Holy Spirit is telling us in 1 John 4:17: "...as he is, SO ARE WE <u>in this world</u>"—NOW. Now we are the sons and daughters of the <u>Living</u> God. First John 5:1 tells us "Whosoever believeth that Jesus is the Christ is <u>born</u> of God." I believe that. I also, then, believe verse 4:

> 4   For whatsoever is born of God overcometh the world: and this is the victory that overcometh the world, even our faith.

Jesus is alive. His Word is alive. We are alive. That means His faith, which has become our faith, is alive. In fact, His faith is in His Word according to Romans 10:17. His faith is a living force. His faith. His hope. His Love. All three are alive in us, ready to do the same works that they did when He was here on earth in His body. Well, He is still here on earth—IN HIS BODY! The exciting thing is His Body is waking up to these truths all over the world.

The whole world is looking for Jesus. Not the news media—yet—but the sick, dying world. Most of them don't know whom they seek, but if they're seeking healing, they are looking for Jesus. If they're trying to save their marriage, they're looking for Jesus. If their children are in trouble, they need Jesus. He is <u>THE</u> Savior. He is <u>THE</u> life. He is <u>THE</u> answer to every question, every despair, every hurt known to man.

He is alive and somebody needs to tell the world about it. Well, that somebody is you and me. We were born into this world for that purpose for this time. His Glory is being manifested for that very purpose. Every piece of equipment. Every book. Every CD and DVD. Every TV broadcast. Every meeting we preach and anything else we can get our hands on is being done toward that one goal—tell the world He is risen. He is alive. He saves. He heals. He is pouring out His Spirit on all flesh. Whosoever will call upon His Name <u>shall</u> <u>be</u> <u>saved!</u>

Whatever condition your household is in, rise up and begin telling everyone around you Jesus is alive and well. Put the whole thing in His hands and join the move of His Glory. Things will change. You will change. Life will explode around you and bring victory like never before.

As you sow your financial seed into ministry this month, speak life into it. Your words are Jesus' words if you speak them filled with Love and faith. It's God's living Word that brings the life into seed. That life is in your praise and worship over your giving.

We receive it in the same spirit of faith, and we speak the Word of Life over it and you when it gets here. Together we can and will get this job done. Shout it right now: "I can do all things in Christ Jesus because <u>He is alive!</u>"

Gloria and I love you and pray for you every day.

Love,

Ken

May 2006

God's Word Is Kingdom Seed!

Dear Partner,

Let's begin this letter by looking at something Jesus said in Mark 4:30-32:

> 30 And he said, Whereunto shall we liken the kingdom of God? or with what comparison shall we compare it?
> 31 It is like a grain of mustard seed, which, when it is sown in the earth, is less than all the seeds that be in the earth:
> 32 But when it is sown, it groweth up, and becometh greater than all herbs, and shooteth out great branches; so that the fowls of the air may lodge under the shadow of it.

He said the Kingdom of God—<u>all of it—everything about it</u>—is compared to seed. I know some people get tired of hearing about seed, time and harvest and some say, "Is that all he can talk about?"

Look again at what Jesus said. <u>If we're going to talk about the Kingdom we have to talk about seed.</u> If we're studying faith, we have to study seed. When we have questions about why did this happen and why didn't that come to pass, the answer in some way is always seed, time and harvest.

I've spent the last 39 years studying these three verses and searching for ways to put them into action in my life and ministry. I'll spend the next 30, if Jesus tarries, looking for ways to make it clear to you and all my Partners. It is the key issue to abundant life.

All life begins with seed. All change and improvement is accomplished through the seed process: Seed—Time—Harvest. That's just the way it is. To struggle with it and to resist it is to flirt with disaster. In fact think about it—the struggle against this process is itself a seed, a seed that in time will produce a harvest of defeat.

How many times over the years has the thought come through your mind: *Jesus, why don't You just heal me?* Or, *Why do I have to go through all this sowing, confessing and standing on the Word? Why don't You just do it?* That's struggling against the Kingdom. You're asking Jesus to step out of His calling as Lord of the harvest and High Priest over our Word seeds and do something that's crosswise to the Kingdom and out of line with the whole Bible. That's not a good thing to do.

Let's go back to Mark 4:32. That is a direct statement of Kingdom fact. Read each word slowly and carefully: "But when it is sown, it groweth up, and becometh greater than all herbs, and shooteth out great branches; so that the fowls of the air may lodge under the shadow of it."

Take this as a covenant promise. When the seed is sown, <u>it will grow up!</u> Let that get down into your spirit. It will—not it might, or it could. It will not only grow up, but it <u>will</u> also become greater. Greater than what? Greater than any problem. Greater than any need. Greater than anything the devil and his bunch can throw at you.

Remember now, Jesus started this whole thing by saying in verse 14, "The sower soweth the word." <u>God's Word is Kingdom seed.</u> It is life to all who find it and health to all their flesh (Proverbs 4:22).

Now that we have Kingdom seed, how do we water it? With Kingdom water. Word seed is watered by Word water. Look at Ephesians 5:25-26:

> 25   Husbands, love your wives, even as Christ also loved the church, and gave himself for it;
> 26   That he might sanctify and cleanse it with the washing of water by the word.

God's Word is the water of Life. Now 1 Corinthians 3:6-7:

> 6   I have planted, Apollos watered; but God gave the increase.
> 7   So then neither is he that planteth any thing, neither he that watereth; but God that giveth the increase.

There it is. That's the process. Plant, water, and God gives the increase. Now can you see why Jesus doesn't just come in and do things where there are no seeds to harvest? In Revelation 21:6 Jesus said, "I will give unto him that is athirst of the fountain of the water of life <u>freely</u>." It's not hard. It's free. But it does require obedience. It <u>must</u> be sown. It <u>must</u> be watered. It <u>will</u> grow up, and it <u>will</u> become greater. That's a promise. Straight from the Throne of Grace.

I'll close with this: Word Life is <u>THE Life</u> in Jesus. That Life grows from an inward seed of God's Word to overcoming, overwhelming Life, Light, and Glory. It raised Jesus from the dead. That Jesus Life is in us now! Word-promise seed watered by Word-praise water is guaranteed victory in Jesus. Get busy. It's harvest time. <u>Shout amen!</u>

At the time I'm writing this letter, we are only two days from flying the Citation X home! Ten years of sowing, watering, standing—and now the shout!

The big thing about this is that, through it all, our faith has grown to an all-time high. <u>It grew up and became greater</u> than the price of that piece of equipment, and it will continue to grow. The bigger it gets, the more souls we'll bring into the Kingdom.

That's the way it works. I remember the very first thing I used my faith to receive was a pair of socks. It worked. From socks to preaching the word of faith from the top of the world to the bottom and all the way around. And we're just getting started. What a way to live!

Gloria and I love you and pray for you every day.

Love,

Ken

June 2006

The Blessing!

Dear Partner

I call you to remembrance of something I wrote to you last month and we will continue in this letter. I asked:

> How many times over the years has the thought come through your mind: *Jesus, why don't You just heal me?* Or, *Why do I have to go through all this sowing, confessing and standing on the Word? Why don't You just do it?* That is struggling against the kingdom. You're asking Jesus to step out of His calling as Lord of the harvest and High Priest over our word seeds and do something that is crosswise to the kingdom and out of line with the whole Bible. That's not a good thing to do.

Remember that? All of that sowing, confessing, and standing on the Word has to do with the law of faith. Let's look at James 1:6-8:

> 6 But let him ask in faith, nothing wavering. For he that wavereth is like a wave of the sea driven with the wind and tossed.
> 7 For let not that man think that he shall receive any thing of the Lord.
> 8 A double minded man is unstable in all his ways.

That's the reason faith is so important. Faith to the Word seeds in the kingdom is the same thing water is to natural seeds. They don't grow without it. That is why nothing just happens by itself. Even things that are the will of God for your life won't come to pass without faith being released.

With all that as our base, let's look at an area in which very little faith is being released even though it is already ours and waiting to be put to work.

Ask yourself:

Self, do you have faith in the Name of Jesus? "Yes!"

Self, do you have faith in the Word of God? "Yes!"

The blood of the Lamb? "Yes!"

Self, do you have faith in The Blessing? "What blessing?" That would be most people's answer.

Let's look at Genesis 1:26-28:

> 26 And God said, Let us make man in our image, after our likeness: and let them have dominion over the fish of the sea, and over the fowl of the air, and over the cattle, and over all the earth, and over every creeping thing that creepeth upon the earth.
> 27 So God created man in his own image, in the image of God created he him; male and female created he them.
> 28 And God blessed them, <u>and God said unto them,</u> Be fruitful, and multiply, and replenish the earth, and subdue it: and have dominion over the fish of the sea, and over the fowl of the air, and over every living thing that moveth upon the earth.

Adam's blessing was to expand the Garden of Eden until it encompassed the whole earth. That's what that blessing was to do. We know what happened when Adam blew it off. It became a curse and cursed every living thing from the ground up.

Now let's read Genesis 12:1-3:

> 1 Now the Lord had said unto Abram, Get thee out of thy country, and from thy kindred, and from thy father's house, unto a land that I will show thee:

> 2 And I will make of thee a great nation, and I will bless thee, and make thy name great; and thou shalt be a blessing:
> 3 And I will bless them that bless thee, and curse him that curseth thee: and in thee shall all families of the earth be blessed.

Now Genesis 13:1-2, 14-16:

> 1 And Abram went up out of Egypt, he, and his wife, and all that he had, and Lot with him, into the south.
> 2 And Abram was very rich in cattle, in silver, and in gold.
> 14 And the Lord said unto Abram, after that Lot was separated from him, Lift up now thine eyes, and look from the place where thou art northward, and southward, and eastward, and westward:
> 15 For all the land which thou seest, to thee will I give it, and to thy seed for ever.
> 16 And I will make thy seed as the dust of the earth: so that if a man can number the dust of the earth, then shall thy seed also be numbered.

The Blessing was now on Abraham by covenant.

The Blessing was working. Silver and gold were in the Garden. The Blessing also was to subdue and have dominion—in this case against thieves and murderers. In Genesis 15 God and Abram entered into a covenant of blood that guaranteed The Blessing to all of Abraham's seed. We see that in Genesis 26:12-13:

> 12 Then Isaac sowed in that land, and received in the same year an hundredfold: and the Lord blessed him.
> 13 And the man waxed great, and went forward, and grew until he became very great.

Now look at the 24th verse:

> 24   And the Lord appeared unto him the same night, and said, I am the God of Abraham thy father: fear not, for I am with thee, and will bless thee, and multiply thy seed for my servant Abraham's sake.

He's talking about The Blessing. The Blessing, then, is manifest in Jacob's life. Genesis 28:3:

> 3   And God Almighty bless thee, and make thee fruitful, and multiply thee, that thou mayest be a multitude of people.

Notice here the same words as were spoken when the Father created Adam. It's the same blessing. From there it was on Joseph's life. He knew he was blessed when he was just a boy because of God's presence and the dreams that came to him.

Genesis 37:8 says his brothers hated him even more because of his dreams and his words. The interesting thing is all of those brothers were the seed of Abraham. They had The Blessing, but they had no faith in it. Therefore it did not manifest.

Joseph believed he was blessed and The Blessing took care of him in spite of all the devil could throw into his life. In Genesis 39:2 Potiphar, the man who bought Joseph, was blessed. In Genesis 39:20-23 the prison into which Joseph was thrown was blessed. In Genesis 41 all of Egypt was blessed because Joseph was made prime minister. He became prime minister because he believed he was blessed. He was taught to believe that Abraham's blessing was his.

The Blessing was why Job was so blessed. The Blessing kept him through all the hell he went through.

Now we can see the power behind the ministry of Jesus. Jesus operated The Blessing in full force. We know that from Galatians 3:16:

> 16 Now to Abraham and his seed were the promises made. He saith not, And to seeds, as of many; but as of one, <u>And to thy seed, which is Christ.</u>

All of this from Adam to Jesus to the Cross was for this purpose—to get <u>The</u> <u>Blessing</u> on <u>you</u>! Shout Amen!

Verse 13:

> 13 Christ hath redeemed us from the curse of the law, being made a curse for us: for it is written, Cursed is every one that hangeth on a tree.

Shout again!

Now verse 29:

> 29 And if ye be Christ's, then are ye <u>Abraham's seed,</u> and heirs according to the promise.

Joint heirs with Jesus. Heirs of Adam's original blessing. Jesus is the second and last Adam!

I didn't have to tell you to shout that time!!

<u>The</u> <u>Blessing</u> has always had one purpose, and that's to create a Garden of Eden wherever and whenever it is released into operation. Regardless of how big a mess the place is in when you get there.

We call it Adam's blessing and then Abraham's blessing, but actually it's Jesus' Blessing. We saw that in Galatians 3:16.

<u>Jesus'</u> <u>Blessing</u> is mine! I'm blessed with <u>The</u> <u>Blessing.</u>

Faith in <u>The</u> <u>Blessing</u> must be developed by hearing the Word of God, just like faith in everything else. Then it is sown into the heart and released through confession of the mouth:

How are you? "I'm blessed!"

What about this debt? "The Blessing will overcome it!"

"I'm the seed of Abraham. I belong to Christ Jesus. The Almighty God is my Father. I'm supposed to prosper. I'm supposed to be healed. That's all part of The Blessing. It's The Blessing of Jesus and I'm His. I am The Blessed. I have dominion and subdue the earth. I multiply and prosper and all those who come in contact with me are blessed."

Self, do you have faith in The Blessing? "Yes, I do! I can do all things in Christ Jesus which strengthens me. He loves me and has blessed me—and with His own Blessing."

As you sow your financial seed this month, sow it knowing it is blessed to multiply and bless the whole earth. Together, as Partners, we are doing that. I'm blessed. You're blessed. We are all blessed. Not with a bunch of different blessings. They are all part of *The* Blessing.

Meditate on these scriptures over and over until the truth of it all rises up in you and begins to manifest around you. Meditate the 23rd Psalm, the 91st Psalm, and also Isaiah 54. You'll see it—The Blessing. It belongs to you.

Gloria and I love you and pray for you every day.

                                              Love,

                                              Ken

July 2006

The Love Connection

Dear Partner

In last month's letter we talked about The Blessing. It began in the Garden of Eden when God spoke to Adam and empowered him to multiply and replenish the earth. That word translated *replenish* in Hebrew means "to fill up." So let's read it that way. Genesis 1:28:

> 28   And God blessed them, and God said unto them, Be fruitful, and multiply, and [fill up] the earth, and subdue it: and have dominion over the fish of the sea, and over the fowl of the air, and over every living thing that moveth upon the earth.

How was Adam to do such an awesome thing? How could one man be responsible to not only fill the whole earth with everything in the Garden of Eden but to also subdue it and have dominion over it? The whole earth!

How could he do that? God <u>BLESSED</u> him. His job was to have faith in <u>The Blessing</u>. Adam did not have to do anything <u>physically</u> to carry out God's command. That would have been impossible, as we see later after he had sinned and lost <u>The Blessing</u>. Look at it. Genesis 3:17-19:

> 17   And unto Adam he said, Because thou hast hearkened unto the voice of thy wife, and hast eaten of the tree, of which I commanded thee, saying, Thou shalt not eat of it: cursed is the ground for thy sake; in sorrow shalt thou eat of it all the days of thy life;
> 18   Thorns also and thistles shall it bring forth to thee; and thou shalt eat the herb of the field;
> 19   In the sweat of thy face shalt thou eat bread, till thou return unto the ground; for out of it wast thou taken: for dust thou art, and unto dust shalt thou return.

Without The Blessing, however, he was almost helpless. Even though he lived almost a thousand years, he never moved more than a few miles away from the place where he began. He couldn't overcome anything that was arrayed against him. I guess not! What had been The Blessing was now the curse. Everything that had been working for him was now working against him. The ground was now producing thorns and thistles. He was filled with fear instead of faith. Death ruled over him, and everything around him was dying instead of living. You and I know the feeling well!

Thank God, He didn't leave it that way! Jesus stepped up and said, "I'll fix it!" And He did. He came and did what the first Adam did not do. He took dominion over the devil, death and all the curse. He became a curse for us in order to get The Blessing back into the earth in full force.

Look at 2 Timothy 1:9-10:

> 9 Who hath saved us, and called us with an holy calling, not according to our works, but according to his own purpose and grace, which was given us in Christ Jesus before the world began,
>
> 10 But is now made manifest by the appearing of our Saviour Jesus Christ, who hath abolished death, and hath brought life and immortality to light through the gospel.

According to verse 9, The Blessing was in Christ Jesus and belonged to Him before the world began. Just because Adam blew it off didn't mean it was gone. It was just gone from him. Adam fell. Jesus didn't! When He came into the earth, He walked in The Blessing of Abraham which, according to Galatians 3:16, was that original Blessing.

To put it as simply as possible, the power of The Blessing was to create, change, multiply or do whatever it had to do to create a garden of Eden. That's still its purpose. God never changes. His purposes never change.

That garden was His purpose in the beginning, and it still is. We see it in the first chapter of the Book and in the last chapter of the Book. Look at Revelation 21:1-7 and 22:1-3, the final two chapters of the last book of the Bible.

1 And I saw a new heaven and a new earth: for the first heaven and the first earth were passed away; and there was no more sea.

2 And I John saw the holy city, new Jerusalem, coming down from God out of heaven, prepared as a bride adorned for her husband.

3 And I heard a great voice out of heaven saying, Behold, the tabernacle of God is with men, and he will dwell with them, and they shall be his people, and God himself shall be with them, and be their God.

4 And God shall wipe away all tears from their eyes; and there shall be no more death, neither sorrow, nor crying, neither shall there be any more pain: for the former things are passed away.

5 And he that sat upon the throne said, Behold, I make all things new. And he said unto me, Write: for these words are true and faithful.

6 And he said unto me, It is done. I am Alpha and Omega, the beginning and the end. I will give unto him that is athirst of the fountain of the water of life freely.

7 He that overcometh shall inherit all things; and I will be his God, and he shall be my son.

1 And he showed me a pure river of water of life, clear as crystal, proceeding out of the throne of God and of the Lamb.

2 In the midst of the street of it, and on either side of the river, was there the tree of life, which bare twelve manner of fruits, and yielded her fruit every month: and the leaves of the tree were for the healing of the nations.

3 And there shall be no more curse: but the

throne of God and of the Lamb shall be in it; and his servants shall serve him.

How does all this affect our daily lives? First of all, the last Adam is in charge. It's <u>His</u> <u>Blessing.</u> Because of that, through Him <u>The Blessing</u> has come on us. We are His Body. Everything in Him and on Him is in us and on us. He not only has made available <u>The</u> <u>Blessing</u> but He has also provided us the <u>FAITH</u> with which to activate it.

We are redeemed from the curse and blessed with <u>The Blessing.</u> That's true, but nothing happens until faith is released. That's the reason it's impossible to please the Father without it. So what is the Love connection? Faith works by Love! The stronger the faith, the more <u>The Blessing.</u> No Love, no faith. No faith, no Blessing. That's just the way it is.

Was there any sickness in the Garden? No. So, when sickness tries to invade, faith does what the first Adam failed to do. It shouts, "Get out of my garden! <u>The Blessing</u> of Jesus is mine. My health is divine. You cannot take it away from me." In the face, then, of every symptom, faith in <u>The Blessing</u> is released, along with faith in the Name and blood of Jesus, by a strong confession of 1 Peter 2:24: "By His stripes I am healed."

Was there any poverty in the Garden of Eden? Absolutely not! Is poverty under the curse? Definitely yes! Then release your faith through the same process as healing or any and everything else that Jesus bore for us on the cross.

That's the way it works. Love Himself released it in the Garden. Love's words of <u>Blessing</u> were the very first words ever heard by a human ear. Be blessed. Be fruitful. Multiply. Have dominion over the earth and <u>subdue</u> it. Love said it. Love suffered to get it back to us. Love is standing behind it today with all power both in heaven and earth.

Without Love we can do <u>nothing.</u> But we are not without Him. Love said, "I will never leave you nor forsake you even to the end of all things." To walk in Love is to walk in <u>The Blessing</u>—walking in <u>the Garden</u> regardless of what's going on elsewhere.

Impossible to bless the whole earth? No! You and I, through Love Himself, are doing it now. Together we are going, preaching, teaching and healing through the gospel, building up His Body in the power and anointing of <u>The Blessing</u>. Faith gardens of Eden are sprouting up in the lives of believers everywhere. Oh, how awesome and marvelous it is in our eyes what Jesus is doing.

As you sow your financial seed this month, see yourself planting seeds in your Garden of Eden. Bless it by laying your hands on it and saying, "I bless you with <u>The Blessing</u>. Grow up and become great in my garden."

Thank you for being our Partner. Gloria and I love you and pray for you every day.

<u>Be Blessed!</u>

Love,

Ken

Together we are going, preaching, teaching and healing through the gospel, building up His Body in the power and anointing of THE BLESSING. Together we can do everything the Lord Jesus has assigned us to do.

August 2006

Hope Deferred Makes the Heart Sick!

Dear Partner

A few weeks ago Gloria and I ministered at Word of Faith International Christian Center in Detroit, where Bishop Keith and Deborah Butler are pastors. What a marvelous place to preach.

My spirit, a few days before, had begun to stir. And by the time we got to that meeting there was a roar in me like a lion. I've never experienced anything like this before. It's not something bad about to happen—it's something good. So good, in fact, that I can't describe it.

I keep hearing the voice of my spiritual father, Oral Roberts, saying, "Something good is going to happen to you," so I started saying it out loud. The more and the louder I say it, the bigger it gets inside me. I don't yet know what it is, but I do know Who it is. His Name is Jesus, and <u>He</u> is happening all over the world.

Start saying that with me: "Something good is about to happen to me today, and His Name is Jesus."

Actually, that's the way Bible <u>hope</u> works. Hoping for something is not wishing for it. Faith will not join forces with wishing. Wishing is completely in the realm of unbelief. You can spot it immediately. For instance you might ask someone, "Are you going to receive your healing in the service tonight?" Unbelief will answer, "Well, I sure hope so." That's wishing—not hope. Faith is the substance of things hoped for, and that answer has no substance at all. First Corinthians 13:13 says that hope is a living thing. Let's look at that:

> 13   And now abideth faith, hope, charity, these three; but the greatest of these is charity.

Living things will work together. Faith works by Love. Hope works by faith.

When faith is strong, hope is strong. Faith cometh by hearing and hearing by the Word of God. At the same time that faith is getting stronger, it is filling hope with substance—spiritual substance, strength and boldness that only comes from acting on God's Word.

Ask that same question about receiving healing of someone who has been meditating and confessing healing scriptures every day for weeks—someone who has been listening to healing messages on tapes or CDs—or, better yet, DVDs—and going to a healing, Word church. You'll get an immediate smile and a bold "Yes! I will! Isn't Jesus wonderful?" He may be in pain when he says it, but faith-filled hope will get bigger than the pain. The pain will eventually have to bow its knee to the Name of Jesus.

Real, Bible hope never says "I guess," or "Maybe it will someday," or "If it's God's will it might." Those are all badges of unbelief. No one can just will those badges away. It takes a quality decision to put the Word first place in one's life and stay with it. Constantly! That's the meaning of the Word *patience* in Romans 15:4:

> 4   For whatsoever things were written aforetime were written for our learning, that we through patience and comfort of the scriptures might have hope.

Hebrews 6:12 says that we inherit the promises of God through faith *and* patience—not just faith. In <u>consistency</u> lies the power. The staying with it—the Word—and never, ever allowing the thought that it's not working to stay in our minds. The Word works whether we can feel it working or not. It works when it's put to work.

Put the Word to work and keep it working by lining up your thoughts, words and actions with faith, hope and love. These are the forces of <u>Life.</u> <u>Jesus is alive!</u> <u>His Word is alive!</u> <u>His Name is alive!</u> <u>The Blessing is alive!</u> <u>You are alive!</u> <u>I am alive!</u> Sickness and disease are dead. They are in the world of darkness supported by the spirits of darkness. We are children of light.

First Thessalonians 5:4-5:

4	But ye, brethren, are not in darkness, that that day should overtake you as a thief.
5	Ye are all the children of light, and the children of the day: we are not of the night, nor of darkness.

Ephesians 5:8:

8	For ye were sometimes darkness, but now are ye light in the Lord: walk as children of light.

Romans 13:12

12	The night is far spent, the day is at hand: let us therefore cast off the works of darkness, and let us put on the armour of light.

<u>Shout amen, somebody!</u>

Light <u>always</u> overcomes darkness. Darkness cannot ever overcome the light unless someone turns off the light and allows darkness to come in through doubt and unbelief. Then and only then can a believer be defeated. Repent! Immediately. Get back on the Word. Take authority over your mind, over your mouth and over your flesh. NOW!

Today is the day of salvation. Not tomorrow. I know your flesh wants to wait, but your flesh will kill you. Take it by the "ear" and put it on its knees and repent. Make the decision and put your faith back to work.

Marvelous things are all around you. Jesus is right there and ready. He's more than willing and oh, so able to do everything that's promised in His Word. This is our time. The Glory is here. Together we can do everything the Lord Jesus has assigned us to do.

The roar of victory in Christ Jesus is at an all-time high in my spirit. Writing this letter to you and all of our Partners has stirred it to an even higher level of expectancy.

Sow your financial seeds this month with an expectant heart. Expect that seed to grow in your church, in this ministry and wherever else the Lord of the Harvest directs you to sow.

Expect a financial overflow, a Glory overflow and a marvelous manifestation of Jesus in your life. John 14:21:

> 21 He that hath my commandments, and keepeth them, he it is that loveth me: and he that loveth me shall be loved of my Father, and I will love him, and will manifest myself to him.

Gloria and I love you and pray for you every day.

Love,

Ken

September 2006

The Lord of the Harvest Is Here Now!

Dear Partner,

Wow! What a time to be alive! Sure, it's dangerous. The devil is scrambling for his life on earth. But in the lives of those who know who they are in Christ Jesus, he's losing at every turn. It's harvest time, and the Lord of the Harvest, Jesus Himself, is on the move.

Let's look at Luke 10:1-2:

> 1 After these things the Lord appointed other seventy also, and sent them two and two before his face into every city and place, whither he himself would come.
> 2 Therefore said he unto them, The harvest truly is great, but the labourers are few: pray ye therefore the Lord of the harvest, that he would send forth labourers into his harvest.

Notice in verse 1 "where He Himself would come." Let there be no doubt about it: He is here.

Have you sown your seed? Then get your mind on the harvest.

What's the first thing most people think about when they think about harvest? Sure, it's what am I going to do when I get my money? That is why it is so important to get the dream going. "Well, Brother Copeland, I guess He knows what I need." That's no dream. That's a fear-based cop-out. Sure He knows what you need, but no one ever thinks that way when he is looking forward in faith toward the Lord of the Harvest.

First of all, let's Word-base the hope or dream. Remember, faith is the substance of things hoped for, and faith comes by hearing and hearing by the Word of God. Second Corinthians 9:8-11:

> 8 And God is able to make all grace abound toward you; that ye, always having all sufficiency in all things, may abound to every good work:
> 9 (As it is written, He hath dispersed abroad; he hath given to the poor: his righteousness remaineth for ever.
> 10 Now he that ministereth seed to the sower both minister bread for your food, and multiply your seed sown, and increase the fruits of your righteousness;)
> 11 Being enriched in every thing to all bountifulness, which causeth through us thanksgiving to God.

Who is able to make all grace <u>abound</u> toward you? The Lord of the Harvest. Who is the One who <u>ministers</u> seed to the sower? The Lord of the Harvest. Who ministers bread to you and multiplies your seed sown? Yes, Jesus—the Lord of the Harvest!

Isn't Jesus your Lord? Then start thinking like it. Begin seeing yourself always having <u>all</u> sufficiency in <u>all</u> things. See yourself <u>abounding</u> to every good work and dispersing abroad—everywhere. See the money and goods just gushing out from you to the poor and needy.

See yourself preaching to great crowds of people and thousands of them receiving their salvation and healing. How can you do that if you're not in the ministry? You're doing it now! You're our Partner!

Once that picture is in place, begin to be more explicit. In fact, settle it now. "The first thing I'm going to do is tithe." Remember, now you're looking out over your field that's ready to harvest, but you haven't been paid for your crop yet. You know it's coming, because the Lord of the Harvest is Lord over your crop. But you're thinking like the money is already in your hand.

"Lord, where do You want my tithe to go?" Now don't see yourself tithing in the same way you always have. Go back to that word *abounding.* ABOUND! See your pastor jumping up and down when you hand him your tithe.

"Now, the next thing I'm going to do is give the offerings I've always wanted to give." Have some fun seeing yourself prospering ministries and your family members. See yourself blessing people everywhere you go—in some cases secretly—and enjoy the excitement and joy on people's faces with only Jesus getting the credit for it. This is life in the Glory lane. You'll begin to get blessed just thinking about being a blessing.

The bigger the dream gets on the inside, the more real it becomes. That's when it begins to take upon itself faith, or substance, and begins its journey from being hope in the spirit realm to manifesting in the material world. Reality does not begin after you can see it. It begins in the world of faith.

The process I've described is actually what Jesus outlined when He said, "Seek ye first the kingdom of God...and all these things shall be added to you."

The next thing is to begin praising and giving thanks on the same level of excitement as you will when the crop is in and the money is in the bank. Praise and keep on praising. Don't quit. Don't be moved ever by what you see or what you feel. Be moved only by what you believe—the Living Word of God!

I have used the harvesting of finances as the example, but it's the same process regardless of what your harvest dream is. Is your harvest healing? The Lord of the Harvest is the Healer. Is your harvest the salvation of your family? The Lord of the Harvest—Jesus—is the Savior. See yourself doing all the things you haven't been able to do. Going strong with no pain. Picture yourself getting others healed. Remove the image of your family members being unsaved and unpleasant from your mind. Think about how it's going to be when they come abounding into the kingdom of God. Begin treating them now as though they were already there.

Love is the key element in all of this. Begin now by saying, "Love Himself is the Lord of the Harvest. Love is the reason there is a harvest."

Begin saying and thinking constantly, "Love has said to me..." and repeat a scripture promise. "Love has said to me, 'I am able to make all grace abound toward you because I love you.'"

Isn't that wonderful and oh, so powerful? Love has said to you and to me, "I redeemed you from the curse of the law, being made a curse for you, so that <u>The</u> <u>Blessing</u> of Abraham might come on you...because I love you."

Take hold of that. Go through the New Testament and read it to yourself from Love Himself, the Lord of the Harvest.

Like I said, What a time to be alive!

As you sow your seeds of faith this month sow them with Love Himself on your mind. "Love, You said to me in Your Word to give, and it will be given to me again. I believe that, so I am bringing my gift to You. You are the Lord of my harvest. Take it and bless it and use it for Your kingdom." Then stop and dream awhile.

Gloria and I love you and we pray for you every day.

Love,

Ken

October 2006

Ministers of the Harvest

Dear Partner

Just as I sat down to write this letter, the thought struck me: *This year of the Glory is almost over and the best is yet to come.* We have seen more wonderful things happen this year than any other in this ministry. More people who have accepted Jesus as Savior. More miracles and healings. More financial breakthroughs. More of everything good. Of course the devil has tried to keep up with more of everything bad, but as always he's fallen way short.

Over the past few weeks I have noticed a sudden increase in supernatural timing. I have known for years this was coming and have been eagerly looking for it. The prophet Amos declared it in Amos 9:13:

> 13 Behold, the days come, saith the Lord, that the plowman shall overtake the reaper, and the treader of grapes him that soweth seed; and the mountains shall drop sweet wine, and all the hills shall melt.

It's even stronger in *The Amplified Bible:*

> 13 Behold, the days are coming, says the Lord, that the plowman shall overtake the reaper, and the treader of grapes him who sows the seed; and the mountains shall drop sweet wine and all the hills shall melt [that is, everything heretofore barren and unfruitful shall overflow with spiritual blessing].

Those days are here! Start looking for sudden, compound manifestation of supernatural harvest. For example, this past August our family got together at our prayer cabin in Arkansas for a few days of vacation together. One morning at breakfast John said to Jeremy, "The Lord spoke to me and said for me to give you my watch." George said to John, "The Lord spoke to me and said for me to give you my watch."

That sounds simple, but behind both of those watches there was a lot of history that touched all three of those men deeply. The point here is the timing of the Lord of the Harvest to see to it that the sowing of one seed was the harvest of another. Jeremy had given me his watch a few weeks earlier which had blessed me big-time.

What's happening here? <u>A sign of the times!</u> <u>The day has come.</u> The watches are not what's important. Even the family love flowing like it did is not the key issue. The important thing is the Lord of the Harvest is making Himself known in our midst. He is moving in our family in small things getting us ready for much larger things.

Notice here how important quick-to-do-it obedience is to the timing. In order to walk in this, one must be looking and listening for the Holy Spirit's direction to move, give, speak a word of love, encourage, help and sow into someone's life—ALL THE TIME! The miracle of the watches happened in our family, and that's wonderful. But the week before, I was in the middle of another Amos 9:13 that was not family and involved seed and harvest 50 times larger than those watches.

<u>The</u> <u>Blessing</u> is on! Get into the flow. It's harvest time.

The biggest thing about this harvest is not material. That's big and has to come. But the big thing is the harvest of souls into the kingdom. Your anointing to be a witness is greater than ever before. Be bold to talk about Jesus wherever you are, not in a religious way but as your best friend. Talk about Him to strangers and friends alike as part of your family.

The hardest, most impossible-looking cases are suddenly turning around. Prepare yourself to help them—not only members of your own family but strangers as well. They are members of someone's family and you are the harvester. Believe for it! Pray. Make yourself available. Don't shy away from an opportunity.

Remember, you're not only a sower. You are also a reaper—a harvester working under the direction of <u>The</u> Lord of <u>The</u> Harvest.

Not just *a* harvest—THE Harvest. Jesus is gathering in everything that belongs to Him. People, land, finances—everything. You and I are part of the greatest harvest of all time. Get in it. It will swallow up everything that's wrong in your life.

All of this is 2 Corinthians 9:8-11 coming to pass:

> 8 And God is able to make all grace abound toward you; that ye, always having all sufficiency in all things, may abound to every good work:
> 9 (As it is written, He hath dispersed abroad; he hath given to the poor: his righteousness remaineth for ever.
> 10 Now he that ministereth seed to the sower both minister bread for your food, and multiply your seed sown, and increase the fruits of your righteousness;)
> 11 Being enriched in every thing to all bountifulness, which causeth through us thanksgiving to God.

Read verse 8 again, only this time read it very slowly and let every word sink in deep. Now verse 10. Notice it does not say He provides seed for the sower—No. It says He ministers seed to the sower—He ministers bread for your food and ministers the multiplying of your seed sown. Now in order to minister seed to someone, Jesus—The minister—must have ministers. Are you available? Man, I am!

Verse 8 has to come to pass big-time for me to be a minister of His through which seed will be ministered to the sower who is just becoming a sower. I have to be blessed overwhelmingly to minister food to the hungry and minister the multiplying of someone's seed sown.

Meditate on this. That's what this ministry is. That's what you are. We are ministers in the hands of the Master—The Lord of The Harvest.

As you sow your financial seeds this month into your church, and into this and other places as The Lord of the Harvest directs, minister it. Don't just send it. Write a note saying, "I minister this offering to you from Jesus with love and faith." Mean it. Don't say things like, "I know it's small and won't mean much to you." Don't speak like that over your seed. Nothing is small when it is filled with faith and compassion.

Minister it. Bless it. Then watch it grow. It's Amos 9:13 time. It's 2 Corinthians 9:8-11 time. It's Harvest time. Shout and be glad!

Gloria and I love you and pray for you every day.

Love,

Ken

November 2006

COMPASSION HAD A PLAN!

Dear Partner,

The question kept coming up in my thinking: *Why is it such a big issue with our heavenly Father and with our Lord Jesus that we live in His love?* I could answer that in any number of ways, but I was looking for the key issue behind THE Commandment. The Holy Spirit was quick to answer.

Let's look at Psalm 78:37-38:

> 37   For their heart was not right with him, neither were they stedfast in his covenant.
> 38   But he, being full of compassion, forgave their iniquity, and destroyed them not: yea, many a time turned he his anger away, and did not stir up all his wrath.

Now let's turn to Psalm 86:15:

> 15   But thou, O Lord, art a God full of compassion, and gracious, longsuffering, and plenteous in mercy and truth.

And again we see in Psalm 111:4 that THE LORD our God is full of compassion:

> 4   He hath made his wonderful works to be remembered: the Lord is gracious and full of compassion.

God is Love and He is full of compassion. Compassion is to have so much mercy and tenderness for someone else that it actually causes pain. It is the deepest desire to show love and goodness. Jesus was moved with compassion and He healed the sick.

Now we can look at the creation of man in a very different way. Genesis 1:1-25 tells us how God created this universe in all of its splendor. He created the earth. Then He prepared Eden, the most beautiful, awesome place He could imagine—no one can understand with the human mind how overwhelmingly beautiful that place was. Compassion did all of that in preparation for His own family.

Then in Genesis 1:26 Compassion reproduced Himself. The creation of man was an act of compassion. Love in action is compassion. So man, created in God's image and crowned with His Glory, had to have been filled with compassion.

Now let's look at The Blessing. This was the first thing Compassion said to His offspring:

> 28   And God blessed them, and God said unto them, Be fruitful, and multiply, and replenish the earth, and subdue it: and have dominion over the fish of the sea, and over the fowl of the air, and over every living thing that moveth upon the earth.

Compassion said, "Be Blessed." The Blessing was a manifestation of compassion—the overwhelming desire to do good—commissioning His child with the command and power to have overwhelming desire to do good and give birth to good and love-filled offspring throughout the entire earth.

Neither the human spirit, soul or body was created for hate, sin, sickness or unrighteousness of any kind. There was nothing in man created to deal with death. Pain was unheard of. Sin caused weakness—what was that? Adam never had any idea of any of this. He was created to be filled with compassion, not with stealing, killing and destruction. In short, man was made for The Blessing—not the curse.

What now? Death had come upon all men. The spirit of death was in charge of everything.

Even the earth was under the pain and strain of it all. It also was created by Love for Love. It was intended to be the home of compassion and everything good. Instead, it began to produce thorns and painful things and became the enemy of the one it was supposed to bless.

It looked so hopeless. But Compassion had a plan!

The Son of Compassion Himself came into this painful mess and took upon Himself the sin, sickness, weakness and pain. He went into the depth of death and bore the punishment due to every human being.

Then Compassion moved! Compassion raised Him from death. Compassion seated Him at His own right hand and reinstated <u>The Blessing</u>. He gave Him His Name, which is above every name, and at the sound of that Name every knee must bow. Sin must bow. Sickness must bow. Poverty must bow. Satan himself, the spirit of death, has bowed before Compassion's mighty work of redemption.

What now?

The Commandment!

Believe on the Name and love one another as He gave commandment. Love the Lord your God with all your heart, all your soul and all your strength. And love your neighbor as yourself. Remember now, it was Compassion who commanded it. Now let's go to Ephesians 3:14-21:

14	For this cause I bow my knees unto the Father of our Lord Jesus Christ,
15	Of whom the whole family in heaven and earth is named,
16	That he would grant you, according to the riches of his glory, to be strengthened with might by his Spirit in the inner man;
17	That Christ may dwell in your hearts by faith; that ye, being rooted and grounded in love,
18	May be able to comprehend with all saints what is the breadth, and length, and depth, and height;
19	And to know the love of Christ, which passeth

	knowledge, that ye might be filled with all the <u>fulness</u> of God.
20	Now unto him that is able to do exceeding abundantly above all that we ask or think, according to the power that worketh in us,
21	Unto him be glory in the church by Christ Jesus throughout all ages, world without end. Amen.

Look again at verse 19. To be filled with the fullness of God is to be filled with Compassion! There it is. That's the reason the commandment of Love is a commandment. A direct order from Compassion Himself.

You can't be a good steward of The Commandment and it not produce becoming rooted and grounded in love. You can't become rooted and grounded in love and it not produce comprehending the breadth, length, depth and height, and coming into an intimate relationship with the Anointed One and with the love and compassion of His Anointing. You can't come into that relationship and it not produce becoming filled with the fullness of God who is full of compassion. That puts you and Him right back where He started.

Compassion has reproduced Himself in you and in me. He has never changed His mind. That's what He set out to do in the first place—to fill this earth with His goodness by blessing His family to be as filled with His love and compassion as He is, and then sending them into all the world to be fruitful and multiply. Fill up the earth and subdue with dominion.

How does Compassion dominate? With love, and healing and restoration. In short, <u>The</u> Blessing.

That's who you and I are. That's what we do. This ministry is the way we do it. It's the tool to carry the Word of His love to the whole earth, casting out death and all of its work. Together we can do it.

That's what His Glory is all about. Manifestations of the Glory are manifestations of His compassion. It's been working all year in the most awesome ways ever, and the best is yet to come!

Release your faith for it. Expect it to explode right where you are. Start confessing daily: "I keep The Commandment. I love the Lord my God with all my heart, all my soul and all my strength. I love my neighbor as myself. I believe I receive His compassion released in me everywhere I go. This is a day of compassion and blessing."

The more you say that aloud, the more you stir up the gift of God that is in you. The more you stir, the less room there is for fear. No fear—no torment and worry. Healing is released through compassion. It's in there because you are the temple of the Holy Ghost and He is all of these good things. It will be said of you what was said of Jesus: "You are going everywhere doing good and healing all who are oppressed of the devil."

God bless and keep you in His love. Gloria and I love you and pray for you every day.

Love,

Ken

December 2006

What's the Big Deal?

Dear Partner

I know you hear "Merry Christmas," and such a lot this time of year, but Gloria and I and all of us here at Kenneth Copeland Ministries really mean it. God has blessed us with a record year, and all of you—our Partners—stood with us, prayed for us, and invested the finances into what we are doing so that along with the powers of heaven we were able to get our job done.

What a glorious year! As I said, it was a record breaker in just about everything we did in every department of this ministry. I'll have a report on it all sometime in 2007. It may take awhile to get it all together, but that's a good thing.

Let's talk about Christmas. Look at Luke 2:7-14:

> 7 And she brought forth her firstborn son, and wrapped him in swaddling clothes, and laid him in a manger; because there was no room for them in the inn.
> 8 And there were in the same country shepherds abiding in the field, keeping watch over their flock by night.
> 9 And, lo, the angel of the Lord came upon them, and the glory of the Lord shone round about them: and they were sore afraid.
> 10 And the angel said unto them, Fear not: for, behold, I bring you good tidings of great joy, which shall be to all people.
> 11 For unto you is born this day in the city of David a Saviour, which is Christ the Lord.
> 12 And this shall be a sign unto you; Ye shall find the babe wrapped in swaddling clothes, lying in a manger.
> 13 And suddenly there was with the angel a multitude of the heavenly host praising God, and saying,

14 Glory to God in the highest, and on earth
peace, good will toward men.

First of all, who was this angel and why was he there? This was Jesus' personal angel—<u>the</u> angel of <u>the</u> Lord. He was not just any angel, but the highest ranking angel in the angelic service. Look at Revelation 1:1: "The Revelation of Jesus Christ, which God gave unto him, to show unto his servants things which must shortly come to pass; and he sent and signified it *by his angel* unto his servant John." See the phrase "by his angel"? It was the same one.

We've all heard the words of his message so many times those words have little to no impact on our thinking. The first thing to notice is <u>The Glory</u>. Not just any glory, but THE GLORY of THE LORD. <u>That's a big thing.</u> It became so bright in that "round about area" that people came out of their houses in great wonder. It was suddenly brighter than the noon sun in the middle of the night!

Yet his very next words stopped all fear. Fear is the enemy to the workings of The Glory.

Now listen carefully to his message: *<u>Look!</u> I bring you the gospel of GREAT JOY!* Good tidings = the gospel. Not of mere joy, but <u>great</u> joy. <u>That's a big deal!</u> Remember, he is talking here about the joy of the Lord which is our strength. Great joy—not just to the Jews, but to <u>all</u> people. <u>Now, that too, is big.</u> *This day a Savior is born!* Not someday, but today. *Christ*—now there is a key word to his message. The Anointing has come. The only thing that can remove burdens and destroy yokes is finally in the earth again, and neither the devil nor anyone else can get it out.

I am also convinced that this angel had been there since the inception of Jesus in the womb of Mary to watch over her and then to protect Jesus' birth—including the cleansing of that manger. A manger is dirty. It is no place for a baby to be born. Someone had to sanctify it. I believe that was the job of angels.

Then something else startling happened. While the general of all the angels was speaking, a multitude of angels broke into praise so great heaven couldn't hold them back. Their message was what all of heaven was ecstatic about. *On earth peace*—not natural peace from wars and rumors of wars, but peace between heaven and earth. As far as they were concerned, the war that started when satan took Adam's authority over the earth was as good as over. They were calling things that be not as though they were—like God. They knew that after 4,000 years of this conflict in little more than 30 years the battle would be won. No wonder they were so thrilled.

Good will toward men. Not good will *among* men as most people read that, but *toward* men. From God to man. What's that about? Go to Genesis 6:5-6:

> 5   And God saw that the wickedness of man was great in the earth, and that every imagination of the thoughts of his heart was only evil continually.
> 6   And [the Lord regretted] that he had made man on the earth, and it grieved him at his heart.

Don't misread verse 6. It did not say the Lord regretted He had made man. It said He regretted He had made him on the earth. He was grieved—in deep pain and anguish in His great heart of love and compassion—that His own created family had come to the place of never having one thought of Him. And the worst part was He created them to live in heaven on earth—not in a cursed, sin-filled world of death and pain.

No wonder heaven was shouting. Jesus is here! He's going to take it all back from the devil, including the keys of death and hell. The first words of faith shouted by those angels after Jesus was born were the words of satan's destruction. They knew He would abolish death and bring life and immortality to light through the gospel (2 Timothy 1:10).

The Blessing! The Blessing! It's coming on all people through Christ Jesus. Well it did! That's why it's so very important to celebrate the birth of Jesus. No wonder the devil hates the sound of the word CHRIST-MAS. *Christ-* (the Anointed One and His Anointing) *mas* (celebration). Celebration of the coming of the burden-removing, yoke-destroying power of the All Mighty God—The Glory. Not the celebration of "the holidays." No. The day life came back into the earth. <u>The</u> <u>Life</u> Himself.

Well, He got His job done. He lived The Blessing. He sacrificed Himself so we could be just like Him. Then He prayed the Father, and the Holy Ghost, The Blessing Himself, came and heaven poured itself out into the earth. He's here, and He's carrying out His great dream of peace on earth, good will <u>toward</u> men. He loves you just as much as He does Jesus (John 17:23). He is standing ready to work His dream out in you and through you. Not a smaller version of that dream, but the very same life-giving, healing, prospering blessing that Adam heard—those first words more thrilling than any human had ever heard: "Be fruitful, and multiply, and replenish the earth, and subdue it: and have dominion over the fish of the sea, and over the fowl of the air, and over every living thing that moveth upon the earth."

<u>Shout it now: "I'm Blessed. The Blessing is working in me now! It's working in me healing and giving me strength. I'm strong in the Lord and in the power of His might to fulfill His mighty dream through me!"</u>

As you sow your financial seeds this month, do so in the same overflowing praise as the hosts of heaven did the day Jesus was born. Celebrate His coming for the real reasons.

Gloria and I love you and pray for you every day. We pray especially for your very best Christmas ever. Our prayers also are for a fabulous 2007. The Word of the Lord came to me about 2007 a few weeks ago declaring it is "the year of the open door" according to Revelation 3:7:

> 7 ...he that openeth, and no man shutteth; and shutteth, and no man openeth.

More about that later. We love you.

Love,

Ken

P.S. The devil will not be able to close the door on what you're called to do in 2007—The Year of the Open Door!

January 2007

The Door Is Open
Get Up and Go Through It—Now!

Dear Partner

Here we are in another brand-new year. A year of great opportunity in the kingdom of God.

This is a year when nothing will be withheld in the spirit. The only thing that can stop or hold back <u>The Blessing</u> in your life in 2007 is you. Jesus has opened the door, and no man can shut it. The only way the devil can keep you from victory is for you to just sit where you are and not go through the door into the next place—a new room full of His glory.

Let's look at our promise for this year in Revelation 3:6-8:

> 6 He that hath an ear, let him hear what the Spirit saith unto the churches.
> 7 And to the angel of the church in Philadelphia write; These things saith he that is holy, he that is true, he that hath the key of David, he that openeth, and no man shutteth; and shutteth, and no man openeth;
> 8 I know thy works: behold, I have set before thee an open door, and no man can shut it: for thou hast a little strength, and hast kept my word, and hast not denied my name.

I know in years gone by there have been things that should have come to pass and didn't. Things I knew the Lord wanted done, but somehow the door shut right in my face. In most cases faith broke through and victory was mine.

Faith is the victory that overcomes the world. In those few cases in which total breakthrough has not yet come, this is the year it must come to pass. Jesus has opened the door for you and me <u>and has slammed it in satan's face!</u>

What is the biggest door in your life? For most people it's the financial door. For some it may be an area of ministry that needs a breakthrough. For others it's a struggling new business. Maybe it is the healing door. Or the door of salvation of a loved one—or of even a whole family. Whatever it is, <u>The Blessing</u> will bring success and satisfaction in Christ Jesus before this year is done.

Just on the other side of the door of victory is a room filled with good health and prosperity even as your soul prospers. Together, Jesus, you and I are going boldly through that door. I see us standing in our dreams—standing in a room filled with joy unspeakable.

I am especially drawn to that 8th verse in Revelation 3:

> 8 I know thy works: behold, I have set before thee an open door, and no man can shut it: for thou hast a little strength, and hast kept my word, and hast not denied my name.

Remember, the Apostle John by the Holy Spirit wrote that verse. The same man by the same Spirit wrote the Gospel of John, as well as First, Second and Third John. First John 3:23-24 shines light on what we have just read:

> 23 And this is his commandment, That we should believe on the name of his Son Jesus Christ, and love one another, as he gave us commandment.
> 24 And he that keepeth his commandments dwelleth in him, and he in him. And hereby we know that he abideth in us, by the Spirit which he hath given us.

That's our part. That's our strength. Being a good steward of the commandment of Love and living by faith keeps us in the zone of victory where the evil one touches us not. That is the promise we also see in 1 John 5:18.

The sum of all of this put together is I am totally convinced that everything is coming to a head both in the spirit and in the world this year. For those who insist on staying on the road of sin and death, <u>the door to destruction is open wide.</u> This will be a terrible year with a horrible harvest of one disaster after another for those who refuse to close those doors in their lives. However, for those who choose Jesus and His ways of Love and faith, the future is the brightest it has ever been since His resurrection. Deuteronomy 30:19 has come alive in my heart and mind greater than ever before:

> 19   I call heaven and earth to record this day against you, that I have set before you life and death, blessing and cursing: therefore choose life, that both thou and thy seed may live.

<u>The Blessing</u> has been released in us, on us, and through us like never before. It is working to turn our lives and circumstances into the Garden of Eden our heavenly Father planned for us from the beginning. I choose Life. I choose <u>The Blessing.</u> The doors are open and we are going through to victory!

As you sow your financial seed this month, lay your hands on every offering you sow and name it the Seed of the Open Door. Every opportunity to bless someone, say in your heart, "<u>That's a door that Love has opened and I'm going through it.</u>" Begin now by thanking God and being grateful for opening the door of Blessing that cannot be closed and for closing the door of sin and death that cannot be reopened.

This is the day we've all been looking for. Rejoice and be glad in it.

Gloria and I love you and we pray for you every day.

Love,

Ken

P.S. I have included the prophecy the Lord gave in the Washington, D.C. Victory Campaign concerning The Year of the Open Door. Read it. Meditate on it. Take hold of it. Now is our time!

Now Is Our Time!

The year of 2007...what will it be like? Will it be a year of disasters and catastrophes beyond imagination as some have predicted? Or will it be a continuance of the glory of heaven being manifest?

The year of 2007 will have some very serious catastrophes. There will be some things happening that the world will not know how to handle. But you may rest in Me, saith the Lord, because the manifestation of My glory will be so great in the year 2007, and [there will be] such overflowing revival throughout this nation and around the world that you're hardly even going to notice the natural catastrophes that happen. And the things that the devil is trying to do will get caught up in the swell and the explosive power of My Spirit being manifest, saith the Lord. Hallelujah.

2007 will be known as The Year of the Open Door. My Word states in Revelation 3 that I open doors no man can shut. I shut doors no man can open.

There are those of you who over the years have set out with commitment and resolve to do things that I have assigned you to do, and over a period of time it looked like the devil just slammed the door in your face. Some because of catastrophic things happening in your family, others because of sickness and disease that has attacked, and others because of financial disasters and just plain ol' not enough money to get it done, that the devil was able, as I said, to just slam the door in your face. But you hear Me now, saith the Lord, I am opening your door! I am opening your door! I am opening your door, and in 2007 neither the devil nor anybody else will be able to close it on you!

Don't quit! Don't give up! The kingdom of heaven is at hand. Don't give up on this nation. Don't give up on your church. Don't give up! Don't quit! Don't stop! 2007 is the year of doors open and held open. Go through them with great faith and stay on the Word! Stay on the Word! Stay on the Word! You stay with Me, I'll stay with you, and together we will see victory beyond anything you or anybody else has ever seen before! Hallelujah. Oh, hallelujah. Glory, glory, glory.

Oh, hallelujah. Hallelujah. Hallelujah. Hallelujah. Yes, bless the Lord. Yes, yes, yes, yes, yes. Amen. Amen. Amen. Amen. Amen. Oh, glory to God.

And by that same token, saith the Lord, there are certain doors that the devil has been holding open—doors of war, doors of destruction, doors of all kinds of disobedience and blaspheming lies and tongues. Well, I'll tell you, in 2007 you and I together are going to slam the door on him. We are going to slam it in his face. We are going to walk on him and you are going to find out what I meant in My Word when I said set your feet on him and walk on him. He has been put under your feet. He is becoming the footstool that I said he would be. And now is our time, saith the Lord. Hallelujah. Yes. Bless the Lord.

Given by Kenneth Copeland
November 11, 2006
Washington, D.C. Victory Campaign

February 2007

The Blessing's Mission

Dear Partner

For some months now we've been learning about The Blessing. The Bible is the history of The Blessing and its effect on the race of man from the Garden of Eden, when it was the very first words a man ever heard, until Jesus went to the cross so that The Blessing could come on the Gentiles and we might walk in its power today.

The intended purpose of The Blessing was to expand the Garden of Eden until it encompassed the entire earth and filled it with the glory of heaven and all its goodness. God the Father has never changed. Neither has His purpose and plan changed. Man changed—The Blessing didn't. It never will. God spoke it forever (Genesis 1:28):

> 28 And God blessed them, and God said unto them, Be fruitful, and multiply, and replenish the earth, and subdue it: and have dominion over the fish of the sea, and over the fowl of the air, and over every living thing that moveth upon the earth.

Genesis 1:28 was God's perfect plan for all men for all time. Jesus was and is The Blessing in action. He was and is the perfect will of God for all men for all time.

Is The Blessing alive in the earth today? Yes. For whom? All men? Absolutely yes.

Did The Blessing come on Jesus just so He could live in a Garden of Eden? After all, He was the Son of heaven. No. He ministered The Blessing to remove the effects of the curse. He was blessed in order to be a blessing. Let's look into that phrase a little deeper. It sounds good, but what does it mean?

The Blessing was God's plan for all men, but all men are not blessed.

Is it His will to bless them? Yes. Then why doesn't He do it? He has. Then why are they not walking in it? They are not connected to Him, or they are connected to Him through Jesus and don't know who they are or what belongs to them. That's the reason Jesus came—to reconnect man to God. It's His will to bless the righteous and the unrighteous, the just and the unjust. Jesus said in Luke 6:35:

> 35 But love ye your enemies, and do good, and lend, hoping for nothing again; and your reward shall be great, and ye shall be the children of the Highest: for he is kind unto the unthankful and to the evil.

He is kind to the unthankful and to the evil. Now let's look at Luke 6:27-34:

> 27 But I say unto you which hear, Love your enemies, do good to them which hate you,
> 28 Bless them that curse you, and pray for them which despitefully use you.
> 29 And unto him that smiteth thee on the one cheek offer also the other; and him that taketh away thy cloak forbid not to take thy coat also.
> 30 Give to every man that asketh of thee; and of him that taketh away thy goods ask them not again.
> 31 And as ye would that men should do to you, do ye also to them likewise.
> 32 For if ye love them which love you, what thank have ye? for sinners also love those that love them.
> 33 And if ye do good to them which do good to you, what thank have ye? for sinners also do even the same.
> 34 And if ye lend to them of whom ye hope to receive, what thank have ye? for sinners also lend to sinners, to receive as much again.

In verses 32, 33 and 34 we see the phrase, "What thank have ye?"

That is not just a figure of speech meaning you have no reward. It means just what it says. Thanks from whom? Now that's the key issue to this whole chapter.

Jesus started this lesson on The Blessing in verse 20:

> 20 And he lifted up his eyes on his disciples, and said, Blessed be ye poor: for yours is the kingdom of God.

The poor are not blessed because they are poor! No! Jesus came to preach the gospel to the poor to remove the poverty (Luke 4:18). Once The Blessing is released by faith and the kingdom of God is activated in one's life, poverty and lack are removed. Why?

Look at verse 33 again—"To do good." To whom? To those unthankful and evil ones about whom Jesus was speaking. He wants to do good to them. Your Father longs to help them in any way He can, but He has no way to get to them _unless_ you and I bless them. That's when our Father says _thank you._

Oh my! Think about that. Almighty God Himself saying, "Thank you for being My connection to that person. I want to 'bless' them and be kind and merciful to them, but I have no connection except through you. Thank you for showing them My love."

Now look at verse 38, and the whole chapter comes together:

> 38 Give, and it shall be given unto you; good measure, pressed down, and shaken together, and running over, shall men give into your bosom. For with the same measure that ye mete withal it shall be measured to you again.

Overflow! Now two things are very clear.

1. The Blessing is the perfect will of God for your life.

2. The Blessing has a mission to abundantly reveal the goodness

and lovingkindness of our heavenly Father. Oh, how He has been misrepresented in the light of all this. John 3:16 takes on a whole new perspective—for God, who is Love, so loved the world:

> 16 For God so loved the world, that he gave his only begotten Son, that whosoever believeth in him should not perish, but have everlasting life.

Now look at Luke 6:27-31:

> 27 But I say unto you which hear, <u>Love your enemies,</u> <u>do good</u> to them which hate you,
> 28 <u>Bless</u> them that curse you, and <u>pray</u> for them which despitefully use you.
> 29 And unto him that smiteth thee on the one cheek offer also the other; and him that taketh away thy cloak <u>forbid not</u> to take thy coat also.
> 30 <u>Give</u> to every man that asketh of thee; and of him that taketh away thy goods ask them not again.
> 31 And as ye would that men should do to you, <u>do ye also to them likewise.</u>

All of those "blessings" in Luke 6, such as in verses 27-31, are seeds that come from a way of living. Jesus was describing the way we should think—all the time. That's just the way He is, and that's the way we must become. We must <u>never ever</u> see these verses as the open door to disaster and injury. Nothing could be further from the truth. Living in <u>The</u> <u>Blessing</u> is dwelling in the secret place of the Most High.

Protection is part of <u>The Blessing's</u> power. That's living in faith. The Body of Christ has a military arm—ministers of God who do not wear the sword in vain. They are both angels and men. "Vengeance is mine... <u>saith the Lord!</u>" He will take care of that part. You are as safe in combat as you are at home in bed—<u>if</u> you trust God and trust The Blessing.

As you sow your financial seed this month, lay your hands on it and call it blessed. You have the power to bless—to release <u>The Blessing</u> that is on you and in you—to reach out in its power to bring God's love into the lives of millions of people. That's what you and I do as Partners together with Jesus. There's never been a time like this before to be able to bring dying, hurting people into a face-to-face encounter with Jesus and His mercy and grace. I mean it. It is a time of joy unspeakable and <u>full</u> of His Glory!

Get in every meeting we are having this year that you possibly can. Tank up and grow up—fill up on His Word. The doors of victory are open. Rise up and go boldly through them.

Gloria and I love you and we pray for you every day.

Love,

Ken

March 2007

Shout the Word, Then Shut Up and Stand!

Dear Partner

For some time now we've been talking about THE Blessing, the very first words ever heard by a human ear. Words of creative power spoken by the Almighty God, Father of all living things.

First words are extremely important. They are the perfect will of God for all men for all time. So, every word and every deed thereafter must be in accordance with the first words.

Jesus came to get that Blessing back in place. Everything He did, everything He said, was THE Blessing in operation. Finally, it was the power of THE Blessing that raised Him from the dead. Why? So that THE Blessing of Abraham might come on every believer through Christ Jesus.

THE Blessing's original purpose was to spread the Garden of Eden from where God created it until it filled the entire earth. Then through the first Adam, sin came into the world and death by sin. That changed everything, but it did not change the will of God or His first words.

THE Blessing still does the same thing it was intended to do—create a Garden of Eden for man. Was there any death in the Garden before Adam sinned? No. So the new birth that Jesus paid for is part of THE Blessing. Was there any sickness? No. So divine healing is part of THE Blessing. Was there any poverty? No. So divine prosperity is part of THE Blessing. Look at 1 Corinthians 15:45 and see how clear this is:

> 45 And so it is written, The first man Adam was made a living soul; the last Adam was made a quickening spirit.

Thank God! THE Blessing is back where it belongs. Not just on Adam but on all who call upon Jesus' Name.

How does one go about activating this mighty force in his life? By the laws of the Spirit that govern faith, hope and love. <u>All three.</u> Each is vital to the operation of the others, and <u>THE Blessing is dependent upon them all working together.</u> Faith cometh by hearing, and hearing by the Word of God.

Faith is the substance of things hoped for.

Faith worketh by Love.

It all starts with a decision. First, the quality decision to keep at all costs the commandment of Love. Then the decision to live by faith. After that, the absolute commitment to the Word of God being final authority in all things. Then comes the settling of it forever by taking Communion—enter covenant with God to do your part and release your faith on His Word that He is going to do His part.

Now that that is done, how is THE Blessing released to change things in our lives?

1. Make the decision

Again, everything begins with a decision. Make the quality decision that <u>this mountain is going to move.</u> You are blessed and it has no business being in your life.

2. Build yourself up (Mark 11:22)

Have faith in God. Begin meditating on scriptures that promise and cover your situation. Wake yourself up during the night for a few minutes to look at one or more of those verses and feed them into your spirit and mind. Smile and say, "I'm so blessed!" Then go back to sleep.

When you get up, do the same again. Repeat that off and on during the day. Put your promises on cards and place them where you can see them—throughout the house, in the car, in your pocket or purse. Keep them constantly before your eyes and in your mouth.

Remember, Jesus said in Luke 6:45 that out of the abundance of the heart the mouth speaks. That abundance is what we're building up to.

3. The moment of release (Mark 11:23)

You'll know when your spirit is full to abundance. Those scriptures you have been meditating on and looking at will begin to spill out your mouth without your having to think about it. The time has come to speak to the mountain, whatever its name is. Whether it is sickness, pain, debt or anything in the world order, faith is the victory over it.

Stand up and point your finger in that mountain's face, shout its name and cast it into the sea. <u>Use Jesus' words</u> in Mark 11:23. Then <u>use the Scriptures.</u> Shout them at that mountain. <u>Don't add a bunch of stuff to it</u>—you'll dilute the Word by adding emotional things. So shout the Word, shut up and stand. How long? Forever!

4. Believe you receive (Mark 11:24)

Immediately write down the time and date. That's the moment the mountain moved as far as you're concerned. "THE Blessing is working" is your confession. If you wake up in the night, say it: "THE Blessing is working." "The mountain is gone." "The Blessing is working in me <u>now</u>." "I am the Blessed."

5. Keep yourself (Mark 11:25; 1 John 5:18)

Put a watch over your mouth. Don't <u>ever</u> say anything crosswise of the Word you have released. Stay in Love. Stay in faith. Be like God who never changes from His Word. Be like Jesus who is merciful to all. Give and stay ready to give at a moment's notice when the Holy Spirit asks you to.

6. Enter into His rest (Hebrews 4:1)

Don't let anything or anyone disturb your rest of faith. Hebrews 4:1 says that is the key to not falling short of the promises upon which you are standing.

7. Shout the victory

Now comes the shout of victory. It may come in the night. It may come while you are in prayer. It may come in the middle of a church service or while you're at work. It <u>will</u> come. Suddenly you just know. You know that you know that you know. It's DONE! <u>VICTORY IN JESUS!</u> It's the sweetest moment of any believer's life.

All of this is yours. The blood of Jesus paid for it in full. Victory belongs to you because you are blessed with His Blessing. It became yours the moment He was raised from the dead. You activated it in your life when that precious moment came and you said those powerful words: "Jesus, come into my life. I receive You as my Lord and Savior." You are blessed. THE Blessing is yours.

You have the power to BLESS. As you sow your financial seeds this month, lay your hands on them and bless and multiply them the way Jesus did the loaves and fishes. That miracle was THE Blessing in operation. Read the first line of 1 Corinthians 14:16. Bless with your spirit. Well, that's another lesson!

Gloria and I love you and pray for you. Be Blessed!

Love,

Ken

April 2007

God Wants You Blessed!

Dear Partner,

I wish I had a way of telling you all the marvelous, wonderful things that are happening all over the world. The Spirit of God is moving in little things, big things and all things in between.

This is the time we've all been looking and believing for, and it's happening big time. Don't miss out on it. Don't get so wrapped up in natural things that the Lord Jesus can't involve you and your family in what He's doing.

This is the time to receive the very best of everything God has.

In last month's letter we outlined the buildup and release of faith that puts THE BLESSING to work in one's life. I hope you keep it so you can refer to it every time you need to activate the faith process and keep it in motion. Faith works. The Word works when it's put to work.

In the life of a born-again believer, God is never the problem. "God just didn't do it" is never the situation. Jesus went to the cross so that THE BLESSING of Abraham would come on everyone who knows Him as Lord and Savior. THE BLESSING is there ready to do what God said when He released it into and on Adam's life. It was there to cause the Garden of Eden to grow and expand until it covered the entire earth.

God has never changed. His Word has never changed or lost its power to produce what He said. However, as always, it takes the power of faith filled with Love to activate it and keep it working until one becomes entire, wanting nothing. The ministry of Jesus as High Priest is to stand behind His Word in our mouths until total victory is accomplished.

The problem has never been on His side. It has always been on our side. He is doing His part. He always has and always will.

Let's look into the part sin plays in all this. What is sin, anyway? I'm not so interested in complex, theological definitions as I am in how it works and what to do about it.

The most important thing to know about sin is that Jesus TOTALLY defeated it. It has no power to resist the Word when <u>any</u> human being resists it. However, that resistance must be in accordance with the Word and not just religious ideas of men.

The simple explanation of sin is anything that hinders or stops <u>THE BLESSING.</u> That seems too simple, but think about Adam's sin. It wasn't complicated. He simply disobeyed God. The reason God told him what not to do was because if he did it, it would stop the very thing he needed most—the glory of God, or <u>THE BLESSING.</u>

The problem with sin is it is always followed by death. Satan is the father of death. Therefore, sin opens the door to the spirit of death, who is the spirit of fear, who is the spirit of antichrist, and so on.

When THE BLESSING is interrupted, it affects not only one's spirit, but everything. Even the natural world around you is hindered. Everything in this earth was created to respond to THE BLESSING. When Adam lost it, the whole earth and everything in it suffered. Jesus had to suffer horribly to break sin's grip and free us from the curse that replaced THE BLESSING. After all that, there is no way He would refuse to stand behind His Word when it is stood upon in faith.

The definition of the Hebrew word translated *sin* is "error" or "failure." The Greek word is "to go astray" or "to miss the mark." Webster's 1828 dictionary defines it as "departure from a known rule... or duty, prescribed by God; any voluntary transgression of the divine law, or violation of a divine command; ...voluntary...neglect of known duty." In other words, Deuteronomy 28:1-2:

> 1   And it shall come to pass, if thou shalt hearken diligently unto the voice of the Lord thy God, to observe and to do all his commandments which I command thee this day, that the Lord thy God will set thee on high above all nations of the earth:

> 2 And all these blessings shall come on thee, and overtake thee, if thou shalt hearken unto the voice of the Lord thy God.

And Deuteronomy 28:15:

> 15 But it shall come to pass, if thou wilt not hearken unto the voice of the Lord thy God, to observe to do all his commandments and his statutes which I command thee this day; that all these curses shall come upon thee, and overtake thee.

The bottom line is this: God wants you blessed!

"Fear not" is a command. To continue in fear stops THE BLESSING. That's sin. Crying about it won't stop it. Being mad at yourself won't stop it. The simple solution is to repent according to 1 John 1:9:

> 9 If we confess our sins, he is faithful and just to forgive us our sins, and to cleanse us from all unrighteousness.

Remember now, to repent is to turn around and go up (or out). It is never based on a feeling of guilt or any other "feeling." It is based on faith in what verse 9 says—He is <u>faithful.</u> Believe it. Receive it. Say it. Then, in this case, turn to 4:18:

> 18 There is no fear in love; but perfect love casteth out fear: because fear hath torment. He that feareth is not made perfect in love.

Now act on that verse, and you've dealt with fear. Take your stand! <u>THE BLESSING</u> is released. It <u>will</u> grow unless you violate it with your words or actions. If you do violate it, <u>repent!</u> <u>Now!</u> How many times? How ever many times it takes. Constantly remind yourself: "My Lord wants me BLESSED." THE BLESSING is working, so keep it that way. Everything around you will come under its influence. In time your whole life—everything—will no longer look like this old, dead world of sin. Instead, it will seem to you as "days of heaven on earth." Deuteronomy 11:21-22:

> 21 That your days may be multiplied, and the days of your children, in the land which the Lord sware unto your fathers to give them, as the days of heaven upon the earth.
>
> 22 For if ye shall diligently keep all these commandments which I command you, to do them, to love the Lord your God, to walk in all his ways, and to cleave unto him;

As you sow your financial seeds of faith this month, remember the open door. No man or devil can stop your harvest from coming <u>this year.</u> It's yours now. Not sometime in the future. It's now. Call it. You're blessed. It cannot refuse your shout of faith.

Thank you from the very bottom of my heart for being our Partner. Gloria and I love you and pray for you every day.

Love,

Ken

May 2007

I Am the Seed!

Dear Partner,

Say it out loud, "I am the seed!"

Let's look at Genesis 26:1-5:

1. And there was a famine in the land, beside the first famine that was in the days of Abraham. And Isaac went unto Abimelech king of the Philistines unto Gerar.
2. And the Lord appeared unto him, and said, Go not down into Egypt; dwell in the land which I shall tell thee of:
3. Sojourn in this land, and I will be with thee, and will bless thee; for unto thee, and unto thy seed, I will give all these countries, <u>and I will perform the oath</u> which I sware unto Abraham thy father;
4. And I will make thy seed to multiply as the stars of heaven, and will give unto thy seed all these countries; and in thy seed shall all the nations of the earth be blessed;
5. Because that Abraham obeyed my voice, and kept my charge, my commandments, my statutes, and my laws.

Notice what the Lord said to Isaac in verse 3: "I will perform the oath." Remember now, verse 2 says the Lord appeared to Isaac personally. So He was speaking to him face to face when He said, "I will perform!" That's how serious He was about THE BLESSING. He called it His Oath. In fact it was a Blood-sworn Oath, wasn't it? <u>He was standing in blood</u> when He swore His Oath to bless Abraham. Abraham obeyed God's voice and kept His commandments, so THE BLESSING now was on the life of Isaac.

This was in a time of famine and lack, yet the Lord said don't leave. Stay here and I will perform. Perform what? The Blood Oath. To do what? <u>THE BLESSING.</u> In the final analysis, Isaac had to have faith not only in God but in THE BLESSING. The bottom line is this: THE BLESSING is God performing His Word. His Word is a Blood-sworn Oath. That's how serious His Word is to us who believe.

Now let's hook this together with Galatians 3:8-14:

> 8   And the scripture, foreseeing that God would justify the heathen through faith, preached before the gospel unto Abraham, saying, In thee shall all nations be blessed.
> 9   So then they which be of faith are blessed with faithful Abraham.
> 10   For as many as are of the works of the law are under the curse: for it is written, Cursed is every one that continueth not in all things which are written in the book of the law to do them.
> 11   But that no man is justified by the law in the sight of God, it is evident: for, The just shall live by faith.
> 12   And the law is not of faith: but, The man that doeth them shall live in them.
> 13   Christ hath redeemed us from the curse of the law, being made a curse for us: for it is written, Cursed is every one that hangeth on a tree:
> 14   That the blessing of Abraham might come on the Gentiles through Jesus Christ; that we might receive the promise of the Spirit through faith.

Verse 11 says the just shall live by faith. Faith in what? THE BLESSING! The Blood-sworn Oath that God Himself swore to Abraham, Isaac, Jacob, Joseph, David, Moses, Jesus—and, through Him, <u>you!</u> And <u>me!</u> It's time to shout amen!

When God spoke THE BLESSING upon Adam, He released the supernatural power that was to control this entire universe. The same creative power that brought the Garden of Eden into being was now on Adam's life to expand and control, or subdue, the earth and have dominion over it. Adam lost it. So God found a man named Abram and swore to BLESS him with this same power from heaven. We read the final results in Galatians 3:8-13. Now look at verses 28 and 29:

> 28 There is neither Jew nor Greek, there is neither bond nor free, there is neither male nor female: for ye are all one in Christ Jesus.
> 29 And if ye be Christ's, then are ye Abraham's seed, and heirs according to the promise.

I don't care where you come from. I don't care what color your skin is—whether you are male, female, black, brown, red, white, yellow or a combination of all the above. Rich man, poor man, beggar man or thief, if you receive Jesus then are you Abraham's <u>seed</u> and heir according to <u>The Promise</u>—the <u>Blood-sworn Oath in the blood of Jesus</u> that Almighty God, the Creator of all things, will perform.

Perform what? THE BLESSING. He made Abraham rich. He's made you rich. Healing is yours. Wonderful peace and joy beyond imagination is yours. All of that is yours while you're here on earth. Heaven is yet to come. The best part of all is Life. God's Life. His Spirit. His Word. His Light. His Love. HIMSELF!! All part of THE BLESSING.

Say it again. "I'm the seed. I'm blessed. I'm healed. I'm rich. I belong to Jesus. Jesus belongs to me. The earth is mine. Heaven is mine. Whatever belongs to Jesus belongs to me. I am His joint heir. I am BLESSED!"

Now don't do anything to mess that up. Walk in Love. Keep the commandment of Love. Think about it all the time. Every time you say, "I'm blessed," think about Love. The love of Jesus is why you're blessed. If you even think anything else, repent. I don't care what the situation is, it is not worth the risk of tearing THE BLESSING down from around you like Job did. Fight for it—fight the good fight of faith. Faith works by Love.

As you sow your financial seed this month, see yourself investing in THE BLESSING. We read in Galatians 3:8 that God preached the gospel to

Abraham when He swore to bless him. Jesus' blood is the guarantee of that Covenant Oath today. That's the gospel you and I are preaching worldwide.

We are blessed to be a blessing, and it's happening BIG-time. Jesus is carrying out the Father's Oath to perform. What a time to be alive!

Gloria and I love you and pray for you every day.

Love,

Ken

June 2007

What Is the Blood-Sworn Oath of God?

Dear Partner,

Let's begin today by reading Genesis 26:2-4:

> 2 And the Lord appeared unto [Isaac], and said, Go not down into Egypt; dwell in the land which I shall tell thee of:
> 3 Sojourn in this land, and I will be with thee, and will bless thee; for unto thee, and unto thy seed, I will give all these countries, and <u>I will perform the oath</u> which I sware unto Abraham thy father;
> 4 And I will make thy seed to multiply as the stars of heaven, and will give unto thy seed all these countries; and in thy seed shall all the nations of the earth be blessed.

Notice in verse 3 the phrase "I will perform the <u>oath</u> which I swore to Abraham your father." Why would the Creator Himself use such strong language to a man? He could have merely said, "I will do it." Since He is God, it wouldn't have been any less true. Lying is <u>impossible</u> for Him.

Hebrews 6:17:

> 17 Wherein God, willing more abundantly to show unto the heirs of promise the immutability of his counsel, confirmed it by an oath.

The meaning of *immutability* in that verse is "not capable of or susceptible to change; never changing or varying." In Texan that translates to "He ain't about to change—ever!"

Now let's read verses 13-17 of that same chapter:

13	For when God made promise to Abraham, because he could swear by no greater, he sware by himself,
14	Saying, Surely blessing I will bless thee, and multiplying I will multiply thee.
15	And so, after he had patiently endured, he obtained the promise.
16	For men verily swear by the greater: and an oath for confirmation is to them an end of all strife [argument].
17	Wherein God, willing more abundantly to show unto the heirs of promise the immutability of his counsel, confirmed it by an oath.

When we hear the term "sworn oath" or "under oath," we think of a courtroom or legal hearing where testimony is given after swearing before God to tell the truth. In Abraham and Isaac's day, it referred to a blood-sworn oath or swearing made in blood. This is an oath with punishment of death if it is broken.

God Himself was <u>standing in blood</u> when He made that Covenant Oath to Abraham in Genesis 15. Standing in blood, He swore by Himself that He would keep this covenant or die. Why? To get THE BLESSING back that Adam forsook. That's how serious THE BLESSING was and is to Him. That's also how doubly serious it should be to you and me.

That swearing by Himself to perform is what produced the coming of Jesus into the earth. God had to have His own blood—sinless—in which to carry out or perform His Oath to Abraham, and through Abraham to Jesus, <u>and through Jesus to you and me.</u>

Wait...wait...don't shout just yet. There's more. Jesus came. The Word (Oath) took upon itself flesh (blood) and walked among us. Sinless and true, He walked before God, commanding and controlling as Adam before Him should have done using THE BLESSING to heal the sick and raise the dead, to stop storms and cast out satan, the leader of devils.

Then the unthinkable happened. God, manifested in the flesh, sacrificed Himself as though He had broken the sworn Oath Covenant. He went to hell and suffered for it. He established the Oath forever, not in animals' blood <u>but in His own precious, sinless blood</u> as a lamb slaughtered. That settled it forever!

Now the <u>man</u> Jesus stands in <u>the</u> Covenant of THE BLESSING between Him and the Almighty Creator Himself. Now <u>THE BLESSING OATH COVENANT</u> can never be broken. It is established in <u>holy</u> blood. It is between God who is immutable and Jesus an immortal man. Sin is impossible between them.

Now shout! You and I can't break that covenant. We can break our fellowship with it, but never can we, or anyone, break the forever Covenant Blood Oath of THE BLESSING. Why all this? So that THE BLESSING could come on the Gentiles through the Anointing (the Holy Ghost power of THE BLESSING) of Jesus that <u>we</u> might receive the promise, the Oath, to Abraham by the Holy Spirit. We are the seed. We are the heirs of this world according to Romans 4:13.

So how do we receive all this? The big problem in the minds of most Christians has always been how does one get God to perform? He has never changed and never will. Abraham did it by faith in that oath. Jesus did it the same way. So did the Apostle Paul and all the people who have known the Lord Jesus down through the centuries. He has <u>never</u> changed. He is the same yesterday, today and forever.

Faith comes by hearing this message of the real meaning of the blood of the Lamb and His sworn Oath over and over and over and over, until your spirit is full to overflowing. THE BLESSING will begin as a seed and grow and grow inside you until it comes through your body healing all your flesh. It will continue and spread outward toward all your circumstances, changing and blessing everything and everyone who will allow it. It will continue to grow and spread just as long as you keep the command of Love and feed your spirit continually on the Word (the Oath of Blood).

Now Mark 11:22-25 really takes on vital importance in our lives:

    22   And Jesus answering saith unto them, Have faith in God.
    23   For verily I say unto you, That whosoever shall

	say unto this mountain, Be thou removed, and be thou cast into the sea; and shall not doubt in his heart, but shall believe that those things which he saith shall come to pass; he shall have whatsoever he saith.
24	Therefore I say unto you, What things soever ye desire, when ye pray, believe that ye receive them, and ye shall have them.
25	And when ye stand praying, forgive, if ye have aught against any: that your Father also which is in heaven may forgive you your trespasses.

No wonder Hebrews 11:6 says it is <u>impossible</u> to please God without faith. Faith is THE BLESSING connection with Him so He can <u>perform</u> His Blood-Sworn Oath in our lives.

Shout, "I'm blessed!" Shout it again. Go around the room and bless everything you can touch. Bless your body a living sacrifice to Jesus—a body for Him to use in your world to perform His Word in the lost and sick. That's our first job as Partners. We are connected by His divine calling according to Ephesians 4:16.

This is the message of the hour for this ministry. We are shouting it worldwide to let people know who they are in Christ Jesus—THE BLESSED of the Lord.

As you sow your financial seed this month <u>BLESS</u> it. Harvest it before you sow it. <u>THE BLESSING</u> makes rich and He adds no sorrow to it.

Gloria and I love you and pray for you every day.

Love,

Ken

July 2007

Who Are You—<u>Really?</u>

Dear Partner,

What is your background?

Where are you from?

That's what they asked when I was younger, when really they wanted to know what produced someone's personality, traits and such. What are you really like—not just on the surface, but for real? Who will you become when the problems arise? Now, of course, they want your DNA.

All of that was relevant until you made Jesus Lord of your life. What happened then?

That changed everything.

First, let's go back to Adam's <u>creation.</u> He was not just formed. He was <u>created.</u> From what? Nothing? No. Absolutely not. <u>Everything</u> started with seed. The first seed ever was the Word of <u>God</u>—<u>The</u> Creator. John 1:1-3 says,

> 1 In the beginning was the Word, and the Word was with God, and the Word was God.
> 2 The same was in the beginning with God.
> 3 All things were made by him; and without him was not any thing made that was made.

In Genesis 1:3 the Bible tells us exactly what that first seed was: "Light BE! Light was!" Then in 1 John 1:5:

> 5 This then is the message which we have heard of him, and declare unto you, that God is light, and in him is no darkness at all.

God is absolute light. <u>Sunshine was not created until day four,</u> so

"Light be! Light was!" was the releasing of THE light, the power of His Glory. That's still the sustaining, holding power of the universe today. Look at Hebrews 1:2-3:

> 2   Hath in these last days spoken unto us by his Son, whom he hath appointed heir of all things, by whom also he made the worlds;
>
> 3   Who being the brightness of his glory, and the express image of his person, and upholding all things by the word of his power, when he had by himself purged our sins, sat down on the right hand of the Majesty on high.

Jesus, the <u>Brightness</u> of <u>His</u> Glory, is upholding all things by that same God-Himself-Glory-Power originally released by His Word—which is, after all, Himself.

Remember, now Jesus is a resurrected man. A <u>glorified</u> man. He was made to be sin. He was raised, <u>created</u> anew by what power? The answer to that question is Romans 6:4—Jesus was raised up from the dead by the Glory of the Father. What is the DNA of Jesus—the resurrected Lord of Glory? Spirit, soul, body through and through: THE GLORY—THE FULLNESS—THE WORD—THE LIGHT—THE LOVE—<u>ALL</u> <u>God</u>!

Yet He is a flesh and bone man. Not flesh and <u>blood,</u> but flesh and bone. Luke 24:39:

> 39   Behold my hands and my feet, that it is I myself: handle me, and see; for a spirit hath not flesh and bones, as ye see me have.

The Glory is flowing in His veins!!

That's who Jesus is. But who are you? Let's look first at 2 Corinthians 5:17:

> 17   Therefore if any man be in Christ, he is a new <u>creature</u> [creation]: old things are passed

away; behold, all things are become new.

So you—your spirit man—has been re-created. You are more than forgiven. Remember, now, how God creates. He never, ever changes. He creates by His Word. First Peter 1:23 is the base of your spiritual DNA:

> 23 Being born again, not of corruptible seed, but of incorruptible, by the word of God, which liveth and abideth for ever.

Ephesians 5:8:

> 8 For ye were sometimes darkness, but now are ye light in the Lord: walk as children [born] of light.

You were, before you were reborn by the Word, darkness. But NOW (say "Now!") you are light. First Thessalonians 5:5 says you are a child of Light. Psalm 104:2 says God covers Himself with light as with a garment. Remember, you and I are born of His seed! Romans 13:12 commands us to do the same thing: "Put on the armour of light." Then 1 John 1:7 makes the same command:

> 7 But if we walk in the light, as he is in the light, we have fellowship one with another, and the blood of Jesus Christ his Son cleanseth us from all sin.

How, then, are we to do that? The clue to it is in Romans 13:9:

> 9 For this, Thou shalt not commit adultery, Thou shalt not kill, Thou shalt not steal, Thou shalt not bear false witness, Thou shalt not covet; and if there be any other commandment, it is briefly comprehended in this saying, namely, Thou shalt love thy neighbour as thyself.

Love! Keep the commandment of Love. Walk in Love and faith. Walking in Love is walking in God who is Light, who is the Word. Are you beginning to see it? First John 2:9-11 spells it out:

> 9   He that saith he is in the light, and hateth his brother, is in darkness even until now.
> 10 He that loveth his brother abideth in the light, and there is none occasion of stumbling in him.
> 11 But he that hateth his brother is in darkness, and walketh in darkness, and knoweth not whither he goeth, because <u>that darkness hath blinded his eyes.</u>

And again in 3:14:

> 14 We know that we have passed from death unto life, because we love the brethren. He that loveth not his brother abideth in death.

The Love book, 1 John, explains all this (remember 1:5, "This then is <u>the</u> <u>message</u>...that God is light"). Right in the beginning it tells the way to walk in the Light with Jesus: Repent by faith—not by feelings of guilt or sorrow.

Abraham <u>believed God,</u> so it was accounted unto him as righteousness. In other words, God dealt with him as though he had not sinned. We <u>are</u> the righteousness of God, and the Blood of Jesus cleanses us from <u>all</u> sin—<u>if</u> we believe God!

Faith is the key. The key is not in feeling guilty, nor in feelings or emotions of any kind. Of course you feel bad. Of course guilt tries to come all over you. But what does the Word of Light say about it? First John 1:9:

> 9   If we confess our sins, he is faithful and just to forgive us our sins, and to cleanse us from all unrighteousness.

What is the key word here? He, Jesus, is <u>faithful</u> and He is <u>righteous</u>—faithful and righteous to forgive, faithful and righteous to cleanse us from <u>all</u> unrighteousness.

When? After you've grieved and sorrowed about it for long enough? After you've done enough good deeds to offset whatever you did to violate His commandment of Love?

No! When you confess it before Him and <u>believe</u> He is faithful and righteous: "Lord, I confess the sin of _____. I did that. It was wrong. I see in Your Word when I confess sin before You, You are faithful and righteous to forgive me <u>and</u> cleanse me from <u>all</u> unrighteousness. I receive Your ministry as my Lord and Savior right now. I receive my forgiveness. I receive my cleansing. I cast all sin out of my life NOW! I stand on Your Word. I am, by faith, forgiven and clean before You. I stand in Your pure, precious blood. I stand in the Light of Your Glory." (Read Romans 8:1-2 right now—out loud.)

Now walk in that Light. Your mind, your body, your feelings may still have symptoms of the sin. The devil will try to pull you back into your feelings, especially when you come into contact with other people. Don't fall for that. Stay in the Light! Stay on the Word! The Blood-cleansing process is working. It's cleansing from <u>all</u> sin.

Let's close by looking at Isaiah 43:25-26:

> 25 I, even I, am he that blotteth out thy transgressions for mine own sake, and will not remember thy sins.
> 26 Put me in remembrance: let us plead together: declare thou, that thou mayest be justified.

Your Lord and Savior is offering you <u>His</u> mind cleansed of all <u>your</u> sin. Now fill His mind with what you want Him to remember about you, not with how badly you <u>feel</u> or how unworthy you are. Fill <u>His</u> mind and yours with words of faith and redemption. With new-creation scriptures. With grace and mercy, love and goodness. Greater is He who is in you than he who is trying to remind you of your sin and shortcomings.

Do you see it? Walk in it. It will walk in you. You are blessed! Jesus is Lord! Believe it.

As you sow your financial seed this month, release your faith for a manifestation of the Glory. It's in you. It's your DNA. Rise up and let it shine.

Gloria and I love you very much. We pray for you every day.

Love,

Ken

"I have to say again how much we appreciate our Partners for helping us lay hold of the Citation X. Having this wonderful ministry tool enables us to say 'yes' at a moment's notice to world-changing inviations."

August 2007

Love—The Key to Life Without Fear

Dear Partner

Have I got a shout of praise in my spirit and in my mouth!

Gloria and I have just returned from China where we met with pastors and spiritual leaders from all over the nation. We had a glorious three days together that I can hardly wait to tell you about. Because of the sensitivity and classified nature of the details, I can't put it in a letter. But I will tell you about it in our Partner services during the Believers' Conventions. I will say this—our God is on the move! And you and I are right in the middle of it all!

The Citation X did a marvelous job getting us there and back refreshed and rested. It was just great. I don't have the words to express to you how very grateful we are to the Lord Jesus and to all of our Partners for providing that wonderful, anointed tool with which to get our job done.

Yesterday while I was praying over this letter, I was reminded by the Holy Spirit of something He said to me about two years ago. It startled me then, and it had the same effect on me yesterday. So simple, but oh so profound! He said, <u>Fear connects to the spirit of fear, and faith connects to the Spirit of faith.</u>

That is so obvious, but at the same time it is a thought that never crosses the minds of most people. This is very serious business. Life and death business. One could just as easily have said, "Fear connects to the spirit of death. Faith connects to the Spirit of life." Remember, now, 2 Timothy 1:7:

> 7 For God hath not given us the spirit of fear; but of power, and of love, and of a sound mind.

We can see in that one verse the plain difference between the spirit of fear and the Spirit of power, the Spirit of Love and the Spirit of a sound mind. A mind under the influence of fear is not a sound mind. Let's look at 2 Corinthians 4:13-14:

> 13 We having the same Spirit of faith, according as it is written, I believed, and therefore have I spoken; we also believe, and therefore speak;
> 14 Knowing that he [the Spirit of faith] which raised up the Lord Jesus shall raise up us also by Jesus, and shall present us with you.

Let's look at this in the light of Romans 8:2:

> 2 For the law of the Spirit of life in Christ Jesus hath made me free from the law of sin and death.

There is no way the spirit of fear can be a part of the Law of the Spirit of Life in Christ Jesus. <u>There is no fear in Christ Jesus.</u> In fact just the opposite is true. The Law of Christ Jesus is the Law of Love, and perfected Love casts out fear. Let's look at that in 1 John 4:18:

> 18 There is no fear in love; but perfect love casteth out fear: because fear hath torment. He that feareth is not made perfect in love.

Notice in that verse that fear has torment. So the spirit of fear is the tormentor. In Matthew 4:24 Jesus healed the sick, tormented, devil-possessed people. Now we can begin to see why this is such a huge and profound statement. Fear connects to the spirit of fear, and faith connects to the Spirit of faith.

One of the major problems in all this is a lack of recognition of fear's presence in everyday life. Most people only recognize fear as fright. But being frightened is only a small part of fear. Unless Love is working casting fear out, then fear is there working to connect and open the door to the spirit of fear—all the time.

Worry is a manifestation of fear. Negative thinking is an expression of fear. Struggling to believe God's Word is a serious sign of fear's presence.

Depression is a big manifestation of fear. Depression's twin brother grief and all forms of loss, large and small, are fear's calling cards.

Fear's job is to hinder, harass, trouble and try to stop the anointing any way it can. Think about it. The spirit of fear and the spirit of antichrist are the same spirit—satan!

Now let's look at the Law of Jesus. First John 3:23:

> 23 And this is his commandment, That we should believe on the name of his Son Jesus Christ, and love one another, as he gave us commandment.

What does faith in the Name of Jesus do? It casts out the devil. What does perfected Love do? It casts out fear. Now look at verse 24:

> 24 And he that keepeth his commandments dwelleth in him, and he in him. And hereby we know that he abideth in us, by the <u>Spirit which he hath given us.</u>

<u>He has not given us the spirit of fear.</u> Remember who the Spirit is that He has given us? We read it in 2 Timothy 1:7. The Spirit of power! The Spirit of Love! And the Spirit of a sound mind!

It's time to shout amen! That's the gift of God. That's the Spirit you've been given. And that's the Spirit who desires to fill every thought, every situation, every moment of your life. Since you have not been given the spirit of fear, refuse to give him any place. Not one thought. Not one word. Not one moment of time. No!

At the very first sign of fear speak to it, "No you don't!" Then remind yourself of John 17:23, "My heavenly Father loves me just as much as He does Jesus. I keep the commandment of Love in my life. The Law of Jesus is the law of my life. There is no place for fear, worry, doubt, depression or any other kind of fear in my life. I am developing the Love of God in my life. I am developing the Spirit of faith—the Law of the Spirit of Life in Christ Jesus."

Now that stirs up the gift of God in your life. And it literally flushes out fear and everything that's connected to it, leaving no room for anything but Love who is God.

Let's close by reading one of the prayers we pray together every day. You see it noted on every letter I write. Ephesians 3:14-20:

14   For this cause I bow my knees unto the Father of our Lord Jesus Christ,
15   Of whom the whole family in heaven and earth is named,
16   That he would grant you, according to the riches of his glory, to be strengthened with might by his Spirit in the inner man;
17   That Christ may dwell in your hearts by faith; that ye, being <u>rooted and grounded in love,</u>
18   May be able to comprehend [because of your sound mind] with all saints what is the breadth, and length, and depth, and height;
19   And to know the love of Christ, which passeth knowledge, that ye might be filled with all the fulness of God.
20   Now unto him that is able to do exceeding abundantly above all that we ask or think, according to the power that worketh in us.

Filled with the fullness of God! Go for it.

As you pray over your financial seed this month, release your faith for the fullness of God to overflow everything that's yours. That's what I'm praying for you all this month.

Gloria and I love you very much and we're holding you up in faith every day.

Love,

Ken

September 2007

It's Time to Shout in the House of Faith!

Dear Partner

What a summer this has been! In fact, this whole year has been a constantly flowing, flood-like moving of the Holy Spirit everywhere Gloria and I have been. In every place—Rome, Nigeria, China, the West Coast Believers' Convention, every TV broadcast—the presence of God has been above and beyond what we've experienced before. My personal prayer and study time is the greatest it's ever been.

It is truly what the Lord said—the year of the open door. To top all that off, I've lost the 30 pounds I've been after all these years. Not only that, it was the easiest thing I've ever done.

Whatever in your life needs changing, now is the time to get it done.

How?

First—get <u>honest</u> with God. Get <u>honest</u> with yourself. *Honest* comes from the word *honor*. Get out of the shadows and stand in the full light of God's Word. First Corinthians 11:31 says

> 31 For if we would judge ourselves, we should not be judged.

We're not talking about self-abasement or self-condemnation. To judge yourself is to look <u>honestly</u> at yourself in the light of the Word—not in the shadow of hiding things you know should be separated from your life. Be blunt. Be strong. Stand up and face it, whatever it is. Call it sin! Say it out loud. Don't be afraid of what the Lord might do—He's known it was there all along. He said to me one day, *Kenneth, when you confessed that sin was not when I found out about it. That's when you got rid of it!*

Now, by faith, receive your forgiveness. At this point, you should be standing before the throne of grace with your Bible in your hand. That's where faith, hope and love come from. Read aloud 1 John 1:6-9:

> 6 If we say that we have fellowship with him, and walk in darkness, we lie, and do not the truth:
> 7 But if we walk in the light, as he is in the light, we have fellowship one with another, and the blood of Jesus Christ his Son cleanseth us from all sin.
> 8 If we say that we have no sin, we deceive ourselves, and the truth is not in us.
> 9 If we confess our sins, he is faithful and just to forgive us our sins, and to cleanse us from all unrighteousness.

Speak to your Lord and <u>Savior</u>: "Lord Jesus, I see here You are faithful and just (or righteous) to forgive me and cleanse me from all unrighteousness. I have confessed <u>all</u> these things openly before You, holding nothing back.

"I know from Your Word You are this moment forgiving me and cleansing me. For You not to forgive me and cleanse me right now, as I confessed these things, would mean You are not faithful. That can't be true. It would mean You are not righteous and just—THAT'S IMPOSSIBLE! You are my High Priest. You are my Lord and Savior.

"At this moment I release my faith, I believe I receive my forgiveness. I believe I receive my cleansing at <u>(time of day)</u> on <u>(today's date)</u>. It is done in Jesus' Name."

The second step is to turn to Isaiah 43:25-26 and read aloud:

> 25 I, even I, am he that blotteth out thy transgressions for mine own sake, and will not remember thy sins.
> 26 Put me in remembrance: let us plead together: declare thou, that thou mayest be justified.

Now receive it: "My Lord Jesus loves me. My heavenly Father loves me as much as He does Jesus according to John 17:23. Not only has He forgiven and cleansed me, but He has also purged His own memory from any wrongdoing in my life. He has done this not just for my sake, but for His own sake. He loves me. He doesn't want to remember any bad things about me."

Look at verse 26 again:

> 26 Put me in remembrance: let us plead together: declare thou, that thou mayest be justified.

There is now a blank page in His memory, and He is inviting you to fill it up with good things from His Word about you. Begin right now and keep filling it up from this moment on: "Oh, thank You, Father. I am so blessed. <u>THE BLESSING</u> of Abraham has come. Blessed is the man whose sins are removed (Psalm 32:1-2; Romans 4:6-8). I'm a new creature in Christ Jesus. All of the old things are passed away. I'm clean in Your loving eyes. You love me and I love You. I love You with all my heart, all my soul, all my strength. I love You, Father, and I love my neighbor as myself because that pleases You. I love You, therefore I love Your children—<u>all of them.</u> Your love is shed abroad in my heart by the Holy Ghost. I walk in Your love."

Every time a symptom of that old life—like guilt, or feelings of grief and sorrow over your sinful past—tries to creep into your mind or your feelings, shout, "<u>No!</u> Jesus is faithful. I'm free from the law of sin and death. My Father has cleansed His mind of that, and so do I. I am blessed, satan, and the Bible is very clear. You cannot curse someone whom God has blessed." Go back through Isaiah 43:25-26 and 1 John 1:6-9 laughing at the devil and telling your Savior how much you love Him.

The third step is to check your diet.

1. What are you feeding your spirit?
2. What are you feeding your mind?
3. What are you feeding your body?

Trash in, trash out. Death in, death out.

God's Word in; faith, hope, love, healing, wealth—THE BLESSING—released. Love in; fear out. Good food in; fat off. Joy released. That's just the way it is. Face it. Embrace it. And life's greatest blessing begins to flow. It's flowing now. Get in it.

"Oh, but Brother Copeland, I've tried before and failed so many times." I know it. So have I. Don't quit. This is your year. Jesus has opened your door of victory, breakthrough and overflow, and the devil cannot shut it on you.

Do it now. Today. It's not enough to know what to do. You must act on what the Lord Jesus has revealed to you in this letter.

Just as soon as you go through these steps I've outlined, bring the Lord an offering—a seed toward your new life. Whether you sow it into this ministry or not is between you and the Lord Jesus.

Think about it. It's clean seed. Fresh before the eyes of the Lord. Now get your eyes off the seed and fix them on the Lord of the Harvest—Jesus of Nazareth, the High Priest who <u>ministers</u> bread to the eater. Who <u>ministers</u> seed to the sower. He <u>ministers</u> the multiplying of your seed sown, and He ministers the increase of the <u>fruits of your righteousness!</u>

It's harvest time, and it's time to shout in the house of faith!

Gloria and I love you very much and we pray for you every day.

Love,

Ken

October 2007

In the Beginning God!

Dear Partner

Let's begin our letter this month at THE beginning, Genesis 1:1—In the beginning God....

In the English Bible the word *God* doesn't give us very much. It simply means "supreme being." One dictionary adds "possibly creator of all things." To some people, *god* means a tree or a rock. To others, it is an object or idol that they look to as god.

Several different names in the Hebrew language are translated *God* in English. In Hebrew these names are very plain in their description of our heavenly Father, but the word *God* gives us none of those insights into His ways, His will or who He actually is. That's where His Word comes in.

Let's look at John 1:1-3:

1 In the beginning was the Word, and the Word was with God, and the Word was God.
2 The same was in the beginning with God.
3 All things were made by him; and without him was not any thing made that was made.

Now we know that God and His Word are the same. We also know there is nothing in existence that He—His Word—did not create.

Now let's go to 1 John 1:5:

5 This then is the message which we have heard of him, and declare unto you, that God is light, and in him is no darkness at all.

So now "In the beginning was the Word, God, Light—the same...."

Let's add to that 1 John 4:7-8:

> 7 Beloved, let us love one another: for love is of God; and every one that loveth is born of God, and knoweth God.
> 8 He that loveth not knoweth not God; for God is love.

So "In the beginning was the Word—Light—Love—God...."

John 1:4 says that God is Life, so in the beginning was the Word, Light, Love, Life, God—the <u>same.</u> ALL <u>things</u> were made by Him—the Word, Light, Love, Life, God—and without the Word, Light, Love, Life, God was not <u>any</u>-<u>thing</u> made that was made.

Think about it. This Bible is the Word of God, the Word of Light, the Word of Love and the Word of Life. Now look at what this divine information does to John 1:14.

The Word was <u>made</u> flesh.

God was <u>made</u> flesh.

Light was <u>made</u> flesh.

Love was <u>made</u> flesh.

<u>This book is not about someone. It *is* Someone!</u>

All of this is very exciting, I know, but what does it mean to us who believe? Go with me to 1 Peter 1:23:

> 23 Being born again, not of corruptible seed, but of incorruptible, by the word of God, which liveth and abideth for ever.

You are <u>born</u> of <u>The</u> Light. That's the very energy that holds this universe together. It's in you now and you can walk in it. As you do, it will continually draw on the Blood of Jesus to cleanse from all sin. Read these words of LIGHT:

Ephesians 5:8:

> 8   For ye were sometimes darkness, but now are ye light in the Lord: walk as children of light.

First Thessalonians 5:5:

> 5   Ye are all the children of light, and the children of the day: we are not of the night, nor of darkness.

Romans 13:12:

> 12   The night is far spent, the day is at hand: let us therefore cast off the works of darkness, and let us put on the armor of light.

How do you walk in all that Light energy? Walk in the Word. At the same time remember God is Love. What happens when we put God's Word first place, final authority in our lives? Look at 1 John 2:5:

> 5   But whoso keepeth his word, in him verily is the love of God perfected: hereby know we that we are in him.

This is talking about committing ourselves completely to being good stewards of the command of Jesus. This is our first calling in life. <u>Job No. 1!</u> When that happens, God—the Word, Light, Love, Life—takes over. That's when perfected Love casts out fear. That's when faith is released. Suddenly the curse has to bow its knee to the Name of Jesus and confess with its mouth that Jesus is Lord and leave your spirit, leave your mind, will and emotions and totally vacate your body. It has to take its hands off your family and get completely out of your finances.

Then what? <u>THE BLESSING explosion!</u> Be fruitful, multiply and fill up the earth around you with His glory. The earth will be subdued and your dominion in Jesus' Name will take over. No wonder James said be a doer of the Word and not a hearer only. He called <u>the Word the perfect law of liberty.</u>

Write these scripture verses down and meditate them. Faith cometh by hearing and hearing by the Word of God who is Light, Love, Life. Faith in the Word itself. Your Bible will become the most precious thing in your life. You will quickly become so attached to it you'll never want to be anywhere without it. It is <u>God</u>—the Word—in your life. His Name is Jesus. He and this Word are one.

Remember, this Book is not about someone. It *is* Someone. This Book is not about Jesus. It is Jesus. It is His Life. It is His power. It is your future, your health, your protection and your prosperity. Read this paragraph again, aloud.

This is the message, John said in 1 John 1:5, from the beginning. It's our message in these last days, and you and I are taking it from the top of the world to the bottom, and all the way around the middle.

As you sow your financial seed this month, lay hands on it and speak <u>the Word</u> of life into it. Then immediately get your eyes on the Lord of the Harvest. Speak words of harvest. Begin declaring His words of harvest and grace abounding toward you.

Keep 2 Corinthians 9:8-10 before your eyes night and day. Keep it in your mouth. When you speak, the harvest hears Jesus. I'm shouting it over your harvest. You shout it over mine. Together we will get it <u>done</u>!

Gloria and I love you and we pray for you every day.

Love,

Ken

November 2007

Believe You Receive

Dear Partner,

"Oh, Brother Copeland, there are some awfully wicked things happening in this ol' world."

I know that. But the most wonderful things that have ever happened are also taking place. It just depends on where you are and with Whom you spend your time.

There is no place on this earth where there is no move of God. He is moving big-time among every tongue and tribe throughout the whole earth. If one could see all the times in the history of God's work in the earth and choose the time in which to live, this would be the time of choice. You and I are right in the middle of it, and some of it is happening because we're here. Are we blessed or what?

Let's look at a phrase from 1 John 4:16:

> 16 And we have known and believed the love that God hath to us. God is love; and he that dwelleth in love dwelleth in God, and God in him.

We have known and <u>believed.</u> Now Mark 11:24:

> 24 Therefore I say unto you, What things soever ye desire, when ye pray, believe that ye receive them, and ye shall have them.

<u>Believe</u> you receive. Now Luke 8:50:

> 50 But when Jesus heard it, he answered him, saying, Fear not: believe only, and she shall be made whole.

Fear not; <u>believe</u> only. Now Romans 10:9:

> 9   That if thou shalt confess with thy mouth the Lord Jesus, and shalt believe in thine heart that God hath raised him from the dead, thou shalt be saved.

<u>Believe</u> in your heart. We could go on and on with example after example, because it's throughout the Bible. In fact it is the purpose of the Bible. Over the years people have struggled, analyzed, discussed, fussed and fought over what believing is, why and how it works.

The first thing one must do in order to begin to understand *believing* in the verses we just read is separate mental acknowledgment from believing. Mental acknowledgment comes from the processing of natural information that is gathered through the five physical sense gates—seeing, hearing, touch, smell and taste. All of the world's education is based on this process.

Believing with the heart, however, is a different thing altogether and utilizes a different system altogether. Simply put, believing with the heart and processing with the mind are two different things. The mind is involved in both, but in one it plays a lesser role than in the other. That's obvious when you think about it.

The first big obstacle is believing something you cannot see. We can, however, settle that issue by listening to Jesus minister to Thomas about this very thing. In John 20:26-29, Jesus very plainly spelled it all out:

> 26   And after eight days again his disciples were within, and Thomas with them: then came Jesus, the doors being shut, and stood in the midst, and said, Peace be unto you.
> 27   Then saith he to Thomas, Reach hither thy finger, and behold my hands; and reach hither thy hand, and thrust it into my side: and be not faithless, but believing.
> 28   And Thomas answered and said unto him, My Lord and my God.

29	Jesus saith unto him, Thomas, <u>because thou hast seen me,</u> thou hast believed: <u>blessed are they that have not seen, and yet have believed.</u>

One system requires no faith and the other depends on it. One system—the faith system—is connected to <u>THE BLESSING,</u> and the other is not. Each system has its source of information that it depends on. The mental processing system depends on the five senses. The heart system is totally dependent on words from God. Romans 10:17 plainly states that. When it comes to believing something we can't feel or see, we make the shift from the mental processing system to the heart, or spirit, system.

Believing something before you see it requires faith. Faith is activated when the decision to believe is made and words such as "I choose to believe that" are spoken. Now that decision can be made and spoken about anything, but only the Word of God has the spiritual life to make the connection with your faith. If that connection is not made, your faith falls flat without bringing anything into being. Faith released in money, horsepower or any other natural power cannot make that connection.

Without that connection, your spirit man lies dormant along with all that <u>su</u>pernatural power Jesus has made available. It's in you, but it can't help when the need is there. That's the reason Jesus said your traditions make the Word of God of no effect (Matthew 15:6). People are saved, healed, prospered, etc., by hearing and believing WORDS.

Let's go back to Romans 10, this time looking at verses 13-17:

13	For whosoever shall call upon the name of the Lord shall be saved.
14	How then shall they call on him in whom they have not believed? and how shall they believe in him of whom they have not heard? and how shall they hear without a preacher?
15	And how shall they preach, except they be sent? as it is written, How beautiful are the feet of them that preach the gospel of peace, and bring glad tidings of good things!

> 16　But they have not all obeyed the gospel. For Esaias saith, Lord, who hath believed our report?
> 17　So then faith cometh by hearing, and hearing by the word of God.

Look carefully at the questions asked in verses 14 and 15:

Q. How then shall they call on Him in whom they have not believed?

A. They CAN'T.

Q. How shall they believe in Him of whom they have not heard?

A. They CAN'T!

Q. How shall they hear without a preacher?

A. THEY CAN'T!

Q. How shall they preach, except they be sent?

A. THEY CAN'T!

In closing, let's look at the "being sent" part. That's primarily pointing out that unless the preacher is sent and anointed to preach by God, he or she can't preach. However, what good is it if God directs a person to go, yet the one He sends lacks such essentials as food, clothing and transportation? God is the spiritual sender and the members of His Body are the natural senders. That's the way the Lord Jesus designed His operation in this earth to "go" into all the world and preach the gospel to every creature. In doing so, the sender reaps the same anointing, the same harvest, the same Blessing, and all the same rewards that the "goer" reaps.

The sender reaps on the same spiritual and natural level as the preacher. One is never less than the other. We actually become one in ministry together. We need one another completely. Partners! We are one with Jesus and we are one with one another. We depend on Jesus and He depends on us. It is the network of <u>THE BLESSING.</u> If you are a preacher, you are Blessed. If you are a sender, you are Blessed.

Read the scriptures in this letter again. Look at them and decide to BELIEVE them. Then say out loud, "I believe that."

Faith will go into action immediately in the spiritual realm just as surely as your natural digestive system goes into operation when you look at an item of food and eat it. You can't "feel" either one, but they do. When you say, "I believe the Love in 1 John 4:16," the faith, Blessing system goes into operation connecting your faith with God's faith and your love with His love.

I'm so thrilled in my spirit writing this, I could go on and on and on and on…

Read the healing verses that way. Read the financial verses, the family verses, the deliverance verses, the joy verses, the strength verses—whatever verses you need. Jesus is the High Priest of God over this Blessing system. That's the way you receive from His ministry. That's what He watches over to perform.

As you sow your financial seed this month, take the time to put THE BLESSING to work. Shout it out loud: "Go, Brother Kenneth! Go, Sister Gloria! I send you in the Name of Jesus to preach the Word. We go together! Together we'll get it done!"

I receive it. We are going and going and going and going and preaching and preaching and preaching…. Well, shout amen, somebody!!

Gloria and I love you very much and we pray for you every day.

Love,

Ken

December 2007

No Word = No faith
Know Word = Know faith

Dear Partner

I want to talk to you this month about a very important New Testament word. It is the word *KNOW*. We will be focusing on the Greek word *ginōskō*. There are other words translated *KNOW*, but they are not our focus right now.

This Greek word, used in the New Testament 185 times, has a core meaning that is very important to anyone who is seriously committed to the Lord Jesus, as you and I are. Because it also has a range of meaning that is not expressed in the English word "to know," it requires several different words to make clear what this word is saying to us. However once we <u>begin to *KNOW* more about "to know," the more we will know.</u>

Let's begin with some of the definitions that are more important to us as they pertain to the word:

1. To be taking in knowledge. To come to know. To recognize, as to know someone's voice.
2. To know or understand completely.
3. To show connection or union. For example, Adam <u>knew</u> his wife.
4. To develop an intimate relationship with—the deepening knowledge that comes from time spent together. (This is the depth of the core of its meaning and very important to us.)

Vine's Expository Dictionary of Biblical Words says of this—"Such 'knowledge' is obtained, not by mere intellectual activity, but by operation of the Holy Spirit...."

I'll say it like this: This knowing, or intimacy with, the Father and His Son Jesus is obtained through revelation of the Holy Spirit from being obedient to the Word and acting on it as quickly as we would the word of a doctor, lawyer or a highly trusted friend.

Far too many men and women truly fall in love, marry and have families, yet never get to know one another. It takes time spent with and deep trust in one another to develop this kind of deep, inner connection or union. This develops in the spirit by love in action— by loving in obedience to God's command all the time, not just when things are OK or when feelings are smooth, etc.

Let's look at this from the Word. First John 4:7-8:

> 7   Beloved, let us love one another: for love is of God; and every one that loveth is born of God, and knoweth God.
> 8   He that loveth not knoweth not God; for God is love.

Those two verses spell it out.

NO LOVE = NO GOD
KNOW LOVE = KNOW GOD

All of the previous definitions of *ginōskō* apply here in one way or another. The more you are obedient to His commandment of love, the more understanding you have of Jesus—the more you understand or know how He thinks and know, or have divine insight into, His acts and ways. Also the more you know Him by spending time with Him in His Word, the harder it is for satan to fool you. Why? Because you know—you recognize—His voice. The more you know Him, the more you know the Father.

Look at the Apostle Paul's fervent prayer in Philippians 3:10:

> 10   That I may know him, and the power of his resurrection, and the fellowship of his sufferings, being made conformable unto his death.

So I know, have deeper understanding, take in more knowledge, come to recognize and completely understand and develop a stronger connection and deeper union not only with Jesus—my Lord, Savior and High Priest of my life—but also with the power of His resurrection and the fellowship, or my partnership, with His sufferings.

Wow! People for centuries have been trying to "figure out" what all that means. They have built great traditions based on their figuring, but have had little intimate knowledge and revelation of any of it. Consequently, strange and failing doctrines have come forth about our sufferings, etc., that rob people of their faith. My part of His suffering is that because of His resurrection power I don't have to suffer. Hallelujah! However, you have to <u>know</u> Him to <u>know</u> that. Spending time with religion just won't get it.

I've spent the past 46 years getting to know Gloria. I've always <u>known</u> she was a wonderful, beautiful person. I've loved her since the first time I saw her. However, I've never loved her like I do now. Why? Because I've never <u>known</u> her like I *know* her now.

The night I met Jesus in November 1962, my life was changed forever. But now after staking my life on His Word in January 1967, I *know* Him. The more I *know,* the more I *must* know. I'll know more 41 years from now than I do now. And I'll know more 41 years after that than I do then. Eternity is not long enough to know all there is to know. But with God as our Father and personal teacher, <u>more</u> is on the way.

Sow toward that knowing. Read Galatians 6:7-8:

7   Be not deceived; God is not mocked: for whatsoever a man soweth, that shall he also reap.
8   For he that soweth to his flesh shall of the flesh reap corruption; but he that soweth to the Spirit shall of the Spirit reap <u>life</u> everlasting.

Look at verse 8: "...shall of the Spirit reap (or harvest) Life"—ZOE, the life of God! Pray that over every offering you give this month into your church, into this ministry and into other ministries and lives—that's loving God. Expect to reap a bountiful harvest of deeper connection and union not only with Him, but also with every person into whom you sow His love.

I close with Ephesians 3:14-20:

14 For this cause I bow my knees unto the Father of our Lord Jesus Christ,
15 Of whom the whole family in heaven and earth is named,
16 That he would grant you, according to the riches of his glory, to be strengthened with might by his Spirit in the inner man;
17 That Christ may dwell in your hearts by faith; that ye, being rooted and grounded in love,
18 May be able to comprehend with all saints what is the breadth, and length, and depth, and height;
19 And <u>to know</u> the love of Christ, <u>which passeth knowledge,</u> that ye might be filled with all the fulness of God.
20 Now unto him that is able to do exceeding abundantly above all that we ask or think, according to the power that worketh in us.

Gloria and I love you and pray for you every day.

Love,

Ken

In 1969, the Lord told Kenneth that he and Jerry would become a team. Today they are still going strong, ministering the uncompromised Word of God.

January 2008

Faith Activates THE BLESSING

Dear Partner

Did you notice how much persecution and abuse the devil stirred up against different ministries during the last part of 2007? We certainly did. Some of it was stirred up against us. Satan was doing his very best to close the doors that Jesus opened in 2007. Well, it didn't work. They are still open, and no man or devil can shut them.

During the 2007 Great Lakes Believers' Convention, Jerry Savelle preached a power-packed message from Romans 15:29. Let's look at it:

> 29 And I am sure that, when I come unto you, I shall come in the fulness of the blessing of the gospel of Christ.

Well you can imagine what that did in me. I immediately grabbed my notebook and wrote the following petition, prayed it and released my faith for fullness of THE BLESSING:

John 16:23: Whatever I ask the Father in Jesus' Name He will grant it me.

Mark 11:24: Therefore whatsoever I desire when I pray, believe it is granted me and I shall have it.

I believe at 8:08 p.m., Aug. 21, 2007—in Jerry Savelle's service, Great Lakes Believers' Convention—I receive according to Romans 15:29 THE BLESSING in fullness
  on Gloria and me
  on our family
  on this ministry—

Blessing without measure.

I believe it is granted NOW! In Jesus' Name.
—Kenneth Copeland

Now that was in August. As you probably know, when Gloria and I were doing the Christmas *BVOV* broadcasts, the Holy Ghost spoke and said 2008 will be the year of the fullness of Blessing—THE BLESSING without measure. If you saw the broadcasts you know what that did for Gloria and me. We were already excited about this for our family and ministry, but the Lord Jesus had just released it for all our Partners and anyone else who would believe it. Jesus opened the door for it in '07. It's here and cannot be stopped.

<u>Faith activates THE BLESSING.</u> The two most notable things in the life of Abraham were THE BLESSING and his faith. Think about it. The two most outstanding things in the Old Testament are The Blessing of Abraham and The Faith of Abraham.

Let's look at Galatians 3:8-9:

8   And the scripture, foreseeing that God would justify the heathen through faith, <u>preached before the gospel unto Abraham,</u> saying, In thee shall all nations be blessed.
9   So then <u>they which be of faith are blessed</u> with faithful Abraham.

You can see in those two verses both The Faith and THE BLESSING. Faith activates THE BLESSING. They which be of faith are blessed.

There are three vital things about faith that must be on our minds night and day:

1. Faith works by Love.
2. THE BLESSING cannot work without faith. (The just cannot live without it.)
3. Faith comes by hearing and hearing by the Word of God.

All the Law and the Prophets hang on "Love the Lord your God with all your heart, all your soul, and all your mind and strength... and love your neighbor as yourself." Every Word of God hangs on that Great Law. Consequently, faith that activates THE BLESSING comes by hearing and hearing by the Word that Love Himself has spoken.

THE BLESSING is and includes everything that Jesus obtained on the cross so that we could have life. The new birth is part of THE BLESSING. Divine healing is part of THE BLESSING. The coming and indwelling of the Holy Spirit is part of THE BLESSING. Divine financial prosperity is part of THE BLESSING. Can you see how all these things are woven together like a spiritual garment?

Once the Law of Love is in place in our daily memory, the Law of Faith begins to activate THE BLESSING. Let's look at John 20:24-29:

> 24 But Thomas, one of the twelve, called Didymus, was not with them when Jesus came.
> 25 The other disciples therefore said unto him, We have seen the Lord. But he said unto them, Except I shall see in his hands the print of the nails, and put my finger into the print of the nails, and thrust my hand into his side, I will not believe.
> 26 And after eight days again his disciples were within, and Thomas with them: then came Jesus, the doors being shut, and stood in the midst, and said, Peace be unto you.
> 27 Then saith he to Thomas, Reach hither thy finger, and behold my hands; and reach hither thy hand, and thrust it into my side: and be not faithless, but believing.
> 28 And Thomas answered and said unto him, My Lord and my God.
> 29 Jesus saith unto him, Thomas, because thou hast seen me, thou hast believed: blessed are they that have not seen, and yet have believed.

<u>Blessed</u> are they that believe without having to see something other than what God has said. Isn't that what the Word says about Abraham's faith? Let's look at Romans 4:16-21:

> 16 Therefore it is of faith, that it might be by grace;

17   to the end the promise might be sure to all the seed; not to that only which is of the law, but to that also which is of the faith of Abraham; who is the father of us all,

17   (As it is written, I have made thee a father of many nations,) before him whom he believed, even God, who quickeneth the dead, and calleth those things which be not as though they were.

18   Who against hope believed in hope, that he might become the father of many nations, according to that which was spoken, So shall thy seed be.

19   And being not weak in faith, he considered not his own body now dead, when he was about an hundred years old, neither yet the deadness of Sarah's womb:

20   He staggered not at the promise of God through unbelief; but was strong in faith, giving glory to God;

21   And being fully persuaded that, what he had promised, he was able also to perform.

That's the way it works. Look at verse 21. Abraham <u>believed</u> what God had promised. What had He promised? THE BLESSING. "And if ye be Christ's then are you Abraham's seed and <u>heirs according to the promise</u>" (Galatians 3:29). What promise? THE BLESSING! It's just as much yours as it was Abraham's. It's just as much yours as it was Isaac's in Genesis 26:3.

THE BLESSING is just as much yours as it was Joseph's, Daniel's, Moses', Job's, Peter's, John's and Paul's. It's just as much yours as it was Jesus' in His earthly ministry, because it is just as much yours <u>as it is His now.</u>

First John 4:17 tells us that as He is, so are we in this world. How is He? BLESSED!! When? After we get to heaven? No! In this world. Now! Shout amen!!

It's here. Blessing without measure. Jesus has opened every door heaven has and has poured it all out. Now it's time for us to stir up our faith like never before and move through this world as a mighty army of Love and healing. A salvation machine going forth bringing faith, hope and Love to this confused, sick, dying mass of people. It's here and we're ready, and together we can do it.

As you sow your seeds of faith this month, release your faith like I did in Brother Jerry's service. Raise your faith sights to a higher level. Not just "blessed enough to get through," but in fullness of BLESSING. Everything Jesus, our High Priest, has. Blessing without measure. It's here. It's for you. Faith <u>will</u> activate it.

Gloria and I love you and pray for you every day. Remember, we're here for you.

Love,

Ken

P.S. Wishing you a <u>happy</u> New Year sounds puny in The Light of Blessing Without Measure. BE BLESSED!—KC

February 2008

What Is the Difference Between Work in Hebrews 4:10 and Labor in Hebrews 4:11?

Dear Partner,

Let's begin this month's letter with Genesis chapter 2, verses 1-3:

> 1 Thus the heavens and the earth were finished, and all the host of them.
> 2 And on the seventh day God ended his work which he had made; and he rested on the seventh day from all his work which he had made.
> 3 And God blessed the seventh day, and sanctified it: because that in it he had rested from all his work which God created and made.

Why did God rest? Was it because He was tired? No. He rested because He was <u>finished.</u> He had spoken and released not only material things, such as the heavens and the earth, but He also released the Word of His power to sustain it all and the life that it supported <u>forever.</u>

The last act of His <u>work</u> was THE BLESSING. That was to keep it all going and growing throughout all eternity. Had Adam not broken the connection, the Father would never have had to "work" again, unless He just had a desire to.

What does all this mean to us and to our lives now? To answer that, let's go to the book of Hebrews. Let's look at the first three verses:

> 1 God who at sundry times and in divers manners spake in time past unto the fathers by the prophets,
> 2 Hath in these last days spoken unto us by his Son, whom he hath appointed heir of all things, by whom also he made the worlds;
> 3 Who being the brightness of his glory, and the express image of his person, and upholding all things by the word of his power, when he had

> by himself purged our sins, sat down on the right hand of the Majesty on high.

First of all, notice that in these verses, and in the entire book of Hebrews, we are dealing with "these last days"—the days in which you and I live. Another way to look at "these last days" is those days after the resurrection of Jesus. The reason this is so important is spelled out in Matthew 28:18:

> 18 And Jesus came and spake unto them, saying, All [authority] is given unto me in heaven and in earth.

And in Philippians 2:9-11:

> 9   Wherefore God also hath highly exalted him, and given him [His] name which is above every name:
> 10 That at the name of Jesus every knee should bow, of things in heaven, and things in earth, and things under the earth;
> 11 And that every tongue should confess that Jesus Christ is Lord, to the glory of God the Father.

There will never be any other kind of "days," because this <u>ADAM</u> will never fail! Once Jesus was raised <u>immortal</u>—or forever untouchable by sin or death—and placed in full authority both in heaven and <u>in earth</u>, the <u>work</u> was <u>finished</u> once and for all. Now let's see where we, the believers, come in. Look at Hebrews 4:1-16:

> 1   Let us therefore fear, lest, a promise being left us of entering into his rest, any of you should seem to come short of it.
> 2   For unto us was the gospel preached, as well as unto them: but the word preached did not profit them, not being mixed with faith in them that heard it.
> 3   For <u>we which have believed do enter into rest,</u> as he said, As I have sworn in my wrath, if they shall enter into my rest: although the

works were finished from the foundation of the world.

4 For he spake in a certain place of the seventh day on this wise, And God did rest the seventh day from all his works.

5 And in this place again, If <u>they</u> shall enter into <u>my</u> rest.

6 Seeing therefore it remaineth that some must enter therein, and they to whom it was first preached entered not in because of unbelief:

7 Again, he limiteth a certain day, saying in David, Today, after so long a time; as it is said, Today if ye will hear his voice, harden not your hearts.

8 For if Jesus had given them rest, then would he not afterward have spoken of another day.

9 There remaineth therefore a rest to the people of God.

10 For he that is entered into his rest, he also hath ceased from his own works, as God did from his.

11 Let us labour therefore to enter into that rest, lest any man fall after the same example of unbelief.

12 For the word of God is quick, and powerful, and sharper than any twoedged sword, piercing even to the dividing asunder of soul and spirit, and of the joints and marrow, and is a discerner of the thoughts and intents of the heart.

13 Neither is there any creature that is not manifest in his sight: but all things are naked and opened unto the eyes of him with whom we have to do.

14 Seeing then that we have a great high priest, that is passed into the heavens, Jesus the Son of God, let us hold fast our profession.

15 For we have not an high priest which cannot be touched with the feeling of our infirmities; but was in all points tempted like as we are, yet without sin.

16   Let us therefore come boldly unto the throne of grace, that we may obtain mercy, and find grace to help in time of need.

It is finished! Death is defeated. Sin is powerless. Sickness is overthrown. The curse is broken. And we're redeemed from it all! The biggest part of all this is THE BLESSING is back where it belonged from the beginning—on Adam.

Jesus is referred to as the last Adam, and that's the reason why. The first Adam was in charge of all the creation. He then misused his authority and turned it all over to God's enemy, satan. THE BLESSING became THE CURSE. Then came JESUS THE CHRIST!! and took it all back. Not only did He take back all that the first Adam had been given, but He also received glory and honor from THE FATHER and received authority over all of heaven as well.

Now comes the big part. We are <u>joint</u> heirs in all this! <u>That place of rest in Hebrews 4 is in Him.</u> It is in that boldness to come to His throne of authority. We belong there just as much as He does. He is our Lord. He is our voice in heaven. We are His voice on this earth.

Now, what is the difference between the labor in Hebrews 4:11 and the work in the tenth verse? Faith always rests. Worry works trying to "get it"—whatever "it" is. The labor is the time spent in the Word meditating and confessing it before the throne boldly (verse 16) and holding fast to it (verse 14) until that rest and peace that passes <u>all</u> understanding <u>rises up from within</u> and quiets the spirit and comforts the soul with <u>all is well.</u> <u>Now rest and let THE BLESSING do its work.</u> James, Jesus' half brother, put it this way: "Let patience (rest) have her perfect work, that ye may be perfect and entire, <u>wanting</u> nothing" (James 1:4).

Don't labor to get healed. Labor to enter into His rest. The healing is part of THE BLESSING. Don't labor to get a bigger house or better car, or whatever. Labor to enter into His rest. Let THE BLESSING do what the Father designed and released it to do in the first place. The answer to every human need is overwhelmingly met in that BLESSING, and faith is the divine connection that releases it. "<u>Blessed,</u>" Jesus said, "are those who have believed and not seen."

This is the year of the fullness of THE BLESSING—BLESSING without measure. Not only are the "doors" of 2007 still open and cannot be shut by devil or man, but the windows of heaven are open and THE BLESSING is poured out for all who will enter into that place of rest (Malachi 3:10).

As you sow your financial seed this month, release your faith for insight into His rest. That's the secret place in Psalm 91. It's the green pasture beside still waters in Psalm 23. Search the scripture promises for it. It's yours. Jesus paid the price so you can enter in and abide there.

I'll close with Ephesians 3:14-20. Read it aloud and let it take you boldly to the throne of His grace:

14   For this cause I bow my knees unto the Father of our Lord Jesus Christ,
15   Of whom the whole family in heaven and earth is named,
16   That he would <u>grant you, according to the riches of his glory,</u> to be strengthened with might by his Spirit in the inner man;
17   That Christ may dwell in your hearts by faith; that ye, being rooted and grounded in love,
18   <u>May be able to comprehend</u> with all saints what is the breadth, and length, and depth, and height;
19   And to know the love of Christ, which passeth knowledge, that ye might be filled with all the fulness of God.
20   Now unto him that is able to do exceeding abundantly above all that we ask or think, according to the power that worketh in us....

Gloria and I love you and pray for you every day.

Love,

Ken

March 2008

Subdue the Curse and Release the Abundance

Dear Partner

In last month's letter we talked about entering into <u>His</u> rest from the fourth chapter of Hebrews. Let's look again at Hebrews 4:10:

> 10　For he that is entered into his rest, he also hath ceased from his own works, as God did from his.

Look at that last phrase: "as God did from his." How did He cease from His own works? Let's go to John chapter 1 and make sure we understand the meaning of the word *work* here. Look at verses 1-3:

> 1　In the beginning was the Word, and the Word was with God, and the Word was God.
> 2　The same was in the beginning with God.
> 3　All things were made by him [His Word]; and without him [His Word] was not any thing made that was made.

His work was done with THE Word. The last work, or Word release, was THE BLESSING. He did not rest because He was tired. He sat down because He was finished.

God created all material things. Then He created all living things. But that's not where He stopped. He wasn't finished until He released the mighty force that would sustain the heavens and the earth and the life it supported <u>forever.</u> That was the finishing touch. THE BLESSING could do anything He could do. It was Him in continual manifestation.

Now let's look at Jesus. He followed in His Father's footsteps. Let's read Hebrews 1:3:

> 3　Who being the brightness of his glory, and the express image of his person, and upholding all

> things by the <u>word of his power,</u> when he had by himself purged our sins, sat down on the right hand of the Majesty on high.

He did, and is doing, exactly the same thing. First, upholding all things by the Word of His power. Then, sitting down, He rested. Tired? No! Finished! Oh, but there's one more thing Jesus did when He sat down. Hebrews 10:12-13:

> 12 But this man, after he had offered one sacrifice for sins for ever, sat down on the right hand of God;
> 13 From henceforth expecting till his enemies be made his footstool.

<u>He sat down expecting THE BLESSING</u> to completely overcome every obstacle, every devil, every bit of the curse and put them under His feet.

Wait a minute, though, before you shout. Where are His feet? In heaven? No, that's not where His enemies are. His feet are in His Body. We are that Body right here in this earth. He is expecting every enemy to be completely subdued and under our control. Didn't the Father say it? Let's look again at Genesis 1:28:

> 28 And God blessed them, and God said unto them, Be fruitful, and multiply, and replenish the earth, and SUBDUE it: and have dominion over the fish of the sea, and over the fowl of the air, and over every living thing that moveth upon the earth.

THE BLESSING not only has the power of abundance but is also the power of God to subdue. That's what the Spirit of God was saying to Malachi in Malachi 3:10-12:

> 10 Bring ye all the tithes into the storehouse, that there may be meat in mine house, and prove me now herewith, saith the Lord of hosts, if I

> 11   will not open you the windows of heaven, and pour you out a blessing, that there shall not be room enough to receive it.
> 11   And I will rebuke the devourer for your sakes, and he shall not destroy the fruits of your ground; neither shall your vine cast her fruit before the time in the field, saith the Lord of hosts.
> 12   And all nations shall call you blessed: for ye shall be a delightsome land, saith the Lord of hosts.

<u>When THE BLESSING is poured out, it subdues the devourer and brings abundance.</u> Can you see the double action there? Subdue the curse and release the abundance of the Garden of Eden.

The Father said to Jesus, "Come sit here with Me and let THE BLESSING work." Jesus, our Lord and High Priest, is saying the same thing to you and me. That's what the Throne of Grace is. It's not a place to bow down or fall before Him. That's not what *boldly* in Hebrews 4:16 means. Ephesians 2:6:

> 6   And hath raised us up together, and made us sit together in heavenly places in Christ Jesus.

Then Revelation 3:21:

> 21   To him that overcometh will I grant to sit with me in my throne, even as I also overcame, and am set down with my Father in his throne.

Now before you put that off into the sweet by-and-by somewhere, remember the overcomer in Revelation 3:21 is the same overcomer in 1 John 5:4-5:

> 4   For whatsoever is born of God overcometh the world: and this is the victory that overcometh the world, even our faith.
> 5   Who is he that overcometh the world, but he that believeth that Jesus is the Son of God?

That's sitting on His Throne of Grace, having ceased from our own works and entered into His rest with Him—EXPECTING! Expecting BLESSING without measure. The fullness of THE BLESSING, as in Romans 15:29.

Sit with Jesus. Hand over all your care and human works. Cast <u>all</u> your care upon Him, for He cares for you. Then hold fast to your confession: "Thank God, I don't have a care. Jesus has taken <u>my</u> care and has called me, 'Come, sit with Me on My throne. THE BLESSING is working. I've <u>taken</u> <u>care</u> of everything!'" Oh, hallelujah! <u>Now you can shout!</u>

Don't allow anything to disturb your rest. The devil cannot come in to your private place. Sinners can't come there until after Jesus is their Lord. Christians walking in unbelief can't disturb you with their unforgiveness and unbelief. That's what Hebrews 4 is all about.

The only way <u>anything</u> can disturb your resting place is for you to <u>GET</u> <u>UP</u> and go out where they are. Don't do it! Let THE BLESSING work. Let patience have its perfect work until you are entire, wanting nothing. That's what persecution is all about. That's what the devil uses to cry out to you, "Come out here and fuss with us. Come defend yourself. You can't just sit there doing nothing."

"What? Doing nothing? I'm not doing nothing. I'm resting. I'm expecting until all my enemies are made my footstool."

As you sow your financial seed this month, sow it from a place of rest. Look down on debt. From your heavenly place of rest look down on lack and boldly declare, "Jesus has <u>taken</u> <u>care</u> of it."

That's what Gloria and I have been doing with all this mess Sen. Charles Grassley's office released to the press about us and other ministries. We have entered our place of rest. This ministry has always been in absolute integrity before God and men, the very best we could keep it. Remember, I prayed publicly in every Partner meeting and committed before Almighty God to keep this ministry pure:

> Pure on the Word of God,
> Pure sexually, and
> Pure financially.

I have and will continue to keep it that way.

Thank God, I don't have a care. Thank you for being our Partner. Gloria and I love you and pray for you every day.

Love,

Ken

April 2008

Persecution and Affliction—THE BLESSING Thieves

Dear Partner

How are you today? Shout, "I'm Blessed!"

In last month's letter we talked about entering into God's rest and staying there during persecutions, afflictions, testing and trials of all kinds. Sitting boldly down on the throne of grace with Jesus and, just like Him, expecting THE BLESSING to work 24 hours a day until your enemies are made your footstool. When you can do this, you're in a great place. Not only are you in a place of divine protection, but you also have proven you're qualified for THE BLESSING to take you to another level.

Remember Proverbs 10:22 says:

> 22 The blessing of the Lord, it maketh rich, and he addeth no sorrow with it.

Rich in salvation. Rich in good health. Rich according to Psalm 112 and 2 Corinthians 9:8-11. And lastly, rich in wealth, riches and honor.

Again Proverbs 10:22, THE BLESSING <u>makes</u> rich. You're not Blessed because you're rich. You're rich because you're Blessed. You're not Blessed because you're healed. You're healed because you're Blessed.

What is satan's motive behind persecution and affliction? First, Jesus said in Mark 4:17:

> 17 And have no root in themselves, and so endure but for a time: afterward, when affliction or persecution ariseth for the word's sake, immediately they are offended.

Notice in His statement that persecution and affliction do not come to teach us something or to make us stronger. That can't possibly be true, because He plainly said in verse 15 that it comes by satan. He is not about to try to make you stronger, or anything else that's good. His only purpose is to steal, kill and destroy. To do that, he <u>must</u> stop the Word in your life. His biggest enemy in this earth is THE BLESSING, and it's in and on <u>you.</u>

Satan's plan is to shame, break down, tempt or create pressure on you any way he can. If you react to that in any way except according to the Word, you increase his access to you. Especially if you get angry and fly off the handle and yield your tongue to doubt and unbelief, you've played right into his hands. He now has a breach in THE BLESSING wall through which he can come into your resting place.

Close the door!! Don't ever violate the commandment of love. THE BLESSING is faith dependent, and faith is love dependent. Remember that Abraham's faith activated Abraham's BLESSING. It still does.

Now let's look at some very interesting scriptures. First, Job 42:10-17:

> 10 And the Lord turned the captivity of Job, when he prayed for his friends: also the Lord gave Job twice as much as he had before.
> 11 Then came there unto him all his brethren, and all his sisters, and all they that had been of his acquaintance before, and did eat bread with him in his house: and they bemoaned him, and comforted him over all the evil that [had come on] him: every man also gave him a piece of money, and every one an earring of gold.
> 12 So the Lord blessed the latter end of Job more than his beginning: for he had fourteen thousand sheep, and six thousand camels, and a thousand yoke of oxen, and a thousand she asses.
> 13 He had also seven sons and three daughters.
> 14 And he called the name of the first, Jemima; and the name of the second, Kezia; and the name of the third, Keren-happuch.
> 15 And in all the land were no women found so

	fair as the daughters of Job: and their father gave them inheritance among their brethren.
16	After this lived Job an hundred and forty years, and saw his sons, and his sons' sons, even four generations.
17	So Job died, being old and full of days.

The key issue verse in this study is Job 1:9-10. Satan's big problem here was THE BLESSING wall. When it went back into place, Job doubled! It's obvious he never allowed that wall to ever be breached again. Remember, that was Adam's, Noah's, then Abraham's BLESSING that did all this.

Now how does that apply to you and me? In the first place, it's still Abraham's BLESSING. THE BLESSING never changes. What it did in Eden, it did around Job. What it did for Job, it will do for you. The only difference is that now the administration of it is in the hands and ministry of Jesus, the second and LAST Adam.

Now look at Isaiah 61:6-7:

6	But ye shall be named the Priests of the Lord: men shall call you the Ministers of our God: ye shall eat the riches of the Gentiles, and in their glory shall ye boast yourselves.
7	For your shame ye shall have double; and for confusion they shall rejoice in their portion: therefore in their land they shall possess the double: everlasting joy shall be unto them.

For your shame you shall receive the double. Those who disrespectfully use and persecute you have qualified you for the double. Put that in your mouth and shout it to the devil and to your own mind and emotions. Stay in your resting place. Don't you dare leave that place of rest and honor.

Finally, let's read James 1:12:

12	Blessed is the man that endureth temptation:

for when he is tried, he shall receive the crown of life, which the Lord hath promised to them that love him.

BLESSED is the man who endures temptations (tests and trials). Notice the phrase "the crown of life." The crown represents the highest authority. The Word says that God crowned Adam with His Glory. That was THE BLESSING, the highest authorized power in the earth. Dominion over all living creatures. This crown is carried through all the way to and including life after we leave this earth. Matthew 25:34:

> 34   Then shall the King say unto them on his right hand, Come, ye blessed of my Father, inherit the kingdom prepared for you from the foundation of the world.

My Lord God and Savior! How can you just sit there? Shout amen, somebody!

As you sow your financial seed this month, don't just look at it as faith seed. It is THE BLESSING seed of faith! Where do I get that? From Acts 20:35, of course:

> 35   I have shown you all things, how that so labouring ye ought to support the weak, and to remember the words of the Lord Jesus, how he said, It is <u>more blessed</u> to give than to receive.

There it is! Release the dream and never, ever violate it.

Gloria and I love you very much, and we pray for you every day to be BLESSED spirit, soul, body, family, financially and socially. This is the year of the fullness of BLESSING. THE BLESSING without measure.

Love,

Ken

May 2008

Sit Down!

Dear Partner

Let's begin this month's letter by looking at three scriptures.

Ephesians 2:1-6:

> 1 And you hath he quickened, who were dead in trespasses and sins;
> 2 Wherein in time past ye walked according to the course of this world, according to the prince of the power of the air, the spirit that now worketh in the children of disobedience:
> 3 Among whom also we all had our [manner of life] in times past in the lusts of our flesh, fulfilling the desires of the flesh and of the mind; and were by nature the children of wrath, even as others.
> 4 But God, who is rich in mercy, for his great love wherewith he loved us,
> 5 Even when we were dead in sins, hath quickened us together with Christ, (by grace ye are saved;)
> 6 And hath raised us up together, <u>and made us sit together</u> in heavenly places in Christ Jesus.

Now let's read Revelation 3:21:

> 21 To him that overcometh will I grant <u>to sit with me in my throne,</u> even as I also overcame, and am set down with my Father in his throne.

Who is the overcomer in that verse? First John 5:5, "Who is he that overcometh the world, but he that believeth that Jesus is the Son of God?"

Look closely at those verses again by reading them slowly and <u>out</u>

<u>loud.</u> Now say it boldly by faith: "Those verses are talking about me!" Say this in thanksgiving and praise: "I was born of His Spirit to sit with Him on His throne!"

Oh, hallelujah! Now it becomes so clear when one reads Hebrews 4:14-16 just what the Word is saying:

> 14 Seeing then that we have a great high priest, that is passed into the heavens, Jesus the Son of God, let us hold fast our profession.
> 15 For we have not an high priest which cannot be touched with the feeling of our infirmities; but was in all points tempted like as we are, yet without sin.
> 16 Let us therefore come boldly unto the throne of grace, that we may obtain mercy, and find grace to help in time of need.

"Come sit with Me on this throne of <u>GRACE</u> until I make your enemies your footstool! Come boldly. I have settled the problem of your sin. I have blotted your sin completely out (Isaiah 43:25-26). As far as the east is from the west I have removed them (Psalm 103:12-13). Come. Sit down. I have declared you BLESSED with THE BLESSING of Abraham. Sit down, rest, and let it work."

Now let's go back to Hebrews 4 again and see why this is so powerful an invitation. Look at verses 10-13:

> 10 For he that is entered into his rest, he also hath ceased from his own works, as God did from his.
> 11 Let us labour therefore to enter into that rest, lest any man fall after the same example of unbelief.
> 12 For the word of God is quick, and powerful, and sharper than any twoedged sword, piercing even to the dividing asunder of soul and spirit, and of the joints and marrow, and is a discerner of the thoughts and intents of the heart.

> 13 Neither is there any creature that is not manifest in his sight: but all things are naked and opened unto the eyes of him with whom we have to do.

You can enter into His rest and SIT DOWN because the Word has you covered. <u>I don't care what kind of situation it is you are resting from, or how terrible or dangerous it is, the Living Word of God covers it, sees through it and will reveal the answer to its defeat.</u> That's when the Healing Word becomes the Sword of the Spirit and produces great victories.

The beautiful part is you don't have to <u>make</u> it work—it is God manifested in faith in this earth. All you have to do is rest. You do, however, have to do that. That's your part.

Sit down! God's wisdom is on the way!

When you think about it, if you knew exactly what to do in that situation it wouldn't be a test or trial. When you take your place of rest in the Word of God, James 1:1-6 has you covered:

> 1 James, a servant of God and of the Lord Jesus Christ, to the twelve tribes which are scattered abroad, greeting.
> 2 My brethren, count it all joy when ye fall into divers [tests, temptations and trials].
> 3 Knowing this, that the trying of your faith worketh patience.
> 4 But let patience have her perfect work, that ye may be perfect and entire, wanting nothing.
> 5 If any of you lack wisdom, let him ask of God, that giveth to all men liberally, and upbraideth not; and it shall be given him.
> 6 But let him ask in faith, nothing wavering. For he that wavereth is like a wave of the sea driven with the wind and tossed.

SIT DOWN with an obedient heart. John 14:1 and 27:

> 1   Let not your heart be troubled: ye believe in God, believe also in me.
> 27 Peace I leave with you, my peace I give unto you: not as the world giveth, give I unto you. Let not your heart be troubled, neither let it be afraid.

Obey the Lord Jesus. Remember, THE BLESSING is working. Fear not! Believe only, and don't allow yourself to do anything to interrupt it.

SIT DOWN saying. Don't just sit there—hold fast your confession. Psalm 91:1-2:

> 1   He that dwelleth in the secret place of the most High shall abide under the shadow of the Almighty.
> 2   <u>I will say</u> of the Lord, He is my refuge and my fortress: my God; in him will I trust.

"I'm in my resting place. The Almighty God is my refuge, He's my fortress and I trust Him! I do not allow anyone or anything to disturb me here beside the still waters in this beautiful green pasture of His Love."

SIT DOWN and rest, shedding your old, religious "unworthy garments" of unbelief. Fill your mouth with Romans 8:1-2:

> 1   There is therefore now no condemnation to them which are in Christ Jesus, who walk not after the flesh, but after the Spirit.
> 2   For the law of the Spirit of life in Christ Jesus <u>hath made me free</u> from the law of sin and death.

Completely bathe your mind by washing it with the water of the Word. "There is <u>now</u> no condemnation to me. I'm in Christ Jesus. The Law of Life in Him has made me free! Free! Free <u>now</u> from the law of sin and death. I was unworthy to even be in His presence, but He bore my unworthiness and gave me His righteousness. I am sitting here in this place of divine rest and protection by His invitation. His precious Blood washed me and wiped out my sin and unworthiness.

"I was born to sit here with Him. He is my Lord and High Priest. I am His joint heir. He has boldly declared me BLESSED. I receive it. I'm BLESSED. THE BLESSING OF THE LORD IS WORKING IN ME NOW! THE BLESSING of the Lord <u>maketh</u> rich and He addeth no sorrow with it. I'm rich in my spirit. I'm rich in my soul. I'm rich in my physical body. I'm rich in my family. I'm rich in my finances. I have a Father! I have a Daddy! He's huge. He loves me. He's GOD! He's rich, rich, rich, rich."

Romans 8:15 says we're supposed to be crying this, so shout it again. Shout all that over every offering you sow this month. A seed-faith BLESSING offering is a powerful tool in the hands of believers who know who they are in Christ Jesus.

Pray for Gloria and me as we take this powerful revelation of THE BLESSING around the world. We love you ever so much, and we pray and release THE BLESSING on you and all our Partners every day.

Love,

Ken

P.S. You're not Blessed because you're rich. You're rich because you're Blessed!—KC

From Believers' Conventions to motorcycle rallies and churches, your faith, prayers and giving see to it that this uncompromised message of faith reaches all over the world.

June 2008

What Is Rich?

Dear Partner

It seems as if the only place we need a definition of the word *rich* is among church people. However, when one discovers the Bible definition of rich, it becomes very evident that though most people think they know what it means to be rich, they don't have any idea of what it really means.

Are Christians supposed to be rich? Yes. Did Jesus provide this as part of what He did for us at Calvary? Yes. Is the Bible referring to financial wealth? Yes.

Let's look first at Proverbs 10:22:

> 22   The blessing of the Lord, <u>it maketh</u> rich, and he addeth no sorrow with it. [Note: THE BLESSING made it.]

It's obvious in this verse that THE BLESSING is the source of the wealth of the believer. Now let's look at Psalm 73:12:

> 12   Behold, these are the ungodly, who prosper in the world; <u>they</u> increase in riches. [Note: They made it.]

Look at the difference here in where the wealth is coming from. One is the world; the other is THE BLESSING of the Lord. One has sorrow with it; the other does not.

There are two very different forms of economy in the earth. One is referred to as the world and came into the human family from two of the three sons of Noah. Let's look at Genesis 9:1:

> 1   And God blessed Noah <u>and his sons,</u> and said unto them, Be fruitful, and multiply, and replenish the earth.

That's exactly what the Lord God said to Adam in the beginning. Two of Noah's sons, Ham and Japheth, did the same as Adam and departed from God's way of doing things. Out of them came the Babylonian system of commerce we know in the world today. That system is basically defined as an attempt to meet the needs of mankind without God. It tries to satisfy spiritual needs with religion, mental needs with scientific theories, and physical needs with its own market-and-supply, dog-eat-dog, lie-cheat-and-steal way of doing things. Then calls it prosperity. That's Psalm 73:12. They even have their own form of giving that's based on pride and self-recognition. Look at Proverbs 22:16:

> 16 He that oppresseth the poor to increase his riches, and he that giveth to the rich [the oppressor], shall surely come to want.

On the other hand, Noah's third son, Shem, followed God. Remember, now, he had THE BLESSING by covenant. The rainbow covenant. Shem became the king, or lord mayor, of Jerusalem. His title was Melchizedek. He is the priest of the Most High God in Genesis 14:18 who after the slaughter of the kings (verse 17) met Abram with bread and wine and received his tithe. He transferred THE BLESSING of the Lord to Abram, who became Abraham. THE BLESSING then became known as THE BLESSING of Abraham through a covenant of blood between God and him.

Remember we answered the question "Does God want every believer rich?" with YES! This is one of the places where that answer comes from. Look at Galatians 3:8:

> 8 And the scripture, foreseeing that God would justify the heathen [Ham and Japheth] through faith, preached before the gospel unto Abraham, saying, In thee shall all nations [ALL men from Ham and Japheth] be blessed.

Now look at Galatians 3:13-14, and we'll see God's perfect will behind Jesus going to the cross:

> 13 Christ hath redeemed us from the curse of the

> law, being made a curse for us: for it is written, Cursed is every one that hangeth on a tree:
> 14 That the blessing of Abraham might come on the Gentiles [nations] through Jesus Christ; that we might receive the promise of the Spirit through faith.

"But, Brother Copeland, I thought the new birth was the reason Jesus went to the cross." It was! Being born again is part of THE BLESSING. His bearing our sickness and diseases is part of THE BLESSING.

Now let's look at 2 Corinthians 8:9:

> 9 For ye know the grace of our Lord Jesus Christ, that, though he was rich, yet for your sakes he became poor, that ye through his poverty [the curse] might be rich.

This is referring to being rich in money. Of course it also includes spiritual wealth and all other kinds of prosperity—spirit, soul and body. But this verse is talking about abounding in this grace along with abounding in faith, utterance, knowledge, diligence and love for the ministry (verse 7).

All of this sets the stage for us to see and understand the Bible meaning of *rich*. The New Testament definition of a prosperous believer is in the next chapter referring to "this grace also." Second Corinthians 9:8-10:

> 8 And God is able to make all grace abound toward you; that ye, always having all sufficiency in all things, may abound to every good work:
> 9 (As it is written, He hath dispersed abroad; he hath given to the poor: his righteousness remaineth forever.
> 10 Now he that ministereth seed to the sower both minister bread for your food, and

multiply your seed sown, and increase the fruits of your righteousness).

Verse 9 leads us to Psalm 112, which also defines "BLESSED is the man." Let's look at it:

1. Praise ye the Lord. Blessed is the man that feareth the Lord, that delighteth greatly in his commandments.
2. His seed shall be mighty upon earth: the generation of the upright shall be blessed.
3. Wealth and riches shall be in his house: <u>and his righteousness</u> endureth for ever. [Note: Notice house, wealth, riches <u>and righteousness.</u>]
4. Unto the upright there ariseth light in the darkness: he is gracious, and full of compassion, and righteous.
5. A good man showeth favour, and lendeth: he will guide his affairs with discretion.
6. Surely he shall not be moved for ever: the righteous shall be in everlasting remembrance.
7. He shall not be afraid of evil tidings: his heart is fixed, trusting in the Lord. [Note: Trusting in the Lord, not wealth.]
8. His heart is established, he shall not be afraid, until he see his desire upon his enemies.
9. He hath dispersed, he hath given to the poor; his righteousness endureth for ever; his horn shall be exalted with honour.
10. The wicked shall see it, and be grieved; he shall gnash with his teeth, and melt away: the desire of the wicked shall perish.

This is a rich man. Verse 2: His family is also BLESSED and strong in the commandments. This means they love and care for one another. Verse 3: He has a house. It must be a nice house, because it's full of wealth and riches. Living in a house filled with wealth and riches, <u>and his righteousness</u> endures. His wealth came from heaven's economy—THE BLESSING, God's power to get wealth—not from the Babylonian system of sorrow. Verse 5: He is a giving man—not stingy. THE BLESSING provides through Jesus <u>wisdom</u> to guide his affairs with discretion or good judgment. Verse 6: This man knows his source.

Verses 7 and 8 outline why he is so strong and immovable. Bad news from the Babylonian system just bounces off his armor. He's in the secret place. He's resting on the Word of his faith:

> 7   He shall not be afraid of evil tidings: his heart is fixed, trusting in the Lord.
> 8   His heart is established, he shall not be afraid, until he see his desire upon his enemies.

Verse 9: Giving activates THE BLESSING which causes receiving. Abraham's faith activates Abraham's BLESSING. That's why Jesus said it's more BLESSED to give than to receive. <u>You're not BLESSED because you're rich. You're rich because you're BLESSED.</u> If you have activated the new-birth part of THE BLESSING by receiving Jesus as your Lord and Savior, you are by heaven's decree <u>rich.</u> You are <u>THE BLESSED,</u> so you are <u>THE RICH.</u> Activate it! <u>Now!</u>

Verse 10 is where all the devil's persecution comes against God's people being wealthy. Don't let it move you. Their desire to destroy you and your ministry is part of their sorrow, but their desire to persecute will melt away if you stay in the Love Walk, remain faithful and let THE BLESSING work. Don't ever be moved by bad news! Don't ever feel <u>sorry</u> for yourself. That's from the Babylonian world of darkness, and it will slow or stop THE BLESSING if allowed to enter in (Mark 4:19).

This is a revelation of your future. It's a picture of the way Jesus, <u>our Melchizedek,</u> sees us. His order is to receive our tithes and BLESS US (Hebrews 7:1-8)!

Study these scriptures. Meditate them day and night. Get the CDs or DVDs. Go to kcm.org and feed your spirit continually until this is the way you see yourself. This is your life. God has given you the power to get wealth through the awesome price Jesus paid to get it to you. Activate it. It's just waiting for your faith.

As you sow your BLESSING SEED this month, lay your hands on it and declare, "I have the faith of Abraham. I activate THE BLESSING of Abraham in my life <u>NOW!</u> I'm rich because I'm BLESSED. I'm rich now. It's only a matter of time until wealth and riches will fill my house according to Psalm 112:3.

Gloria and I love you and pray for you every day.

Love,

Ken

July 2008

Don't Join the Recession—It Doesn't Belong to You!

Dear Partner

There is no recession in the kingdom of God!

"Well I know that, Brother Copeland, but what about here where we live?" That question lets me know that person is "living" in this world, looking to this world for provision. The kingdom of God I mentioned in the opening statement of this letter is not referring to heaven. It is referring to wherever Jesus is king, both in heaven and in earth.

When God created this earth and placed Adam in it, He released THE BLESSING to provide <u>everything</u> for every living thing He had created. That was His perfect will then, and it's His perfect will now. He never changes.

It is no harder to believe God in "bad times" than it is in "good times." The problems come from not using your faith when things seem good or easy. Then when something happens that causes trouble, spiritually lazy people are not ready. Then it looks worse than it actually is. Especially when one listens to the news media and all the noise the world makes. The world system and everyone in it stays in trouble all the time. That system is fear-based and full of sorrow. Proverbs 10:22 says:

> 22   The blessing of the Lord, it maketh rich, and he addeth no sorrow with it.

Notice in that verse THE BLESSING <u>MAKES.</u> The world says, "I have to <u>make</u> a living. I <u>make</u> my way in this world. I <u>make</u> my money," etc. In the kingdom we live by faith. We work, according to Ephesians 4:28, that we may have to give to him who needs.

"But what about my needs?" Jesus dealt with that question in Matthew 6:24:

> 24   No man can serve two masters: for either he

> will hate the one, and love the other; or else he will hold to the one, and despise the other. Ye cannot serve God and mammon.

You cannot serve the world's way and the kingdom's way at the same time. The world's way is me working to meet my needs, always thinking about what I don't have.

Let's read on. Verse 25:

> 25 Therefore I say unto you, Take no thought for <u>your life,</u> what ye shall eat, or what ye shall drink; nor yet for your body, what ye shall put on. Is not the life more than meat, and the body than raiment?

Stop thinking about it! Verses 26-34:

> 26 Behold the fowls of the air: for they sow not, neither do they reap, nor gather into barns; yet your heavenly Father feedeth them. Are ye not much better than they?
>
> 27 Which of you by taking thought can add one cubit unto his stature?
>
> 28 And why take ye thought for raiment? Consider the lilies of the field, how they grow; <u>they toil not,</u> neither do they spin:
>
> 29 And yet I say unto you, That even Solomon in all his glory was not arrayed like one of these.
>
> 30 Wherefore, if God so clothe the grass of the field, which today is, and tomorrow is cast into the oven, shall he not much more clothe you, O ye of little faith?
>
> 31 Therefore take no thought, saying, What shall we eat? or, What shall we drink? or, Wherewithal shall we be clothed?
>
> 32 (For after all these things do the Gentiles seek:) for your heavenly Father knoweth that ye have need of all these things.

33	But seek ye first the kingdom of God, and his righteousness; and all these things shall be added unto you.
34	Take therefore no thought for the morrow: for the morrow shall take thought for the things of itself. Sufficient unto the day is the evil thereof.

How do I seek the kingdom, or God's way of doing things? You don't just try it; you put His ways the first and only way you do things. He depends on His Word. You depend on His Word—for everything. He uses His faith. You use His faith. He is love. You are love. He released THE BLESSING expecting it to do the work. You release THE BLESSING and expect the very same thing. That's where the "all these things shall be added unto you" part of verse 33 comes in.

This is the way a believer lives all the time, regardless of what's happening in the world. When THE BLESSING is working all the time, it is preparing ahead of time for whatever the curse is trying to do.

Remember what Jesus said? "Your heavenly Father knows you have need of all these things." He knows you have need of fuel for your car, as well as food for your table. THE BLESSING is unlimited unless it doesn't have the spiritual resources with which to work—Faith, Hope and Love.

"No! High gas prices don't move me! My God meets my needs according to His riches in glory!"

Buy a tank of gas for someone else! That's the kingdom way. That's what THE BLESSING needs to "fuel" it and keep it going. Ephesians 6:8: "Whatsoever good thing any man doeth, the same shall he receive of the Lord...." Now we can understand what Jesus was saying when He said it is more BLESSED to give than it is to receive. Giving sets THE BLESSING in motion so that you have something to receive.

Don't ever stop BLESSING. That's your way of life. When trouble comes, keep giving. Keep BLESSING someone. Stay constant, consistent, steady and on course. Be like Jesus and don't look to the right or to the left. Stay on the Word. Stay in faith. Stay in Love.

It works! Notice I did not say I work. No, it works. The Word works. Faith works. Love works. THE BLESSING works. It maketh rich. You're not BLESSED because you're rich. You're rich because you're BLESSED. Galatians 3:13:

> 13   Christ hath redeemed us from the curse of the law, being made a curse for us: for it is written, Cursed is every one that hangeth on a tree.

Second Corinthians 8:9:

> 9   For ye know the grace of our Lord Jesus Christ, that, though he was rich, yet for your sakes he became poor, that ye through his poverty might be rich.

Galatians 3:14:

> 14   That the blessing of Abraham might come on the Gentiles through Jesus Christ; that we might receive the promise of the Spirit through faith.

Proverbs 10:22:

> 22   The blessing of the Lord, it maketh rich, and he addeth no sorrow with it.

What more do you need? Stand up and shout, "I'm BLESSED! I'm BLESSED! I have a Father! He's the God of Solomon! He's the God of all creation. And He's my God! NOTHING IN THIS WORLD ORDER CAN OVERCOME ME—1 John 5:4 says so."

When I say shout, I mean it. Shout it with every fiber of your being. Wake up your faith even if it wakes up your neighbors. Now go back over it and SHOUT it. NOW!

Just a quick note to let you know how deeply Gloria and I appreciate the Citation X you and the other Partners brought into this ministry. We had two meetings in Europe in April—one in Bournemouth, England, and the other in Basel, Switzerland. When we return from our meeting in Lagos, Nigeria (April 25), we will have flown that airplane 283,356 miles since we took delivery of it in March 2006. We have literally preached the Word all over the world with it. We're BLESSED. And it's not because we have the airplane. We have the airplane because we're BLESSED!

God swore to Abraham that He would BLESS those who would help Him BLESS. Equally. You have helped us take THE BLESSING to the world. Therefore you are BLESSED with the same BLESSING. The same anointing. The same rewards. Receive it. It's yours.

As you sow your BLESSING seeds this month, go back over all the scriptures in this letter and BLESS your seed. When we receive it, we here at Kenneth Copeland Ministries BLESS your seed. We BLESS you.

Gloria and I love you and we pray for you every day.

Love,

Ken

August 2008

My Heart Is Fixed—Trusting God

Dear Partner,

You've heard me say this many times, and no doubt I will say it many times more: Faith begins where the will of God is known. I remind myself of this on a regular basis—especially when my mind is being challenged. Whenever those challenges come, our response should always be to cast down imaginations and bring <u>every</u> thought into captivity. Let's look at that instruction in 2 Corinthians 10:3-6:

> 3 For though we walk in the flesh, we do not war after the flesh:
> 4 (For the weapons of our warfare are not carnal, but mighty through God to the pulling down of strong holds;)
> 5 Casting down imaginations, and every high thing that exalteth itself against the knowledge of God, and bringing into captivity every thought to the obedience of Christ;
> 6 And having in a readiness to revenge all disobedience [of thought], when your obedience is fulfilled.

Stay ready to capture every thought. Don't allow your thought life to get away with one word of unbelief. By fixing your mind on the <u>Word of God,</u> you base yourself firmly on the <u>will of God.</u> That's because His Word and His will are the same. Faith lives and thrives in that atmosphere.

I love the 112th Psalm, which is the Holy Spirit's portrait of a prosperous believer. Look at verses 7 and 8—no, let's read the entire Psalm:

> 1 Praise ye the Lord. Blessed is the man that feareth the Lord, that delighteth greatly in his commandments.
> 2 His seed shall be mighty upon earth: the generation of the upright shall be blessed.

3		Wealth and riches shall be in his house: and his righteousness endureth forever.
4		Unto the upright there ariseth light in the darkness: he is gracious, and full of compassion, and righteous.
5		A good man showeth favour, and lendeth: he will guide his affairs with discretion.
6		Surely he shall not be moved for ever: the righteous shall be in everlasting remembrance.
7		He shall not be afraid of evil tidings: his heart is fixed, trusting in the Lord.
8		His heart is established, he shall not be afraid, until he see his desire upon his enemies.
9		He hath dispersed, he hath given to the poor; his righteousness endureth for ever; his horn shall be exalted with honour.
10		The wicked shall see it, and be grieved; he shall gnash with his teeth, and melt away: the desire of the wicked shall perish.

In verse 7 we are told the heart of the prosperous believer is "fixed." Something fixed is something set solid, like concrete or rock. God's Word is the solid rock upon which my heart and mind are fixed immovable. All else is sinking sand.

"Yeah, but you just don't know what all they accused me of!"

Every time you have that thought, cast it down. Do it out loud, with the Word: "I don't care what they have said, are saying, or ever will say about me. Their words don't move me. I'm BLESSED! I am the righteousness of God in Christ Jesus! In Christ I am the seed of Abraham and an heir according to His promises. I believe what God in His Word says about me. I'm supposed to BE BLESSED! I'm supposed to BE healed. I'm supposed to BE free! I'm supposed to BE rich."

"Yeah, but...."

"DON'T 'YEAH, BUT' ME! I CAST YOU DOWN!!"

If it comes again, do it again. How long? How many times? As long and as many times as it takes. There is no more important thing you can do with your time and thoughts. This is the battleground where life's most precious victories are won or lost.

In order to come to the place of prosperity and victory that your heavenly Father planned for you and promised you in Christ Jesus, you must first change your <u>whole way of thinking</u> to line up with those promises.

So many people were taught all of their lives that things are bad and there's nothing you can do about it: "We're just poor folks." Or, "You know, sickness just runs in our family." NO! It doesn't! We are the family of God! Healing and good health run in our family.

The negative thoughts and ideas so many people hear all their lives have been thought and said so often over the years they are "just there." How do we change all that mess?

Jesus gave us the key in Matthew 6:31. He said, "Therefore take no thought, saying…." That's the unchangeable process. A thought is taken or activated by saying it. The only way to change our way of thinking is to think something different and say it. To do that, we must first go to a different source of thoughts. Isaiah 55:7 says that an unrighteous man can and should forsake his thoughts. Then, verses 8-9:

> 8 For my thoughts are not your thoughts, neither are your ways my ways, saith the Lord.
> 9 For as the heavens are higher than the earth, so are my ways higher than your ways, and my thoughts than your thoughts.

Don't stop reading there. Look at verse 11:

> 11 So shall my word be that goeth forth out of my mouth: it shall not return unto me void, but it shall accomplish that which I please, and it shall prosper in the thing whereto I sent it.

His Word, His thoughts, have been given to us with which to change our entire <u>way of thinking</u> to His <u>way of thinking</u>. Also remember this: We have been raised up and made to sit with Him in heavenly places in Christ Jesus. We're at home thinking His thoughts and living in His ways. So the next thing is to make the <u>decision to think this thought.</u> Then say that thought and take it.

Decide.

Think.

Then say.

Now do it again.

Then do it again. Decide. Think. Then say. Again, and again, and again, and over, and over, <u>until you don't have to decide to think it and say it.</u> It just flows out your mouth. That's what you're looking for. That thought from God's own mind, His thought and Word, has become yours. It has gotten down into your heart and has become part of you.

Not only that, but His thought and Word in your heart has taken upon itself faith. Now when it comes out your mouth, it activates THE BLESSING. Before, what you were saying without having to think about it was activating the curse. Sure, sickness <u>ran</u> in the family. The family handed down those thoughts and words and gave the force of fear, sickness, disease and poverty a free, unchallenged place to work. But <u>NOW</u> in THE NAME of Jesus, we've been redeemed from the curse! Jesus was made a curse for us so that THE BLESSING of Abraham might come on us in Him.

The faith of Abraham activated THE BLESSING of Abraham. It still does. What did Abraham believe? He believed God. What did God say? He said Abraham was BLESSED. Abraham believed he was BLESSED!

I believe I am BLESSED! I think I AM BLESSED! I say I AM BLESSED! I take the thought and say it. THE BLESSING is working for me now. I have made the decision to think, to take the thought by saying it. I don't just think I'm BLESSED, but I now know I'm BLESSED. I'm supposed to

BE BLESSED. I'm supposed to BE WELL. I'm supposed to BE HAPPY and filled with JOY. I'm supposed to BE RICH.

As you sow your BLESSING seed this month, lay your hands on it and declare, "I'm BLESSED. Therefore, I BLESS this seed. I BLESS it to You, Lord Jesus. For Your work, I BLESS the harvest in Your Name. I'm supposed to receive BLESSING overflow, pressed down, shaken together, and running over. It's mine. That's Your <u>way of thinking</u>, Lord Jesus. You're the One who said that. I take that word as my thought. I say it. It's mine. That's now <u>my way of thinking</u>."

Well, that's the <u>Bible way</u> it's done. It works. I know. Gloria and I started 41 years ago broke, sick and defeated. All because of our defeated <u>way of thinking</u>. Then we took His thoughts and thought them. We took His words and put them in our mouths. We are <u>so</u> BLESSED. No dirty plan the devil has tried to destroy us with has been able to prosper. To God be the glory forever!

Thank you so very much for being our Partner and standing with us. Our victory is your victory. Together, we can do everything Jesus calls us to do. We love you and pray for you every day.

Love,

Ken

September 2008

Why the Commandment of Love?

Dear Partner,

Let's look first of all at John 13:34:

> 34 A new commandment I give unto you, That ye love one another; as I have loved you, that ye also love one another.

Jesus not only commanded us to love one another but to love "as I have loved you." Why so strong? Didn't He know how much He was demanding of us to love on His level? Certainly He did. He gave His life to give us the power and equipment in the Spirit so we could love as He loved. It is of vital importance that we get to the bottom of this. He suffered hell so we could carry out His <u>command.</u> So it must be first place in His life. If it's first with Him, then it's first with me.

Let's think for a moment about something He said in John 14:21:

> 21 He that hath my commandments, and keepeth them, he it is that loveth me: and he that loveth me shall be loved of my Father, and <u>I will love him, and will manifest myself to him.</u>

It's very obvious in this scripture that without our walking in His command to love as He loves, He cannot manifest Himself to us. What was He talking about when He said He would "manifest" Himself? To *manifest* means "to show" or "to reveal." I can think of a lot of ways I would like for Him to manifest Himself to me. However, that's not what's important. The important thing is His will—what is it and how is it He wants to reveal Himself.

Let's go back to the beginning. Genesis 1:28:

> 28 And God blessed them, and God said unto them, Be fruitful, and multiply, and replenish

the earth, and subdue it: and have dominion over the fish of the sea, and over the fowl of the air, and over every living thing that moveth upon the earth.

In Genesis 2:8 we get a profound look at God's perfect will for all men for all time:

> 8   And the Lord God planted a garden eastward in Eden; and there he put the man whom he had formed.

<u>God took seed from heaven</u> and planted a garden in the earth, and <u>He</u> made it grow. Then He created the man and put him in the garden. How plain does it have to be to understand that?

And that was only the beginning. That was supposed to be the worst condition man would ever know. Think about it. Heavenly seed produces heavenly crops. Do you think heaven has become old and ugly over the last several thousand years? Absolutely not. God is there. It could only have gotten better.

In fact, the Word says in 1 Corinthians 2:9 that no man has ever dreamed what God has prepared for those who love Him. Those who what? LOVE! Before the foundation of the world, God—who is Love— in His compassion and desires for His family, made every human being ever to be born richer and more grand than anyone could ever dream. He is able (and willing) to do exceeding abundantly above all that we ask or think (Ephesians 3:20). That includes you and me! Especially if Jesus is your Lord and Savior.

Let's dig a little deeper into our question—why the <u>commandment</u> of love?

We know from what Jesus said that He <u>never ever</u> did or said <u>anything</u> but what His Father said or did. John 5:17:

> 17   But Jesus answered them, My Father worketh hitherto, and I work.

Then John 5:19:

> 19 Then answered Jesus and said unto them, Verily, verily, I say unto you, The Son can do nothing of himself, but what he seeth the Father do: for what things soever he doeth, these also doeth the Son likewise.

Now verse 30:

> 30 I can of mine own self do nothing: as I hear, I judge: and my judgment is just; because I seek not mine own will, but the will of the Father which hath sent me.

Then again in John 14:24:

> 24 He that loveth me not keepeth not my sayings: and the word which ye hear is not mine, but the Father's which sent me.

Now, let's take the next step into knowing why He commanded instead of asking or suggesting.

Let's go over to Acts 3:25-26. Remember now, what Jesus said. He said and did what His Father said and did.

> 25 Ye are the children of the prophets, and of the covenant which God made with our fathers, saying unto Abraham, And in thy seed shall all the kindreds of the earth be blessed.
> 26 Unto you first God, having raised up his Son Jesus, <u>sent him to bless you,</u> in turning away every one of you from his iniquities.

He came to this earth to carry out the promise sworn to Abraham. <u>He sent Him to BLESS you!</u> That's the manifesting of Himself to you. He is THE BLESSING. That's who He is and that's what He is. No man or woman has ever imagined in his heart or mind how abundantly

Jesus has BLESSED us. John 10:10 says <u>more</u> abundantly. More means more—more means more—more means more—more—more—and so on, forever.

Remember now, Peter said, "You are children of the prophets and the covenant...in Him shall all the <u>kindreds</u> (that includes you and me) be <u>BLESSED</u>" (see Acts 3:25).

Now let's look at Luke 24:44:

> 44 And he said unto them, These are the words which I spake unto you, while I was yet with you, that all things must be fulfilled, which were written in the law of Moses, and in the prophets, and in the psalms, concerning me.

Praise God! Those words must be fulfilled. Now look at verses 50-51!

> 50 And he led them out as far as to Bethany, <u>and he lifted up his hands, and blessed them.</u>
> 51 And it came to pass, <u>while he blessed them,</u> he was parted from them, and carried up into heaven.

You and I know exactly what He said. He said what His Father said to Adam. Be BLESSED! Be fruitful. Multiply. Fill up the earth. Subdue it. Have dominion over it. Fill it with what? The Garden of Eden. Abraham's promise was the Eden BLESSING. <u>Read Isaiah 51:1-3</u> and then shout, "He has planted a Garden of Eden for me. It's mine. Jesus is mine! Abraham's BLESSING is mine. I'm saved! I'm healed! I'm rich!"

The last words Jesus spoke on this earth were the first words the Father spoke to Adam. He is the Alpha and the Omega. BLESSED beyond measure was His will at the beginning, and it's His will now. He has never changed and never will. If you've seen Jesus, you've seen the Father.

As He spoke those words, He ascended to sit down in His place of authority over all heaven and earth as Lord and High Priest <u>forever</u> after the order of Melchizedek, who received Abraham's tithe and BLESSED him. Forever He will run this earth and all of the Father's creation by the power of THE BLESSING—THROUGH US. We are the key to His success.

For Him to perfectly please the Father He has to carry out the Eden Blessing in the earth. That's His manifesting of Himself. Love planted that garden. Love created the man and put him in it. Love sent Jesus into the earth to get THE BLESSING back for mankind—more specifically, you!

Faith works by Love. Without faith it is impossible to please God. Now you know why. We are THE BLESSING connection to the earth the same as Adam was. Without obedience to the Commandment of Love, THE BLESSING is stopped. When we walk in Love as He loved us, then the BLESSING stream can flow. Not only to us but through us.

In closing let's go back where we began. John 14:21:

> 21 He that hath my commandments, and keepeth them, he it is that loveth me: and he that loveth me shall be loved of my Father, and I will love him, and will manifest myself to him.

Look at it. That's the whole picture. He "that hath my commandments" (that's you and me), the Father, Jesus and the manifestation of THE BLESSING.

You've been wildly rich, and wonderfully healed and well, all this time. It's yours. Lay hold of it. It's the hope set before you. However first things first. Make a quality decision right now to be a good steward of the Commandment of Love for now and forever.

Jesus took His place to receive our tithe and BLESSED us (Hebrews 7:1-8) forever. Now it's time for us to take our place as good stewards of the Commandment. That means I leave no excuse to violate the Commandment of Love. There may be reasons to violate it, but I WILL NOT DO IT! I must either fix the reason or ignore it. THE BLESSING is far too important and too precious to damage it. It cost too much. It saved me from a devil's hell.

Settle it forever by taking Communion. Then stand at attention and declare it before God the Father, before the Lord Jesus Christ and all His angels. Declare it before the devil and all his demons and fallen beings: "I am BLESSED. I am steward and keeper of Jesus' Commandment of Love. He loves me. My Father loves me, and Jesus—THE BLESSING—manifests Himself to me. I receive it now. I'm not BLESSED because I'm saved. I'm saved because I'm BLESSED. I'm not BLESSED because I'm healed. I'm healed because I'm BLESSED. I'm not BLESSED because I'm rich. I'm rich because I'm BLESSED. That's who Jesus is and that's who I am. <u>THE BLESSED</u>."

This is our message. Together we can and will shout it to the whole world.

As you sow your BLESSING seed this month, speak and declare those words over it. It is heavenly seed just as sure as the seed God planted in Genesis 2. Wow!

My, it is such a joy and a thrill sharing these things this month. Gloria and I love you, and we pray for you every day.

Love,

Ken

October 2008

What's the Big Deal?

Dear Partner

What a great summer. Three power-packed FULLNESS of BLESSING Believers' Conventions and all kinds of miracles happening everywhere you look. AND the best is yet to come. The rest of this year is really going to be something! Do whatever it takes to stir up the gift of God in you. The spirit of power, love and a sound mind. Stir yourself on the Word.

If you were in one or more of the conventions, go through it again with the CDs and DVDs. Get the conventions you missed and go through them—all three of them. If you missed them all, by all means get the DVDs and have your own conventions. All three of them were the most anointed meetings I've ever been in. Each one took us all to a higher level in the spirit and set our feet on higher ground. All the speakers seemed to preach beyond themselves. I know I did. It was simply marvelous.

In last month's letter we talked about why Jesus commanded us to love one another even as He loves us. We are His Body—His fullness according to Ephesians 1:16-23. Without us He cannot complete His mission as High Priest. He needs us strong. He needs us healthy. He needs us always having all sufficiency in all things, abounding to every good work (2 Corinthians 9:8). In other words, He needs us rich.

THE BLESSING of the LORD, it maketh rich, and THE BLESSING is totally Love dependent. Look at that phrase again from Proverbs 10:22: THE BLESSING of THE LORD. The English word LORD—capital L small capital ORD—is the translation of THE Name of the Almighty Most High God. YHVH. Why is that so important to know in Proverbs 10:22? YHVH, or LORD, is God, and God is Love. So THE BLESSING of Love maketh rich.

Wow! That really clears things up, doesn't it? That makes John 13:34-35 more clear than ever:

34	A new commandment I give unto you, That ye love one another; as I have loved you, that ye also love one another.
35	By this shall all men know that ye are my disciples, if ye have love one to another.

How will all men know? Because of THE BLESSING on us.

Now let's look at something on the opposite side of love—STRIFE. Everyone knows strife is not love, <u>but what's the big deal?</u> It goes on all the time.

Well, let's go to the Word and find out.

First of all, what does *strife* mean? It means discord, lack of agreement or harmony. Strife emphasizes a struggle for superiority. Let's take the time and space to look at a number of scriptures.

Hatred stirreth up strifes: but love covereth all sins. *Proverbs 10:12*

A wrathful man stirreth up strife: but he that is slow to anger appeaseth strife. *Proverbs 15:18*

A froward [disobedient] man soweth strife: and a whisperer separateth chief friends. *Proverbs 16:28*

The beginning of strife is as when one letteth out water [like a crack in a dam]: therefore leave off contention, before it be meddled with [before it becomes a fight]. *Proverbs 17:14*

He who loves strife and is quarrelsome loves transgression and involves himself in guilt; he who raises high his gateway and is boastful and arrogant invites destruction. *Proverbs 17:19,* The Amplified Bible

Cast out the scorner, and contention shall go out; yea, strife and reproach shall cease. *Proverbs 22:10*

Where no wood is, there the fire goeth out: so where there is no talebearer, the strife ceaseth. As coals are to burning coals, and wood to fire; so is a contentious man to kindle strife. *Proverbs 26:20-21*

An angry man stirreth up strife, and a furious man aboundeth in transgression. *Proverbs 29:22*

For ye are yet carnal: for whereas there is among you envying, and strife, and divisions, are ye not carnal, and walk as men? *1 Corinthians 3:3*

For I fear, lest, when I come, I shall not find you such as I would, and that I shall be found unto you such as ye would not: lest there be debates, envyings, wraths, strifes, backbitings, whisperings, swellings, tumults. *2 Corinthians 12:20*

Now the works of the flesh are manifest, which are these; adultery, fornication, uncleanness, lasciviousness, idolatry, witchcraft, hatred, variance, emulations, wrath, strife, seditions, heresies, envyings, murders, drunkenness, revellings, and such like: of the which I tell you before, as I have also told you in time past, that they which do such things shall not inherit the kingdom of God. *Galatians 5:19-21*

Look at the company strife keeps!

Let nothing be done through strife or vainglory; but in lowliness of mind let each esteem other better than themselves. *Philippians 2:3*

He is proud, knowing nothing, but doting about questions and strifes of words, whereof cometh envy, strife, railings, evil surmisings. *1 Timothy 6:4*

So now what's the big deal? Let's look at two more scriptures. First, 2 Timothy 2:23-26:

> 23 But foolish and unlearned questions avoid, knowing that they do gender strifes.

> 24 And the <u>servant of the Lord must not strive;</u> but be gentle unto all men, apt to teach, patient,
> 25 In meekness instructing those that oppose themselves; if God peradventure will give them repentance to the acknowledging of the truth;
> 26 And that they may recover themselves out of the snare of the devil, <u>who are taken captive by him at his will.</u>

That's the big deal. Satan takes people who are in strife captive at <u>his</u> will. I don't care how much they pray, fast, go to church and pray in tongues. Without Love—who is God—it doesn't work. Our praying without love, according to 1 Corinthians 13, is just a lot of noise.

Finally, James 3:14-16:

> 14 But if ye have bitter envying and strife in your hearts, glory not, and lie not against the truth.
> 15 This wisdom descendeth not from above, but is earthly, sensual, devilish.
> 16 For where envying and strife is, there is confusion and every evil work.

Where strife is, there is how much evil work? All of it. Every evil work. In the midst of the confusion, satan—not Jesus—is in command.

That's a BIG DEAL. Not only to you and me, but also to our Lord and Savior who loves and cares for us so deeply. In that confused, evil environment He can't get through, but the devil has access to one's innermost counsel. Every strife word unrepented of opens the door to fear. Fear connects to the spirit of fear. Faith connects to the spirit of faith. Faith works by Love. Fear works by strife.

Take the first step. Examine yourself. Take authority over your earthly, sensual, devilish flesh and repent according to 1 John 1:9. Confess the sin of strife. Confess the sin of unforgiveness.

Next, believe you receive your forgiveness and cleansing from all sin. Right then! Not after you feel forgiven. He is faithful to forgive and cleanse the moment you confess the sin in faith. Feeling guilty is a symptom of sin in your feelings and emotions.

Begin to praise and shout the victory: "Thank God I'm free from strife. Satan, I enforce 1 John 5:18 on you. You cannot take me captive. I obey the commandment of Love. You touch me not. I'm free from confusion. I'm a forgiver. I'm not a condemner."

The more you say that, the more 1 John 4:18 is released. Fear is leaving. Love is growing. And that changes everything.

As you sow your Blessing seed, know this—in fact, say this: *I know now my seed is alive and THE BLESSING is working.*

It's working in me.

It's working through me.

It's working around me.

It's blessing everyone with whom I come in contact.

Jesus needs me, and now I'm ready.

Gloria and I love you and we pray for you every day.

Love,

Ken

P.S. Pray! Vote! Pray! Jesus needs us to vote His way! —KC

November 2008

What Are You Going To Do—Now?!

Dear Partner,

How long have we been together? Some only a short time. Others five years, 10 years—and a number 30 years and more. We know of families that have been our Partners for many years, the parents have since gone home to be with the Lord, and now the children and their families have continued their partnership.

The wonders and joys of the family of God doing the works of God together never cease to amaze me. The Scripture says it will continue until we all come together in the unity of our faith. We are closer to that happening than ever before. Stronger and stronger. Bigger and bigger. Blessed without measure. That's the image our heavenly Father has had of His family since before the foundation of the world. It is finally coming to pass. And thanks be to Jesus, you and I are right in the middle of it all.

In this letter today, let's go back to some familiar but oh, so important things that have to do with remaining strong and steady in such an unstable atmosphere as what's going on around us.

Is it OK for us to just fall apart like everyone else when unexpected things happen? No! It is not OK!

"How then, Brother Copeland, can I keep it together when all of a sudden the company I work for goes broke or lays me off? Especially if it's for no reason."

First of all, get over that "for no reason" idea. No one—not you, nor me, nor anyone else—can ever grow and improve at what we do as long as that idea is allowed to remain. Let's look at Proverbs 26:2:

> 2   As the bird by wandering, as the swallow by flying, so the curse causeless shall not come.

Now from the *Amplified* translation:

> 2   Like the sparrow in her wandering, like the swallow in her flying, so the causeless curse does not alight.

Your very first response should always be, "I'm going to stay in Love, stay in faith and do what the Word says and not what I feel!" Always then examine yourself according to 1 Corinthians 11:28-32:

> 28   But let a man examine himself, and so let him eat of that bread, and drink of that cup.
> 29   For he that eateth and drinketh unworthily, eateth and drinketh damnation to himself, not discerning the Lord's body.
> 30   For this cause many are weak and sickly among you, and many sleep.
> 31   For if we would judge ourselves, we should not be judged.
> 32   But when we are judged, we are chastened of the Lord, that we should not be condemned with the world.

"Lord, did I open the door to this? If I did, I need to know it." Now here's where it gets down deep inside your inner being: "If I did, then I repent with my whole heart, and I am willing to do whatever it takes to fix and change me. Not the boss-man. Not anyone else. ME!"

So much of the time, after shining the light of the Word on yourself, you come to the conclusion that "if I'd been them, I would have fired me too." Now you've just become stronger in the Lord and in the power of His might. You have just become much more valuable to the plan of God and also to the workplace.

It doesn't matter what "they" think. "They" cannot hold you back. You are redeemed from the curse of anything that the world and its system can do to hold you back. The only thing that holds back and hinders the success of any believer is joining in with that system and doing all the things the world does.

Let's see where promotion comes from. Psalm 75:5-7:

> 5 Lift not up your horn on high: speak not with a stiff neck.
> 6 For promotion cometh neither from the east, nor from the west, nor from the south.
> 7 But God is the judge: he putteth down one, and setteth up another.

In Scripture, the word *horn* is a symbol of strength, power, glory, honor and dignity. It represents an animal whose horn or horns represent its power and importance.

Psalm 75:5-7 is simply saying for God to promote you, you must stop trying to do it your own way. There's no such thing as your own way. If it's not God's way, then it's the world's way—the way in which being held back by people, fear, politics, racism, etc., is everyday stuff. Even if one is a born-again child of God, if he does what causes lack, he will surely have lack in abundance. Reacting to loss in anger, fear or self-exaltation like the gentiles do only acts to open the door wider to the destruction.

What can we do to grow up and become stronger before these kinds of things happen? Meditate and prepare your mind and emotions to react properly before they happen. Do you think Joshua never gave a thought about how to fight a war God's way until he got into combat? Let's see. Joshua 1:1-8:

> 1 Now after the death of Moses the servant of the Lord it came to pass, that the Lord spake unto Joshua the son of Nun, Moses' minister, saying,
> 2 Moses my servant is dead; now therefore arise, go over this Jordan, thou, and all this people, unto the land which I do give to them, even to the children of Israel.
> 3 Every place that the sole of your foot shall tread upon, that have I given unto you, as I said unto Moses.
> 4 From the wilderness and this Lebanon even

5 unto the great river, the river Euphrates, all the land of the Hittites, and unto the great sea toward the going down of the sun, shall be your coast.

5 There shall not any man be able to stand before thee all the days of thy life: as I was with Moses, so I will be with thee: I will not fail thee, nor forsake thee.

6 Be strong and of a good courage: for unto this people shalt thou divide for an inheritance the land, which I sware unto their fathers to give them.

7 Only be thou strong and very courageous, that thou mayest observe to do according to all the law, which Moses my servant commanded thee: turn not from it to the right hand or to the left, that thou mayest prosper whithersoever thou goest.

8 This book of the law shall not depart out of thy mouth; but thou shalt meditate therein day and night, that thou mayest <u>observe</u> to do according to all that is written therein: for then thou shalt make thy way prosperous, and then thou shalt have good success.

Look in verse 8 at the word *observe,* or "see into." "See" yourself responding in love. See yourself never ever being in lack. See yourself strong and victorious, always with heaven's plan. Don't <u>ever</u> see yourself as a victim. You are victorious in Jesus always.

"But, Brother Copeland, won't meditating on these things just bring them on me?" Only if you do it in fear. Notice that before God told him to meditate day and night, He first told him what to meditate on: "There shall not any man be able to stand before you all the days of your life.... Only..."! <u>Only</u>—what? "Only be strong and of good courage that you may observe to do according to the Law—My Word, My way! My way is always greater than the enemy's way. Do it My way and prosper. Do it 'their' way and fail."

All of this takes time. I know you "don't have time," but you will if you get laid off. Make the time. I don't have time to go back to recurrent flight training twice a year, so I make time. Why? So I don't do something stupid and crash. Take time out of your entertainment. Especially TV. Very quickly you'll begin enjoying your time in your "life simulator" so much you wouldn't give that time up for anything. Especially after it saves your life a few times and puts you in the right place at the right time—PROMOTION!

As you sow your financial seeds, speak out loud: "My promotion—my harvest—my BLESSING does not come from the east or the west or the south. My lifting up comes from my Father in heaven. He has BLESSED me in Christ Jesus. Never let it be said that any man promoted me but the God of Abraham. Nothing in this world order can hold me back or arrest my harvest. I receive it. It's mine. I'm BLESSED—I'm BLESSED—I'm BLESSED."

Now shout and give all the glory and praise to the One who gave Himself for you—Jesus! High Priest forever!

Stand with Gloria and me in prayer and faith. We're preparing for a very busy, marvelous year in 2009. We love you and pray for you every day.

Love,

Ken

December 2008

Keep Your Eyes on Me (Jesus)
and You'll Get the Job Done!

Dear Partner,

Sunday, October 19, 2008, I was praying over John 16:13-15:

> 13   Howbeit when he, the Spirit of truth, is come, he will guide you into all truth: for he shall not speak of himself; but whatsoever he shall hear, that shall he speak: and he will show you things to come.
>
> 14   He shall glorify me: for he shall receive of mine, and shall show it unto you.
>
> 15   All things that the Father hath are mine: therefore said I, that he shall take of mine, and shall show it unto you.

I know there's no problem with the Holy Spirit's hearing, so it must be with mine. He will and does show us things to come that glorify Jesus. And how to glorify Him in things that don't. So I opened my ears to hear. And I immediately heard these words:

Don't pay attention to or make any plans based on what the media says or what [politicians] say. Stand on My Word in John 16. Pay attention to Me. I [the Holy Spirit] will obey verses 13-15. I will show you things to come. I will lead you through troubled times. I already have THE plan for you, and it's very good. Follow it. It will not only get you through, it will place you in a very high place—a rich place—a strong place of victory.

You will have to discipline yourself and be diligent to listen to Me. All the other voices will have a plan, a word, an idea for your future and security. Don't listen to Babylon's system. It has fallen apart. My system is stronger than ever. My kingdom is flourishing, and THE BLESSING is the place to be.

Keep your eyes on My Word. Listen to it. It will guide you and I will perform it. Love Me. Love My people as I have loved you. Walk in it. Love

<u>never fails</u>, and neither does My plan.

Be very cautious to stay completely clean from covetousness. First Timothy 6:10 must live in the forefront of your thinking. If you will do these things and continue therein, you will come into your wealthy place. A place lifted up. A place in Me already planned and prepared for you now. Here. Not heaven—not yet. But it will seem like heaven right in the midst of all the trouble, and you'll be able to reach out to untold numbers of suffering people with the Good News of the gospel.

I'm coming very soon. Sooner than you think. Keep your eyes on Me and you'll get the job done.

Let's look at 1 Timothy 6:10:

> 10   For the love of money is the root of all evil: which while some coveted after, they have erred from the faith, and pierced themselves through with many sorrows.

The love of money and covetousness are the same thing. People commit that sin who don't have money or anything else. Having money and things is not the problem. Loving it is. Being afraid you'll not have any is a problem! Planning your actions and your future around money and things is a big problem.

Our planning and desires must be based on obeying God and being available to His Spirit to be used of Him any way, any time, anywhere He needs us. That plan works and it's well-financed and abundantly supplied. That plan does not depend on politicians and government solutions. Politicians need to learn to depend on Jesus and His BLESSING plans for our country.

To receive His plan and direction promised in John 16:13-15, from what we've just learned it's obvious our focus must be on becoming aware of loving money. Covetousness.

First, as always, our words. What are we saying? What are our word habits in this area? I was shocked when I first began to open my ears to what was coming out my mouth. One of the first things I heard myself say was how much I love my car. The Lord did not give me that car to "love." He gave it to me to enjoy.

"Augh, Brother Copeland, isn't that just being picky?"

No. That's becoming aware. That's training. Correct yourself and line up with the Word. Look at something that has blessed you and instead of saying how much you love it, praise God for it and say, "That's the work of the Lord and it's marvelous in my eyes. I really do enjoy it and I'm ready, Lord, to sow it anywhere, anytime You call for it."

Now you have not only lined up with Psalm 118:23: "This is the Lord's doing; it is marvellous in our eyes," but also again with verse 17 in 1 Timothy 6:

> 17   Charge them that are rich in this world, that they be not highminded, nor trust in uncertain riches, but in the living God, who giveth us richly all things to enjoy.

That leads us to the second step of our training. See how awareness works? It has led us right into the flow of the Word and plan.

That 1 Timothy 6:10 could not be saying that having money and loving it—or being covetous of it—are the same thing is clearly laid out in verses 17-19. As I said, verse 17 is our direction:

1. Don't get high-minded, proud and start showing off how much faith you have because you received a new car, etc.

2. Don't ever put trust in things. Watch your emotions. Does the thought of losing things or money stir up fear? Rebuke it. Your God loves you and He has an abundance of things. Seek Him, His Word and His plan, and all these things will be added to you.

3. Do good! Never! ever! use people to get things! Use things to love people. That is the result of training your words and thoughts. I don't love things. I love God and I love people.

4. Stay willing and ready. That sets you up for verse 19. Your storehouse will always be full no matter what comes in the world and its Babylonian system.

5. Lay hold on eternal life. That's ZOE in Greek—the Life of God. The very force that makes God, God. It came into you when you were born again. Realize it by faith. Everything you need now, or ever will need, is laid up for you. Get on Mark 11:22-25. Put Jesus' words to work immediately. That's what the Holy Spirit has come to perform—the Word of THE BLESSING.

Galatians 6:6-10 makes laying hold on and harvesting life very simple and very plain. Sow <u>SOMETHING!</u> Act on the Word. Do it now. If bad news of <u>any</u> kind comes, act on the Word. Don't react to evil tidings. I don't care how "serious" the news or how bad the word is, it's not big enough to overcome ETERNAL LIFE. That's <u>Word Life.</u> That's <u>faith Life.</u> That's <u>the Life of God</u> = LOVE. It NEVER fails!

Lay your hands on your seed of Life and shout, "BLESSED! FEAR STOP! NOW! I obey Jesus and I <u>believe</u> only, and I shall be made <u>whole</u>."

Now, go through and with all your heart believe and claim the 112th Psalm. That's you! That's you right now!

1. Praise ye the Lord. Blessed is the man that feareth the Lord, that delighteth greatly in his commandments.
2. His seed shall be mighty upon earth: the generation of the upright shall be blessed.
3. Wealth and riches shall be in his house: and

	his righteousness endureth for ever.
4	Unto the upright there ariseth light in the darkness: he is gracious, and full of compassion, and righteous.
5	A good man showeth favour, and lendeth: he will guide his affairs with discretion.
6	Surely he shall not be moved for ever: the righteous shall be in everlasting remembrance.
7	He shall not be afraid of evil tidings: his heart is fixed, trusting in the Lord.
8	His heart is established, he shall not be afraid, until he see his desire upon his enemies.
9	He hath dispersed, he hath given to the poor; his righteousness endureth for ever; his horn shall be exalted with honour.
10	The wicked shall see it, and be grieved; he shall gnash with his teeth, and melt away: the desire of the wicked shall perish.

Gloria and I, and over 500 people here at KCM, are believing and pulling for you in prayer and faith. All the other Partners are standing with you as you pray and believe for them. Together WE'LL GET THE JOB DONE.

We all love you very much.

Love,

Ken

P.S. This is the greatest Christmas going into the wildest, most BLESSED year of God's glory we've ever seen! Have a joyous Christmas and a fabulous 2009. —Kenneth and Gloria

Preaching the Word of THE BLESSING is our job for 2009!

January 2009

Have a BLESSED 2009!

Dear Partner

What about 2009?

Well, what about it? What do <u>you</u> see happening? What are <u>you</u> hearing? What is <u>your</u> understanding about all this?

Let's go back over the verses of Scripture that we talked about in last month's letter. In John 16:13-15 Jesus said:

> 13   Howbeit when he, the Spirit of truth, is come, he will guide you into all truth: for he shall not speak of himself; but whatsoever he shall hear, that shall he speak: and he will show you things to come.
> 14   He shall glorify me: for he shall receive of mine, and shall show it unto you.
> 15   All things that the Father hath are mine: therefore said I, that he shall take of mine, and shall show it unto you.

October 19, 2008, I was reading those verses, and it struck my thinking that Jesus is responsible for me being led and guided every step of my life. He's my Lord. He's my Savior. He's my High Priest forever. He sent His Spirit, THE SPIRIT OF TRUTH, to carry out that responsibility.

<u>Jesus is speaking.</u> The Holy Spirit is relaying that word to me, inside me. It can't possibly be that Jesus refuses to speak to me. He's speaking The Word of Heaven's plan, THE BLESSING, into my life faithfully. He is a faithful High Priest. The Holy Spirit does not have a hearing or a speaking problem. The problems are with me—with my hearing the voice of His Spirit leading and guiding my spirit.

I immediately acted on those verses and releasing my faith and attention to hear, I said, "I believe Jesus is speaking into my life. I believe

THE Holy Spirit is listening and speaking into my spirit and showing me <u>things to come</u>!"

Then I said, "I turn my attention toward His Word. I open my ears to hear. I open my eyes to see. I open my understanding by committing myself to acting on what He leads me to do. I hold out nothing for myself. My will does not count for anything except that I <u>will</u> to put His plan first place. His will is final authority."

No sooner had I done this than THE Word of the Lord came, and I heard Him plainly give words of wisdom and instruction. (I've included another copy of that word.) I didn't try to hear with my natural ears (the paddles on the sides of my head). No, I turned inward, listening to my inner man—my spirit. I did what Habakkuk did in Habakkuk 2:1-3:

1	I will stand upon my watch, and set me upon the tower, and will watch to see what he will say unto me, and what I shall answer when I am reproved.
2	And the Lord answered me, and said, Write the vision, and make it plain upon tables, that he may run that readeth it.
3	For the vision is yet for an appointed time, but at the end it shall speak, and not lie: though it tarry, wait for it; because it will surely come, it will not tarry.

To do this, especially if you've not done it very often, you will need to get still and quiet. Just begin to praise and worship and give thanks because your heavenly Father loves you so much. He loves you just as much as He loves Jesus. He's not holding out on you. With all His heart He wants you to know everything you need to know about being victorious and greatly BLESSED in every area of life. Jesus paid for it all on the cross so you could know everything He knows about your glorious future in Him. He then sent the Holy Spirit to reveal it to you.

Believe that. Believe it now. This very moment. In that atmosphere of praise and worship, you <u>will</u> hear from heaven.

Now let's go over to the 13th chapter of Matthew and check out something else Jesus said along these same lines. First, in verse 9 He said, "He who hath ears to hear, let him hear." Now, that makes it very clear that He's not choosing to whom He will speak. <u>The choice is a step of faith.</u> Our choice.

Then He acts on what He just said by saying in verse 18, "<u>You hear,</u> therefore the parable of the sower...." Now look very carefully at the first phrase of verse 19. "When <u>any one</u> hears <u>the word of the kingdom</u>...." That's what we're listening for: The Word of faith, The Word of God. The Word of the anointing. The Word of healing. THE BLESSING of THE LORD!

Now, here comes the bottom line of what He is saying in the teaching of this letter. Let's very carefully and aloud read verse 15:

> 15 For this people's heart is waxed gross, and their ears are dull of hearing, and their eyes they have closed; lest <u>at any time</u> they should see [the Word of the kingdom] with their eyes, and hear [the Word of the kingdom] with their ears, and should understand [the Word of the kingdom] with their heart, and should be converted [change what they see, change what they hear and change the way they think and what they say], and I should heal them.

The word *should* there means "as soon as they do this"—it also means "will."

Wait a minute now before you shout. I know that's wonderful, but look at verse 16:

> 16 But <u>BLESSED</u> are your eyes, for they see: and [BLESSED are] your ears, for they hear.

Now go ahead and shout: "Any time is NOW! MY EYES ARE BLESSED! MY EARS ARE BLESSED!"

That's not just with reference to healing of the physical body. The word translated *heal* in that verse means "healings" plural. Jesus is saying, "Whatever is wrong, whatever is broken, whatever is lacking, I came that you might have life and have it more abundantly. Life till it overflows." Your ears are BLESSED! Your eyes are BLESSED! You are THE BLESSED!

What about 2009? What do you <u>see</u> happening? Look through BLESSED eyes. What are you hearing? Listen through BLESSED ears. What is your understanding about all this? Understand with a BLESSED heart.

As you sow your BLESSING seed this month, lay your hands on it and declare, "I'm BLESSED to see. I'm BLESSED to hear. I'm BLESSED to understand. I sow this seed to the spirit, and I receive and reap everlasting life. ZOE life. THE BLESSED life."

We make no plans based on what the news media says or what the politicians say. The Lord Jesus always reveals to us things to come. We're not in a recession. We're BLESSED. We're not in a depression. We're in the kingdom of God, where there is no depression.

Read this letter over and over until these words get bigger inside than the words of Babel coming from the outside.

Preaching this Word of THE BLESSING is our job for 2009. We're preaching it from the top of the world to the bottom, and all the way around the middle. We'll preach it with all our might in Christ Jesus! Together we can—and WILL—do it!

Gloria and I and all of us here at KCM love you and pray for you every day.

Love,

Ken

P.S. Have the most thrilling and BLESSED year of your life. —Ken

"Howbeit when he, the Spirit of truth, is come, he will guide you into all truth: for he shall not speak of himself; but whatsoever he shall hear, that shall he speak: and he will show you things to come."
John 16:13

Word of the Lord to Kenneth Copeland, October 19, 2008

Don't pay attention to or make any plans based on what the media says or what [politicians] say. Stand on My Word in John 16. Pay attention to Me. I [the Holy Spirit] <u>will</u> obey verses 13-15. I will show you things to come. I will lead you through troubled times. I already have THE plan for you, and it's very good. Follow it. It will not only get you through, it will place you in a very high place—a rich place—a strong place of victory.

You will have to discipline yourself and be diligent to listen to Me. <u>All</u> the other voices will have a plan, a word, an idea for your future and security. Don't listen to Babylon's system. It has fallen apart. My system is stronger than ever. My kingdom is flourishing, and THE BLESSING is the place to be.

Keep your eyes on My Word. Listen to it. It will guide you and I will perform it. Love Me. Love My people as I have loved you. Walk in it. Love <u>never</u> fails, and neither does My plan.

Be very cautious to stay completely clean from covetousness. First Timothy 6:10 must live in the forefront of your thinking. If you will do these things and continue therein, you will come into your wealthy place. A place lifted up. A place in Me already planned and prepared for you now. Here. Not heaven—not yet. But it will seem like heaven right in the midst of all the trouble, and you'll be able to reach out to untold numbers of suffering people with the Good News of the gospel.

I'm coming very soon. Sooner than you think. Keep your eyes on Me and you'll get the job done.

February 2009

What Are You Looking At?!

Dear Partner

Last month's letter was based on a powerful word from the Lord concerning not only what is happening all around us, but for all of 2009. The year 2009 is just the first year of the rest of our future. He said, <u>*Keep your eyes on Me.*</u>

Why is that so important? Look at the heading of this letter again: "WHAT ARE YOU LOOKING AT?" What are you? You are whatever you've been looking at. Whatever you focus on most is what you become.

This is a strong biblical truth that controls all human learning. Consequently, it is the root of all conduct and behavior. If you keep your eye on your instructor, you will eventually become like him. That's the reason you hire an instructor in the first place.

If you keep your eye on all the failing and falling going on around you, you will follow it. You may say, "I'll never be mean like my mean father was to me." But you will if you don't forgive your father and get your eyes off his meanness and look at how Jesus has forgiven you.

In John 1:35-38:

> 35 Again the next day after John stood, and two of his disciples;
> 36 And looking upon Jesus as he walked, he saith, Behold the Lamb of God!
> 37 And the two disciples heard him speak, and they followed Jesus.
> 38 Then Jesus turned, and saw them following, and saith unto them, What seek ye? They said unto him, Rabbi, (which is to say, being interpreted, Master,) where dwellest thou?

Jesus asked, "What seek ye?" Or, "<u>What are you looking for?</u>" At that time all they wanted to see was where He lived. Had they turned away or looked back, that's all they would have seen. Look on down at verses 50-51:

> 50   Jesus answered and said unto him, Because I said unto thee, I saw thee under the fig tree, believest thou? thou shalt see greater things than these.
> 51   And he saith unto him, Verily, verily, I say unto you, Hereafter ye shall see heaven open, and the angels of God ascending and descending upon the Son of man.

<u>Keep your eyes on Me!</u> To keep your eyes on Jesus will open up heaven, and you'll see heaven's ways of doing things. Judas took his eyes off Jesus and began looking at money. Right in the presence of heaven's light and glory, all he could see was failure. Money finally became more important to him and more precious in his eyes than Jesus.

Look at John 12:1-8:

> 1   Then Jesus six days before the passover came to Bethany, where Lazarus was which had been dead, whom he raised from the dead.
> 2   There they made him a supper; and Martha served: but Lazarus was one of them that sat at the table with him.
> 3   Then took Mary a pound of ointment of spikenard, <u>very costly</u> [approximately $30,000 today], and anointed the feet of Jesus, and wiped his feet with her hair: and the house was filled with the odour of the ointment.
> 4   Then saith one of his disciples, Judas Iscariot, Simon's son, which should betray him,
> 5   Why was not this ointment sold for three hundred pence, and given to the poor?
> 6   This he said, not that he cared for the poor; but because he was a thief, and had the bag, and bare what was put therein.
> 7   Then said Jesus, <u>Let her alone:</u> against the day of my burying hath she kept this.

> 8 For the poor always ye have with you; but me ye have not always.

Mary was the one, remember, who chose the Word and wouldn't let Him out of her sight when Martha was <u>upset</u> about all the cooking she had to do (Luke 10:38-42). Mary was so grateful and faithful to His Word that He had become very precious to her. To her He was worth far more than the most expensive thing she owned. Why? She had kept her eyes on Him and on His Word.

Whatever you focus on the most becomes the most important thing in your life. Let's look at Mark 14:4:

> 4 And there were some that had indignation within themselves, and said, Why was this waste of the ointment made?

What was precious to Mary was seen as a waste to Judas and some of the others present. "Oh, Brother Copeland, I would never think that way about Jesus." You do if you're spending more time worrying about your job than you do in His Word. Or, if your children and their behavior is on your mind more than the promises of Abraham.

"But I just don't have time. My retirement is gone. My company is laying everyone off. I just don't know what I'm going to do. I even had to quit tithing."

You have become what you're looking at. You're looking at the world and the things of the world, and it has become more precious to you than the Word of God. <u>Tithing is the most important thing you could do right now.</u> Put your eyes on the promises of the Most High God to the tither, and <u>tithe something</u> QUICK!

Your Babylonian friends will say, "Tithe? You can't be wasting your money like that. Not now. You'd better hang on to it. Don't you know you're about to lose everything?"

NO! I'm not! The windows of <u>heaven</u> are opened to me! What did Jesus say would happen? We read it in John, chapter 1—you'll see heaven open up.

God told Joshua to "meditate on My Word day and night and you'll 'see' how to do all that's written therein." Joshua was headed into combat. He absolutely could not think and worry about dying in battle. He would lose his vision and along with that his courage. God's Word said, "Be strong and very courageous." Worry said, "The land's filled with giants, and you're going to die and fail God and all of Israel." Joshua stayed with the Word, and he became what it said.

What are you looking at when you stay focused on Jesus? <u>He is the Word</u> of our salvation. <u>He is THE Life,</u> and <u>THE Life is the Light.</u> <u>He is the author of our faith</u> and the finisher, or the developer, of it. Faith is the victory that overcomes the world. <u>He is the minister of grace and mercy</u> that helps in times of need.

He is able to make <u>all</u> grace abound toward you so that you <u>always</u> having <u>all</u> sufficiency in <u>all</u> things may <u>abound</u> to <u>every</u> good work!

<u>He is Lord!</u> <u>He is the Father's Love.</u> He is <u>High Priest</u> forever over THE BLESSING—the Eden Covenant! He doesn't need Wall Street or anyone's government handout to meet your every need according to His riches in glory. Did you get that? <u>His riches!</u> Debt-free, filled-with-joy riches. Not riches filled with sorrow and worry. Proverbs 10:22:

> 22   The blessing of the Lord, it maketh rich, and he addeth no sorrow with it.

<u>He is the kingdom.</u> Put Him <u>first.</u> Be like Mary. Choose Him by choosing His Word. Make it final authority in everything.

Don't look back! Every time you do, you lose momentum. Press forward. Keep Jesus—THE PRIZE, THE HIGH CALLING—before your eyes. Never, ever compromise the Word or your faith to get money. Having done all to stand, STAND! How long? STAND! With what? STAND! How?

> My son, attend to my words; incline thine ear unto my sayings. <u>Let them not depart from thine eyes;</u> keep them in the midst of thine heart. <u>For they are life</u> unto those that find them, and health to all their flesh. Keep thy heart with all diligence; for

out of it are the issues of life. Put away from thee a froward mouth, and perverse lips put far from thee. Let thine eyes look right on, and let thine eyelids look straight before thee. Ponder the path of thy feet, and let all thy ways be established. Turn not to the right hand nor to the left: remove thy foot from evil (Proverbs 4:20-27).

I close with this. If you didn't have what it takes to make it in this dangerous generation, God would have had you born some other time!

The following is the picture of you and me in 2009:

Praise ye the Lord. <u>Blessed is the man</u> that feareth the Lord, that delighteth greatly in his commandments. His seed shall be mighty upon earth: the generation of the upright shall be blessed. <u>Wealth and riches shall be in his house:</u> and <u>his righteousness endureth</u> for ever. Unto the upright <u>there ariseth light in the darkness:</u> he is gracious, and full of compassion, and righteous. A good man showeth favour, and lendeth: he will guide his affairs with discretion. Surely <u>he shall not be moved for ever:</u> the righteous shall be in everlasting remembrance. <u>He shall not be afraid of evil tidings:</u> his <u>heart is fixed, trusting in the Lord.</u> His heart is established, <u>he shall not be afraid,</u> until he see his desire upon his enemies. He hath dispersed, he hath given to the poor; his righteousness endureth for ever; <u>his horn shall be exalted with honour.</u> The wicked shall see it, and be grieved; he shall gnash with his teeth, <u>and melt away:</u> the desire of the wicked shall perish (Psalm 112).

That's the way God sees you, and that's the way Gloria and I see you. We love you and pray for you every day.

Love,

Ken

March 2009

Stay on God's Side of Everything!

Dear Partner,

I want us to look at a key scripture today that will be of great help in the middle of all this whirl of ideas, reports, media junk, Wall Street junk, and all the other stuff flying around these days about the economy. We've talked about this principle before. Today, we're going to look at it from a different angle.

Remember I wrote to you about "What are you looking at"? We are whatever we focus our eyes on the most. To be like Jesus, we must keep our eyes on Him. Not just religious ideas *about* Him, but *on* Him. If we've seen Him, we've seen the Father. To see either One, we have to keep our eyes on the Word.

The scripture to which I'm referring is Proverbs 4:20-27:

20   My son, attend to my words; incline thine ear unto my sayings.
21   Let them not depart from thine eyes; keep them in the midst of thine heart.
22   For they are life unto those that find them, and health to all their flesh.
23   Keep thy heart with all diligence; for out of it are the issues of life.
24   Put away from thee a froward mouth, and perverse lips put far from thee.
25   Let thine eyes look right on, and let thine eyelids look straight before thee.
26   Ponder the path of thy feet, and let all thy ways be established.
27   Turn not to the right hand nor to the left: remove thy foot from evil.

Let's break this down into steps toward our goal—to be like Jesus and not like the world. He is not confused, and neither should we be.

He's not sick, and neither should we be. He's not worried about the economy, and neither should we be.

The first step is to obey verse 20. <u>God's Word is right!</u> Whether it sounds right and looks right, or not. So then, we must commit to it. We must never try to alter the Word to fit our lifestyle. We change our lifestyle to fit the Word!

Step two is to keep it in front of our eyes! Not just when we think we need it, but constantly. It must replace all the other things that try to get our attention.

Once those two steps are in place, step three becomes a reality: Keep His words in the midst of our hearts. Jesus laid all this out in Mark 4:14-20. He taught there what would happen if the devil is allowed to sidetrack our attention. He also taught what would happen if we kept the Word in our hearts—harvest! Some thirty-, some sixty- and some a hundredfold! That's to what verse 22 is referring.

The next step is to become aware of how vitally important the spiritual forces resident in our born-again spirit are to our life and health. Keep our eyes off things that rob us of our peace. Don't listen to questions that gender strife. Stay on the faith side of everything. To do that we must always stay on the Love side—God's side. <u>NEVER, EVER</u> take sides against God or His Word!

By keeping the Word in our eyes and in our hearts, the next step becomes a way of life. Because out of the abundance of the heart the mouth speaks. We are to put away a disobedient mouth, or a mouth of unbelief.

Verses 25, 26 and 27 are back to what we are to continually fix our eyes upon. However, if we don't hold fast to steps one and two—put the Word in authority and keep our eyes on it (on Jesus)—how will we know the left hand from the right? What good will it do to "ponder the path[s] of [our] feet" if we don't know which path is right?

Now we have identified the real problem—<u>confusion!</u> There is a way that seems right to (natural) man, but the end thereof is death—disaster. (See Proverbs 14:12 and 16:25.) <u>The definition of the word</u>

confusion is "a mixture of several thoughts, ideas or things being blended and mixed together creating disorder in the mind."

When the Lord commanded me to never again go into debt, I couldn't <u>see</u> how Gloria and I could even live, much less accomplish what He had called us to do. Why? So many other ideas made it hard to believe that. All that stuff mixed and blended together brought confusion.

Before I learned that from the Word, borrowing looked like the "path" to take. It looked like, in most cases, the only path available.

That all changed once Gloria and I saw it in the Word. We had no understanding of it, but we had already put step one firmly in place. The Word said it, and we changed our "way" of doing things to fit that Word. That's when the Spirit of Truth Himself began to train us. Eleven months later we were debt free, and have been ever since. We didn't get the training and understanding first and then make the commitment that the Word was right. It doesn't work that way. Faith is the key issue in all things of God.

<u>Why can't the world see these things?</u> They've been confused ever since the tower of Babel. Their entire way of life is based on a system of confusion. The answer is simple. At the tower of Babel God scrambled their imaginations. Let's look at it. Genesis 11:1-7:

> 1 And the whole earth was of one language [Heb. = one purpose], and of one speech.
> 2 And it came to pass, as they journeyed from the east, that they found a plain in the land of Shinar; and they dwelt there.
> 3 And they said one to another, Go to, let us make brick, and burn them thoroughly. And they had brick for stone, and slime had they for mortar.
> 4 And they said, Go to, let us build us a city and a tower, whose top may reach unto heaven; and let us make us a name, lest we be scattered abroad upon the face of the whole earth.
> 5 And the Lord came down to see the city and

	the tower, which the children of men builded.
6	And the Lord said, Behold, the people is one, and they have all one language; and this they begin to do: and now nothing will be restrained from them, which they have imagined to do.
7	Go to, let us go down, and there confound their language, that they may not understand one another's speech.

They all had one language, one purpose, one understanding: Imagine it, believe it, say it and it will come to pass. That's the way God created the earth and everything in it. That's the way it worked. That's the only process anyone had ever heard of. It worked. So who needed God?

That's the way it looked to them, but we know what was going on behind all that. Satan had become god of this world. He's the one behind what they were doing. He was using them to get whatever he wanted done in the earth. A cap had to be placed on that natural system so that it could never succeed in replacing God in the earth. That same system is what we are watching crumble all around us.

So the bottom line is the unsaved person or the carnally minded Christian cannot control their imagination. If you can't imagine it you can't believe it. If you can't believe it you can't say it. If you can't say it, it will not come to pass.

I didn't say they cannot imagine. They can. <u>They just can't control it.</u> Oh, they imagine all right. They can see themselves losing their jobs, losing their homes, losing their health and losing their lives before they're 50 years old. So they worry or meditate on it until they believe it. Then they say it, and say it, and worry, and say it some more, until it comes to pass. And then, "Why does this kind of thing always happen to me?"

The believer's advantage is in the mighty power of God in the weapons of our warfare. Look at 2 Corinthians 10:3-5. Get ready to shout!

3	For though we walk in the flesh, we do not war after the flesh:

4	(For the weapons of our warfare are not carnal, but mighty through God to the pulling down of strong holds;)
5	<u>Casting down imaginations,</u> and every high thing that exalteth itself against the knowledge of God, and <u>bringing into captivity</u> every thought to the obedience of Christ.

Do what to <u>imaginations</u> that rise up against <u>what you know God's Word says?</u> Cast them down! And put them in prison so they can never take root and spoil your faith. You know what the Word says, and you've committed to it. Your eyes are fixed on the Truth. "My needs are met according to His riches in glory!" <u>Now the more you keep looking at it, at Jesus, at your merciful, heavenly, rich Father,</u> the stronger your imagination—or your inner image and purpose—becomes. That's the mighty power in verse 4. It's no longer just <u>your</u> imagination anymore. It's a blueprint for faith. Hope! Now watch Love bring it to pass.

That, my dear Partner, is what 2009 is all about.

As you sow your seed this month, look at the Word, then at your seed and back and forth until you "see" the greatest year of your life all around you. Not just a little better. Go on and dream! Let it grow then let it go! You're in THE BLESSING and that's the place to be.

Gloria and I love you and pray for you, and we believe in you. Together we'll get the job done.

Love,

Ken

April 2009

Abounding in Grace

Dear Partner,

For the past several weeks, the same phrase has been going over and over from my spirit to my mind and out my mouth: "Isaac sowed in famine and reaped a hundredfold the same year." In that same famine (Genesis 26) he not only got back the wells that his father, Abraham, had dug, but he also dug new wells. Of course the devil fought him over every one of them, but he just kept on digging.

Then the Lord led him just across the valley, where he dug a new well. But this time he struck an underground river. Not just a well, but a river. All this in time of famine. THE BLESSING was working, and not only for Isaac. That whole area made it through hard times because the Lord God performed the oath He had promised Isaac's father, Abraham. Let's look at it in Genesis 26:2-3:

> 2   And the Lord appeared unto him, and said, Go not down into Egypt; dwell in the land which I shall tell thee of:
> 3   Sojourn in this land, and I will be with thee, and will bless thee; for unto thee, and unto thy seed, I will give all these countries, and I will perform the oath which I sware unto Abraham thy father.

Notice in verse 2 he was told not to go to Egypt. Stay put. Why? God didn't need him in Egypt. He needed him where the famine was. With that in mind, let's look at Isaiah 51:1-3 and see what the Father had in mind doing in that place in that famine:

> 1   Hearken to me, ye that follow after righteousness, ye that seek the Lord: look unto the rock whence ye are hewn, and to the hole of the pit whence ye are digged.
> 2   Look unto Abraham your father, and unto

> Sarah that bore you: for I called him alone, and blessed him, and increased him.
> 3 For the Lord shall comfort Zion: he will comfort all her waste places; and he will make her wilderness <u>like Eden,</u> and her desert <u>like the garden of the Lord;</u> joy and gladness shall be found therein, thanksgiving, and the voice of melody.

That's the reason why Abraham's covenant is called the Eden covenant. Our Creator planned and planted a garden in Eden and then He created man and placed him in it. That was His plan then and He never changes. That's His plan today. That's His plan for you and me just as much as it was for Adam, Abraham, Isaac, you, me or anyone else who will believe it and act on it.

Let's look at Genesis 26:12-13. Remember, Jesus redeemed us from the curse of the Law so that THE BLESSING of Abraham might come on us. So, we are just as much the seed of Abraham as Isaac was, and heirs according to the same promise we read in verse 3:

> 12 Then Isaac sowed in that land, and received in the same year an hundredfold: and the Lord blessed him.
> 13 And the man waxed great, and went forward, and grew until he became very great.

Shout Amen, Somebody!!

We're not just getting through this mess, we're going to become very great right in the middle of it all. THE BLESSING inside you is not just a well of salvation rising up within. It's a <u>river</u> of <u>living water.</u> The well's for you. The river flows for anyone who needs it <u>**THROUGH YOU!**</u>

"But, Brother Copeland, I thought that was grace to be saved." It is, but grace saves from more than just sin. Let's go to 2 Corinthians 8:7:

> 7 Therefore, as ye abound in every thing, in faith, and utterance, and knowledge, and in

all diligence, and in your love to us, see that ye
abound in this grace also.

In this list it's very clear that faith, utterance, knowledge, diligence and love for their man of God was because of grace and their abounding in each one. It also points out there was available to them a grace for something they did not yet know about. Also obvious is that if one does not know about something that grace from God produces, he cannot abound in it.

So what is the grace they were not developed in? Verse 9:

> 9   For ye know the grace of our Lord Jesus Christ, that, though he was rich, yet for your sakes he became poor, that ye through his poverty might be rich.

Now I know that's shouting ground, but it gets even greater than that. Go over to chapter 9:8:

> 8   And God is able to make all grace abound toward you; that ye, always having all sufficiency in all things, may abound to every good work.

<u>All grace!</u> What? ALLLLLL GRACE! Do you suppose the <u>All</u>-mighty God, Creator of <u>all</u> things, might have at least one grace we don't know about yet? Eternity is not long enough to find out the end of His grace. This, however, is what's so important to you and me.

Look again at the words "all grace" for "all sufficiency in all things." There is grace for "whatever it takes" for you to be totally sufficient in all things. Just for your survival? No! So that you may <u>abound.</u> There's the same word the Holy Spirit used in 8:7, referring to faith, utterance, knowledge, diligence and in their love for their man of God.

It's shining <u>THE</u> light on 8:9. The riches in verse 9 are so we can abound to <u>every</u> good work. That's every grace it takes to help hurting people in time of famine. Whether it's food famine, money famine, or any other kind of lack and poverty, such as sickness and disease which is health famine. It's called the curse, and we're redeemed from it. <u>Where sin abounds, grace does much more abound.</u> There's that "abound" word again.

Abounding time has come. The first word on the list was faith. Without faith none of the rest of it works. However, without Love, faith doesn't work. So what's priority here? Constant intake of THE Word.

1. The preached Word
2. The studied Word
3. The meditated Word
4. The spoken Word
5. The Word acted upon

All of the above, coupled with prayer and obedience to the leading of the Holy Spirit, will <u>always</u> produce 2 Corinthians 9:8-11 and Psalm 112. Those scriptures are the profile of a prosperous believer. It's a picture of <u>you.</u>

Look at them until you have them in your heart, then keep them there. Make yourself available to Jesus every morning: "Lord Jesus, what may I do today to help You BLESS Your people?" Forget about what you don't have. That's His job. Offer Him whatever you do have. Loaves and fishes! Remember? Well, don't ever forget it.

Your and Gloria's and my job right now is to get the message of His Love, Grace, and THE BLESSING to this hurting world as loudly and as fast as we can. Together we can and will get it done. Gloria and I love you and pray for you every day. Especially 2 Corinthians 9:8-11 and Psalm 112.

Jesus, our Melchizedek, BLESS and keep you.

Love,

Ken

2 Corinthians 9:8-11:

8 And God is able to make all grace abound toward you; that ye, always having all sufficiency in all things, may abound to every good work:

9 (As it is written, He hath dispersed abroad; he hath given to the poor: his righteousness remaineth for ever.

10 Now he that ministereth seed to the sower both minister bread for your food, and multiply your seed sown, and increase the fruits of your righteousness;)

11 Being enriched in every thing to all bountifulness, which causeth through us thanksgiving to God.

Psalm 112

1 Praise ye the Lord. Blessed is the man that feareth the Lord, that delighteth greatly in his commandments.

2 His seed shall be mighty upon earth: the generation of the upright shall be blessed.

3 Wealth and riches shall be in his house: and his righteousness endureth for ever.

4 Unto the upright there ariseth light in the darkness: he is gracious, and full of compassion, and righteous.

5 A good man showeth favour, and lendeth: he will guide his affairs with discretion.

6 Surely he shall not be moved for ever: the righteous shall be in everlasting remembrance.

7 He shall not be afraid of evil tidings: his heart is fixed, trusting in the Lord.

8 His heart is established, he shall not be afraid, until he see his desire upon his enemies.

9 He hath dispersed, he hath given to the poor; his righteousness endureth for ever; his horn

shall be exalted with honour.
10   The wicked shall see it, and be grieved; he shall gnash with his teeth, and melt away: the desire of the wicked shall perish.

P.S. The Lord Jesus gave me a strong faith-building message while Gloria and I were at Words of Life Fellowship Church in Miami, February 15. I knew it was not just for them but for all my Partners. It was the strongest anointing to release His BLESSING for times of famine I've ever experienced. —K.C.

May 2009

Remember! It Is God!

Dear Partner

Have you ever seen and heard such confusion? Every day, day in and day out, one thing after another—failure, doom, we're-right-they're-wrong, what now, we don't know....

No wonder the Lord said to us last October: *Don't pay attention to or make any plans based on what the media says or what the politicians say.*

"Why not? I don't plan to let what they say influence my thinking."

You will if you watch and listen to it. You and I must realize that every day we are going to be making a constant flow of decisions we've never had to make before. Believers have never had to deal with a time like this—ever. Our faith and trust in God, and His need of us here in the middle of all this is the key issue to the outcome. "Thy will be done in earth, as it is in heaven" is being brought to pass.

Paying attention to one thing and carrying out another is not the way things work. What you look at and hear most creeps into your thinking. Then into your mouth. Once there you will act on it and most of the time not even realize it. Boundaries and limits begin to form. Wrong seeds begin to grow around you.

Before long Jesus is going one way and you're going another. Something happens you didn't expect, and you find yourself in a mess you're not prepared for: "Why didn't the Lord Jesus warn me about this?"

Look out, now! Are you sure He's not doing His job as your leader, guide and savior? No. That's not the problem. He's leading and guiding all the time. The problem is always ME! You! Who, me? Always? Yes. The problem when we find ourselves unprepared is always that we were paying attention to a bunch of babble when the direction came.

Let's look at Deuteronomy 8:18:

> 18 But thou shalt remember the Lord thy God: for it is he that giveth thee power to get wealth, that he may establish his covenant which he sware unto thy fathers, as it is this day.

God has His plan to establish His covenant of the Eden BLESSING in the earth. You and I are not only part of that BLESSING; we are part of The Plan for its establishment. We are those through whom THE BLESSING flows.

"Remember" means just that. Put "It is God who has empowered me in the earth to get wealth" in the forefront of your mind. Right along with and just behind the commandment of love. It is LOVE Himself who gave us the power to get wealth and the power to establish His covenant in the earth. It is also LOVE who commanded us to live by faith and to fear not. No one can do any of that without remembering it is God!

On the other hand, the ones who take their eyes and ears off the TV babble, quit listening to the doubt and junk being talked on the street and fix their attention on the Word, without even knowing it begin to think like Jesus thinks. Then they begin to talk like Jesus talks. Before long, they'll begin acting like He acts. Anyone who thinks like He thinks and talks like He talks will get His results. However, anyone who thinks like the world and talks like the world, even though a believer, will get the world's results.

How can we get Jesus' results? We are born of His Spirit! We are born of His Word and in His image. He said it: "The works that I do shall [you] do also."

Jesus has been preparing us—you, me, this ministry—as partners for a long time. I believe—no, I know we're ready. We know our God and we do exploits in His Name. The Glory is here. It's here for us. It's in His Word, His Blood and His Name, and THE BLESSING has been released from heaven through the earth to and for us. We'll not only come through all this greater than when it began, but we'll be able to bring many, many souls with us who otherwise would not have made it. Jesus has THE PLAN to establish THE COVENANT of THE

BLESSING—now! For whom?

<u>THE</u> CHURCH!

<u>THE</u> Body of CHRIST!

As you sow your BLESSING seed this month, do so knowing you are a <u>minister</u> of seed—not just helping someone do their job. You are a distributor of seed for the sower and bread for the eater, and a multiplier of seed sown. Together! We are the channel of THE BLESSING, supernatural multiplication. That's who <u>YOU</u> are. That's what you are! Claim it right now and shout it to the rooftops. Someone will hear you and begin to think like you, talk like you and act like you. And they, along with you and me, will get heaven's results.

Gloria and I love you, and we're standing on the Word with you and in prayer every day.

Love,

Ken

June 2009

The Father Himself Loves Me!

Dear Partner,

My, how the Word comes alive when it's put to work in the midst of a hard time or place. Especially when we're surrounded with bad news, gross failure and defeat.

No wonder James wrote to count it <u>all</u> joy when tests, temptations and trials come. Especially when you were already "doing the Word" when the storm hit. Joy just rises up in Gloria and me when the trials come—they don't work on us. Oh! the joy! when we've had great opportunities to get sick, but we already KNEW we were healed. We had to fight the good fight of faith all right, but that's part of the joy.

Fight and WIN! What a thrill when all those around you are crying, "What are we going to do??" And you just keep doing what the Word taught you to do in times past. All the time knowing that whatever you don't know yet, the Greater One living in you does know and has been <u>SENT,</u> assigned, ordered, called and directed by the Most High God to see to it you find out.

Let's refresh ourselves by looking once again at John 16:13-15:

13   Howbeit when he, the Spirit of truth, is come, he will guide you into all truth: for he shall not speak of himself; but whatsoever he shall hear, that shall he speak: and he will show you things to come.
14   He shall glorify me: for he shall receive of mine, and shall show it unto you.
15   All things that the Father hath are mine: therefore said I, that he shall take of mine, and shall show it unto you.

Now add to that verse 23:

> 23   And in that day ye shall ask me nothing. Verily, verily, I say unto you, Whatsoever ye shall ask the Father in my name, he will give it you.

WHAT ELSE DO YOU NEED TO STIR UP THE JOY? Read it again—out loud! Hear it come out your own mouth. "Brother Copeland, is that really for me?" Yes, it is if you believe verse 27:

> 27   For the Father himself loveth you, because ye have loved me, and have believed that I came out from God.

Let's go back, now, to something Jesus said in 16:14-15. Notice here He said, "He [the Holy Spirit that's in <u>you</u>] shall"—He will, it's His will to do this—"take of mine, and shall show it unto you." Why? Look again. It's right there. Because it glorifies Him. It brings Him glory when you and I receive what He knows and act on it and gain great victories in our lives. He wins the battle. He gets the glory. We get the victory. However, that's not the end of it. Our victories equip us to reach out to those around us, and bring victory and peace to them when they need it the most.

Now another thing in this statement of promise that is so huge it takes help to believe it. First, He said in verse 14, "He shall receive of mine and show it unto you." But He didn't stop there. He <u>promised</u> verse 15.

Read verse 15 very slowly, out loud and let it really sink in. "<u>ALL THINGS</u> that the FATHER hath are mine." Again, "<u>ALL THINGS</u> that the Father hath are mine: therefore—said—I—He—<u>SHALL</u> take of mine [all that the Father has!], and <u>shall</u> show it unto you"!!!

OH, DEAR GOD IN HEAVEN! Just writing this has shot a thrill through me that is beyond words to express. What are your greatest problems? Of what are you most afraid? Do you suppose your heavenly Father knows anything about that? Didn't He say He would show you things to come?

Everything—I mean everything—the Father has belongs to Jesus.

Everything He knows. All His wealth. All His power. All His grace. All His wisdom. All of it both in heaven and in earth belongs to Jesus. And He said. All that is the Father's and all that is His, the Holy Ghost will show it (give it) to you—ALL OF IT!

Now stir up your faith. Don't just read these covenant words. Imagine them. See yourself with the victory. Then believe it's done. Now! Then say it: "God loves me. Jesus loves me. It says so right here in John 16:14-15 and 27. He is showing me everything I need to know to reap a hundredfold in famine. He <u>is</u> showing me my victory. I receive it."

If you're having to struggle to get over the pressures that have come go back to verse 27 and read it out loud at least 100 times. "God loves me!" Do it. JUST DO IT! NOW! Don't stop. "I will not be defeated, and I'll <u>never</u> quit. Never!"

Let's close for now with verse 33:

> 33   These things I have spoken unto you, that in me ye might have peace. In the world ye shall have tribulation: but be of good cheer; I have overcome the world.

Everything that looks so big and bad has already been defeated. Jesus' victory over it all belongs to you. That last line is not a suggestion. It's a command. BE OF GOOD CHEER! Jesus said it, so you <u>can</u> do it. Make up your mind and set your jaw hard: "Jesus did this for me and I'm going to be glad about it."

Be cheerful to everyone you meet. What does how you feel have to do with anything? Nothing. He didn't say feel cheerful. He said <u>BE</u> cheerful. All the feelings will get in line, but even if they didn't, who cares? Roll all the cares over on Jesus. Humble your feelings and do what He said. He is Lord. He is Savior. He is also our Melchizedek—the One who receives our tithes and BLESSES US!

Sow your BLESSING seeds this month in cheer for cheerfulness, gratitude and joy. The joy of the Lord is our strength.

May the God of all grace BLESS and keep you prosperous and in good health. Gloria and I love you and pray for you every day.

Love,

Ken

July 2009

From the Top of the World to the Bottom
and All the Way Around the Middle!

Dear Partner

Last night Gloria and I landed in Sydney, Australia, and after 11 hours of flying over 5,000 miles we were still in good shape. There's never any jet lag in the Citation X. We woke up this morning rested and ready. During a trip like that, we both thank God every few minutes for all our Partners.

I don't have the exact figures with me, but we've flown that great piece of equipment you and Jesus put into our hands between 550 and 600 thousand miles all over the world, preaching and teaching THE WORD. The Word of salvation. The Word of healing. THE BLESSING of Abraham that Jesus bought and paid for on the cross.

I get so thrilled with His great grace, it all but overwhelms me. It does overwhelm me from time to time. Like right now! Gloria and I, and every member of our family, know that we have the greatest Partners of any ministry on earth. Your faithfulness to the Lord Jesus and to His Word is one of the anchors of my life.

Let's look into something Jesus said. Every Word He said to us is vital to every part of our lives. We live by every Word.

In Matthew 11:28-30 He said:

28	Come unto me, all ye that labour and are heavy laden, and I will give you rest.
29	Take my yoke upon you, and <u>learn of me;</u> for I am meek and lowly in heart: and ye shall find rest unto your souls.
30	For my yoke is easy, and my burden is light.

There is a command here spoken to us that very few have taken to heart. He commanded several things here, but the Word we'll look at is in verse 29: "learn of Me." Not just learn of Him, but He specifically pointed out what He wants us to learn: "[that] I am meek [gentle] and lowly [humble] in heart."

That's not all, keep reading: "My yoke is easy, and my burden is light." Whatever <u>heavy</u> burden is on you, Jesus did not put it there! No, He didn't <u>put</u> anything on you—period! Anything you have from Him, you <u>received.</u> Don't allow assumptions and religious ideas to tell you that He <u>put</u> something on you to teach you or do anything else "to" you. The Holy Spirit was sent to be our teacher, and it was because Jesus prayed to the Father that He was sent in our behalf.

What else can we learn of Him from these scriptures? What about "<u>I will give you rest</u>"? Does He just help you bear the burdens? No, that's not what He said. He said, "Take My burden which is light." Can you hear what He just said? Oh! I can hear Him: "I'll take your heavy load and give you My light and easy one."

"How do you know that, Brother Copeland?" I have learned that of Him. Not only in my own experience of walking with Him for more than 40 years, but also from His Word in 1 Peter 5:5-10. Let's read verses 6 and 7:

> 6 Humble yourselves therefore under the mighty hand of God, that he may exalt you in due time:
> 7 Casting all your care upon him; for he careth for you.

Notice in verse 7: "He cares for you." That's why He said cast, roll, dump, get out from under <u>all</u> your care. That word means worries, anxieties, concerns, anything <u>heavy</u> on your heart and mind.

Remember He said, "Learn of Me that I am gentle and humble in heart"? He doesn't look at you like you're some lowlife sinner who should be punished or like someone who's lower in class or less valuable to God and heaven than He is. No! A million times NO! He looks at you as an equal. As one so valuable He gave His life for you.

Jesus sees someone whom His Father loves. A <u>joint</u> heir in inheritance—the one to whom the Most High God has given great grace and upon whom He has bestowed His Name. That's who you are! Believe the Love. Receive the Love. You are not a beast of burden. You are born of God—a child of His affection. HE CARES FOR YOU! Look at and learn of Him in verse 10:

> 10 But the God of all grace, who hath called us unto his eternal glory by Christ Jesus, after that ye have suffered a while, make you perfect, stablish, strengthen, settle you.

Now don't let that English word "suffer" get in the way. That's referring to resisting the devil in verse 9. In fact, that's no burden. That's victory. It didn't just say resist him. It said resist him steadfast <u>in the faith.</u>

Read Ephesians 6 and take your stand with <u>God's full</u> armor. Doing what? Guarding your mind against the thoughts of the cares you've given Jesus, and thinking about all the Grace and Goodness He has given you. He has redeemed you, or set a wall of separation between you and the law of sin and death. All worry, burdens, cares, sickness, poverty and fear of death come under the law of sin and death.

While you're standing against those care thoughts, the redemption wall is growing stronger. Perfected Love is happening. It's casting out fear. You're taking your place of rest at the throne of grace. You're becoming settled in the midst of chaos and fear. His desire for you is working to exalt you, mature you, establish you, strengthen and settle you.

All of this is in believing and receiving "all grace abound[ing] toward you." Look at it in 2 Corinthians 9:8:

> 8 And God is able to make all grace abound toward you; that ye, always having all sufficiency in all things, may abound to every good work.

Now look at it in Psalm 112 as if you're looking in a mirror:

> 1 Praise ye the Lord. Blessed is the man that

feareth the Lord, that delighteth greatly in his commandments.
2. His seed shall be mighty upon earth: the generation of the upright shall be blessed.
3. Wealth and riches shall be in his house: and his righteousness endureth forever.
4. Unto the upright there ariseth light in the darkness: he is gracious, and full of compassion, and righteous.
5. A good man showeth favour, and lendeth: he will guide his affairs with discretion.
6. Surely he shall not be moved for ever: the righteous shall be in everlasting remembrance.
7. He shall not be afraid of evil tidings: his heart is fixed, trusting in the Lord.
8. His heart is established, he shall not be afraid, until he see his desire upon his enemies.
9. He hath dispersed, he hath given to the poor; his righteousness endureth for ever; his horn shall be exalted with honour.
10. The wicked shall see it, and be grieved; he shall gnash with his teeth, and melt away: the desire of the wicked shall perish.

That's Jesus' idea of <u>you.</u> That's the way He sees you. That's who you are in Him. Look again. That's <u>you</u>! Read it and shout, "That's me!" That's what great Grace has done for us. James called it "The Perfect Law of Liberty."

That, dear brother...that, dear sister, is THE BLESSING in operation. That's what the precious Blood of Jesus bought and paid for. Not just heaven and a glorious forever, but glorious, heavenly victory while we're here in this earth. The whole creation is crying out, earnestly expecting the manifestation of the sons of God. This world needs us to be who we are in Christ Jesus. BLESSED CONQUERORS and MORE through Him who loves us. That's why we keep preaching this Word all over the world.

As you sow your BLESSING seed this month, lay your hands on it and read 1 Peter 5:5-10, and act and receive each verse. Then Psalm 112.

Then close the Book and declare, "Today this scripture is fulfilled in my life. This is me. This is who God says I am. This is the way Jesus sees me. Therefore this is the way I see me from this day forward." That's your rock, Word foundation. Stand on it. How long? <u>Forever!</u>

Be sure to hold Gloria and me up in prayer. The heaviest part of our schedule is right now through the rest of the year. We're strong, but together with you, we are an overwhelming force in the devil's face.

Gloria and I love you and pray for you every day.

Love,

Ken

In 1975, the Lord commanded Kenneth to "preach the uncompromised Word of God on every available voice." In the early years it was radio, then came television and now the Internet. KCM is reaching the world, declaring, "Jesus is Lord"!

August 2009

We've Got a Long Way to Go
and a Short Time to Get There!

Dear Partner

Not long ago, when I was dealing with a situation in my physical body, the Lord led me to go back to Mark 11:22-25 and put the Words of Jesus in my mouth. So I did that. I took each verse and read it aloud. Then I applied each one to my situation starting with verse 22:

> 22   And Jesus answering saith unto them, Have faith in God.

I read it out loud again and then said, "I obey. I have faith in God." Then I did the same with verse 23:

> 23   For verily I say unto you, That whosoever shall say unto this mountain, Be thou removed, and be thou cast into the sea; and shall not doubt in his heart, but shall believe that those things which he saith shall come to pass; he shall have whatsoever he saith.

"I obey. I, whosoever, say to the mountain of (whatever needs to leave, be changed, etc.), <u>be</u> removed and <u>be</u> cast into the sea. Gone! Out of sight! Now, I refuse to doubt! I believe what I just said comes to pass. Therefore, I have what I said and what I say."

Now verse 24:

> 24   Therefore I say unto you, What things soever ye desire, when ye pray, believe that ye receive them, and ye shall have them.

Read it aloud. As you read it, hear the voice of Jesus—not just your own. These are His Words, coming out of your mouth, speaking directly to you. Then, "I obey. The desire of my heart is…." Stop right there. Don't just blurt out something off the top of your head. Go deeper than that.

The mountain you have cast out of your life has roots in fear, unbelief and other areas that need to be repented of. Do it now.

"My desire is to be totally free of this pain (or debt, or whatever else it is) and I receive it now. Jesus said I shall have it, and so I shall!"

Wait a minute. You're not done yet. There's still verse 25. Without releasing the Love of God to forgive, none of the rest of it has any power to actually remove the mountain. Faith, in verse 22, works by Love.

Why is this so important? Well, think about it. Whose words did you put in your mouth? <u>Jesus'</u>. Who has to back those words for them to come to pass? <u>Jesus</u>. In whose Name does that mountain bow its knee and confess that Jesus is Lord? <u>Jesus'</u>.

Under whose law do you live, the Law of Moses or the Law of <u>Jesus</u>? The Law of <u>Jesus</u>. What is that Law? The Law of Love! It's not a matter of hurt feelings or any other kind of feelings. This is a matter of the spiritual laws that govern life and death in this earth. There are two. "For the <u>Law</u> of the Spirit of life in Christ <u>Jesus</u> [Who? <u>Jesus!</u>] has made me free from the <u>law</u> of sin and death!"

Who is the author of your faith? <u>Jesus.</u> Who is the finisher or developer of your faith? <u>Jesus.</u> Who said have faith in God? <u>Jesus.</u> Who said speak to the mountain? <u>Jesus.</u> Who said believe you receive and you shall have it? <u>Jesus.</u> Who loves you and wants you to prosper and be in good health? <u>Jesus.</u>

Who is faithful and just to forgive us our sins when we confess them? <u>Jesus.</u> Who cleanses us from all unrighteousness? <u>Jesus.</u> In whose light do we walk as He is in the light? <u>Jesus'</u>. THEN WHOSE BLOOD CLEANSES US FROM ALL SIN? <u>JESUS'!!</u>

Who receives and BLESSES our tithe? <u>Jesus.</u> Who gave Himself for us? <u>Jesus.</u> Who gave the commandment: "Love the Lord your God with all your heart, all your soul, and all your mind and strength"? <u>Jesus.</u> Who commanded, "Love one another even as I have loved you"? <u>Jesus.</u> Who? <u>Jesus!</u>

Then do it now!

When you stand praying, forgive! Say it out loud: "I forgive! I hold nothing—NO-THING—against anyone on this earth. Jesus—my Lord—commands it. I obey. Bow your knee, satan. Jesus commands it. You are gone, mountain of _____. Jesus commands it. Thank God, I am free from the law of sin and death!"

Now don't look at anything else. Don't listen to anything else. <u>Above all, don't say anything else.</u> You have just released the highest authority ever given to man on earth. THE BLESSING of Eden in the most powerful Name in the earth. Let it work. Watch over it.

It's building a great wall of separation between you and the curse. The same wall that was around Job. The wall that protected the land of Goshen. The wall of redemption from the law of sin and death. It's the secret place of the Most High. It's the full armor of God. It's the resting place until our enemies be made our footstool.

Stay there. Keep yourself in faith, in love and in the Word. Don't come back into the world of strife where confusion reigns through sin and death. No! You're a soldier in the army of Love. You're THE BLESSED. BLESSED TO BE A BLESSING.

Now, put 1 John 4:18 in your heart. Perfected Love casts out fear. Say it; obey it: "God loves me. I have no fear!" You haven't really said this until you've said it at least 500 times.

"God loves Kenneth!" I said that when it was hard to say because my past was still in my eyes. I said it anyway. Hundreds of times. Thousands of times. Over and over until it exploded into reality. I read the 17th chapter of John again and again, and then went through the same process we just went through in Mark 11:22-25. I read every verse of Jesus' prayer and received it as if He was standing right in front of me praying for me. That was 41 years ago, and I still walk in the light of that prayer.

That qualifies me to get in the devil's face with 1 John 5:18:

> 18 We know that whosoever is born of God sinneth not; but he that is begotten of God keepeth himself, and that wicked one toucheth him not.

"I keep myself in Love and faith, satan. You touch me not!" Now, you can see why! The wall is up! He's stuck on the outside. This is the message you and I must preach, Partner, all over this hurting country and the rest of the world. <u>Gloria and I are reaffirming our commitment to get it done.</u> Together we can and will do it.

As you sow your seed this month, release it in the faith process we've just laid out in this letter. We've got a long way to go and a short time to get there. Jesus is coming! Much sooner than any of us think.

We love you and pray for you every day.

Love,

Ken

P.S. No! Gloria and I are not quitting! We are not retiring! We're putting these kids of ours to work. We're branching out to do more, preach more Word, reach more people. They are all anointed with the anointing of this ministry + plus! + Get in their meetings. —Ken

September 2009

The Ways of Death Produce Death!
The Way of Life Produces Life!

Dear Partner,

Some time ago I wrote to you about a powerful word of instruction and direction from the Lord concerning the financial mess this country and the rest of the world is in. Early in the morning of October 19, 2008, the Lord got me up to give me this word:

Don't pay attention to or make any plans based on what the media says or what politicians say. Stand on My Word in John 16. Pay attention to Me. I [the Holy Spirit] <u>will</u> obey verses 13-15. <u>I will</u> show you things to come. <u>I will</u> lead you through troubled times. I already have THE plan for you, and it's very good. Follow it. It will not only get you through, it will place you in a very high place—a rich place—a strong place of victory [Genesis 26:12-13].

You will have to discipline yourself and be diligent to listen to Me. <u>All</u> the other voices will have a plan, a word, an idea for your future and security. Don't listen to Babylon's system. It has fallen apart. My system is stronger than ever. My kingdom is flourishing, and THE BLESSING is the place to be.

Keep your eyes on My Word. Listen to it. It will guide you and I will perform it. Love Me. Love My people as I have loved you. Walk in it. Love <u>never</u> fails, and neither does My plan.

<u>Be very cautious</u> to stay completely clean from covetousness. First Timothy 6:10 must live in the forefront of your thinking. If you will do these things and <u>continue therein,</u> you will come into your wealthy place. A place lifted up. A place in Me already planned and prepared for you now. Here. Not heaven—not yet. But it will seem like heaven right in the midst of all the trouble, and you'll be able to reach out to untold numbers of suffering people with the Good News of the <u>gospel</u> [Galatians 3:8—THE BLESSING].

I'm coming very soon. Sooner than you think. Keep your eyes on Me and <u>you'll get the job done.</u>

Remember, this came just BEFORE the meltdown began. It was during the presidential campaign when all kinds of political double talk was going on. Looking back, it's easy to see where all the Lord said that morning fits in.

There is, however, one extremely important thing that I want us to look at in this letter. It's the command, "<u>Be very cautious</u> to stay completely clean from covetousness."

Why would the Lord say something like that? Because He is leading us into our wealthy place. A place lifted up—a place in Him already planned and prepared for us now. And covetousness is a huge barrier to THE BLESSING.

"Well, Brother Copeland, I'm not covetous."

Oh, really? How do you know?

"I don't think I am."

The only way to know for sure is to know what THE Word says about covetousness—what it is and what to do about it.

First let's read Luke 12:15:

> 15   And he said unto them, Take heed, and <u>beware</u> of covetousness: for a man's life consisteth not in the abundance of the things which he possesseth.

There it is again: "Beware (or, as He said to me, 'Be very cautious') of covetousness." Jesus said that, so the first step is always obedience. Yes, Sir! I obey!

The rest of that verse does not say it's bad to have abundance. No, it says abundance is not what life is about. Covetousness is not just wanting something that belongs to someone else. It is a way of life planned solely around acquiring wealth for one's own selfish purposes and comfort. The getting of things for all the wrong reasons. Under the influence of this kind of thinking, people make seriously wrong decisions. Remember: "There is a way which seemeth right unto a man, but the end thereof are <u>the ways</u> of death" (Proverbs 14:12).

The man Jesus used to illustrate this made some very bad, deadly decisions. Let's look again at Luke 12, starting with verse 16:

> 16   And he spake a parable unto them, saying, The ground of a certain rich man brought forth plentifully:
> 17   And he thought within himself, saying, What shall I do, because I have no room where to bestow my fruits?
> 18   And he said, This will I do: I will pull down my barns, and build greater; and there will I bestow all my fruits and my goods.
> 19   And I will say to my soul, Soul, thou hast much goods laid up for many years; take thine ease, eat, drink, and be merry.
> 20   But God said unto him, Thou fool, this night thy soul shall be required of thee: then whose shall those things be, which thou hast provided?
> 21   So is he that layeth up treasure for himself, and is not rich toward God.

This man's land is BLESSED. That's wonderful. Then came the question, *What shall I do?* Notice Jesus said that thought came from within himself. It came out of his spirit. It was a good question, but a bad answer. The right answer is in verse 33. Jesus said:

> 33   Sell that ye have, and give alms; provide yourselves bags which wax not old, a treasure in the heavens that faileth not, where no thief approacheth, neither moth corrupteth.

Use what you have to bless people.

Look at what a terrible business decision this man made: "I will pull down my barns." He was going to spend a lot of money pulling down perfectly good barns.

Then, bad decision No. 2: "I will build bigger barns." Now he was going to blow money—a lot of money—instead of selling and bringing in money. What was going to happen to all the goods he had stored in those barns while he was pulling down and building greater? <u>Ruined!</u> More money lost and wasted.

But he doesn't see it. His purpose, which is covetousness, has him blinded. Why? <u>Because it was not God's plan.</u> So whose plan was it? Death's. Sin's. Satan's.

He's trapped and doesn't know it. He's caught up in his vision of retirement. Taking it easy, doing what <u>he</u> wants to do. PARTY! EAT! DRINK! LIVE IT UP!

Oh! My! Look again at verses 19 and 20—he didn't live long enough to carry out his dream. Something—sickness? accident? murder?—who knows? He did all this laying up for himself and was not rich toward God. No prayer life. No praise. No care at all about God's will and plan for his life. So he had no divine protection. He was wide open to destruction.

Compare that life with the life of the BLESSED believer in the 112th Psalm! Verses 3-10 paint a totally different picture of this man who delights greatly in the Lord and in His Word:

> 3 Wealth and riches shall be in his house: and his righteousness endureth for ever.
> 4 Unto the upright there ariseth light in the darkness: he is gracious, and full of compassion, and righteous.
> 5 A good man showeth favour, and lendeth: he will guide his affairs with discretion [makes good decisions, good plans and has right answers].
> 6 Surely he shall not be moved for ever: the righteous shall be in everlasting remembrance.
> 7 He shall not be afraid of evil tidings: his heart

8	is fixed, trusting in the Lord. His heart is established, he shall not be afraid, until he see his desire upon his enemies.
9	He hath dispersed, he hath given to the poor; his righteousness endureth for ever; his horn shall be exalted with honour.
10	The wicked shall see it, and be grieved; he shall gnash with his teeth, and melt away: the desire of the wicked shall perish.

It never was God's plan for you, or anyone else, to provide for your own future. That's His job. It's already planned.

What now? Obey Jesus. Change your <u>way</u> of thinking. He made a very clear outline of what to think, what not to think, and how to change from one to the other. Let's read on in Luke 12:22-32:

22	And he said unto his disciples, Therefore I say unto you, Take no thought for <u>your</u> life, what <u>ye</u> shall eat; neither for the body, what <u>ye</u> shall put on.
23	The life is more than meat, and the body is more than raiment.
24	Consider the ravens: for they neither sow nor reap; which neither have storehouse nor barn; and God feedeth them: how much more are ye better than the fowls?
25	And which of you with taking thought can add to his stature one cubit?
26	If ye then be not able to do that thing which is least, why take ye thought for the rest?
27	Consider the lilies how they grow: they toil not, they spin not; and yet I say unto you, that Solomon in all his glory was not arrayed like one of these.
28	If then God so clothe the grass, which is today in the field, and tomorrow is cast into the oven; how much more will he clothe you, O ye of little faith?

	29	And seek not ye what ye shall eat, or what ye shall drink, neither be ye of doubtful mind.
	30	For all these things do the nations of the world seek after: and your Father knoweth that ye have need of these things.
	31	But rather seek ye the kingdom of God; and all these things shall be added unto you.
	32	Fear not, little flock; for it is your Father's good pleasure to give you the kingdom.

1. Get your mind off yourself—clothes, food, etc. No thought means NO, NONE, ZERO. Stop it—now!

2. <u>Consider,</u> study, think about, control your mind by thinking about the ravens. They don't work. They don't build barns like the covetous man Jesus told us about. Your heavenly Father feeds them. Think, then, about how much He loves you and how much more you are to Him than the birds. He so loved you, He gave His only Son, Jesus, so you could have life abundantly.

3. <u>Consider</u> the lilies. Spend some quality time thinking about "<u>they toil not.</u>" Jesus said the same thing about the birds. The curse of earning bread by the sweat of your brow has been overthrown by the blood and the grace of Jesus.

Now verse 25—thoughts <u>cannot</u> change anything. "Figuring it out" by worrying and feeding on the bread of sorrow only makes it worse by building and developing a double mind or a doubtful mind, strengthening unbelief and fear.

What changes things? FAITH, HOPE and LOVE! Put verse 28 on a card someplace where you can see it every day, and let it build your hope and faith, <u>O</u> <u>you</u> <u>of</u> <u>great</u> <u>faith</u>!

Now the bottom line! Verse 31:

	31	But rather seek ye the kingdom of God; and all these things shall be added unto you.

Put your mind on the plan Jesus has for your life. Pray. Listen. Seek or look for it. Look for ways to help people. That's really what church is for—not just to feed and help you. There are people there who need you.

Now comes verse 32. Fear not! Obey Jesus. Now. Stop the fear of tomorrow, and money and all that goes with it. How? First John 4:18: Perfected love <u>casts out</u> fear. Go back to verses of love in Luke 12—verses 24, 27 and 28. "God loves <u>me.</u> I believe the Love. I receive the Love He has for me. I receive <u>His</u> care for me. I work for and with Him. I don't toil for clothes and food and for my future. He knows I have need of these things. THE BLESSING OF THE LORD, it maketh rich."

Go over and over that. Take <u>that</u> thought and say it. Read it. Take it. Say it. When you begin to say it without having to think about it, you have changed your "way" of thinking from the ways of death to the way of Life. THE BLESSING is working. You are rich—now! It's only a matter of faith processing it and getting it to you.

Gird up, verse 35 says. Get ready. Sow the seed. BLESS someone. Jesus will fill up your barn before you can get it empty. Heaven is ready and already on the go. This is not a great time of lack and recession. This is the time of our harvest. Our brothers and sisters in Christ who don't know this yet need help, and they need desperately to find out what you and I are assigned to do: Preach the Word of Jesus and His healing abundance. Together we can, we are, and we will continue to get it done.

Gloria and I and <u>all</u> the Copeland family, all of us at KCM, love you very much. We are here for you, and we pray for you every day.

Love,

Ken

October 2009

THE BLESSING Is THE Place to Be!

Dear Partner

In last month's letter we looked at Jesus' words in Luke 12:15-30 to take heed and beware of covetousness. Covetousness is a way of thinking based on the world's Babylonian system of meeting the needs of man without God. That <u>way</u> of thinking comes under Proverbs 14:12:

> 12   There is a way which seemeth right unto a man, but the end thereof are the ways of death.

It looks right, sounds right and feels right until it must be the thing to do—but the end result is loss, death and destruction.

What was—and is—the bottom line of Jesus' teaching on this? He is <u>the</u> source of all life and all things. Yes, <u>things</u>! He created <u>all</u> things. <u>All</u> things were created for and by Him (Colossians 1:16; Ephesians 3:9). What did our Father have in mind when He created <u>all</u> <u>things</u>? Let's look at 1 Timothy 6:17:

> 17   Charge them that are rich in this world, that they be not highminded, nor trust in uncertain riches, but in the living God, who giveth us richly all things to enjoy.

He did not give you your car, your home or your new suit to <u>love.</u> He gave them to you to enjoy. He did not give you a good job or good business for you to put your trust in. He gave it to you as a channel of His grace. There are many channels but only <u>one</u> source—Jesus. He is the High Priest of THE BLESSING of Abraham. This puts Philippians 4:19 in a new light:

> 19   But my God shall supply all your need according to his riches in glory by Christ Jesus.

<u>All</u> <u>need.</u> <u>All</u> supply. One source! By <u>Christ</u>—the Anointing of—

Jesus. This <u>must</u> become our way of thinking, not mixed up with the covetousness and "me-first" thinking of the world.

Let's go back now to Luke 12:22-32:

22   And he said unto his disciples, Therefore I say unto you, Take no thought for your life, what ye shall eat; neither for the body, what ye shall put on.
23   The life is more than meat, and the body is more than raiment.
24   Consider the ravens: for they neither sow nor reap; which neither have storehouse nor barn; and God feedeth them: how much more are ye better than the fowls?
25   And which of you with taking thought can add to his stature one cubit?
26   If ye then be not able to do that thing which is least, why take ye thought for the rest?
27   Consider the lilies how they grow: they toil not, they spin not; and yet I say unto you, that Solomon in all his glory was not arrayed like one of these.
28   If then God so clothe the grass, which is today in the field, and tomorrow is cast into the oven; how much more will he clothe you, O ye of little faith?
29   And seek not ye what ye shall eat, or what ye shall drink, neither be ye of doubtful mind.
30   For all these things do the nations of the world seek after: and your Father knoweth that ye have need of these things.
31   But rather seek ye the kingdom of God; and all these things shall be added unto you.
32   Fear not, little flock; for it is your Father's good pleasure to give you the kingdom.

Look again at verse 30. Now say out loud: "My Father knows I have <u>NEED</u> of these things, and <u>my need</u> for these things is met in Christ

Jesus." Say that over and over, until every time you think about food you respond: "My Father knows I have need of that." When you think about clothes, "My Father knows I have need of that, and my needs are met. Thank You, Jesus." I don't care what it is—"My Father knows I have need of that. There's no need for me to even think about it. I believe I receive it now!"

Now, Luke 12:32:

> 32 Fear not, little flock; for it is your Father's good pleasure to give you the kingdom.

"I refuse to fear. My Father loves me as much as He loves Jesus!" (John 17:23). Remember, perfected—or working, developing—love casts out fear. "God loves me! That's the whole point. For God so loved the world, He gave His only Son! I spend my time thinking about that instead of how I am going to get what I need. I don't need to get it. Jesus got it for me. It's mine. He will get it to me. I seek His plan. I walk in His Love. He gave me His faith in His Word."

Meditate on these verses. This is your new way of thinking, and the end thereof is the way of life and BLESSING. It's not based on the condition of the world's economy or their way of health and welfare. They are broke on all counts. The world's system is bankrupt. Their healing system is bankrupt. Their spiritual system is bankrupt. The whole thing is falling in on itself.

God's way of thinking, His way of living, His way of prosperity and health is not A way. It's THE way. It works. Psalm 91:5-12 absolutely comes alive. Look at it:

> 5 Thou shalt not be afraid for the terror by night; nor for the arrow that flieth by day;
> 6 Nor for the pestilence that walketh in darkness; nor for the destruction that wasteth at noonday.
> 7 A thousand shall fall at thy side, and ten thousand at thy right hand; but it shall not come nigh thee.

8	<u>Only with thine eyes shalt thou behold and see the reward of the wicked.</u>
9	Because thou hast made the Lord, which is my refuge, even the most High, thy habitation;
10	There shall no evil befall thee, neither shall any plague come nigh thy dwelling.
11	For he shall give his angels charge over thee, to keep thee in all thy ways.
12	They shall bear thee up in their hands, lest thou dash thy foot against a stone.

<u>Right in the middle of it all,</u> <u>there you stand without a scratch.</u> Not only that, but you are BLESSED and able to help those around you who are losing every <u>thing</u> they have. What a time to preach the gospel of Jesus as Lord, Savior and High Priest of heaven's BLESSING.

Set aside some time to meditate on these verses, even if it's just a few minutes a day. Obey Jesus. Think about the ravens and how God feeds them. Think about how much <u>more</u> you mean to your Father than the birds. Kick out the thoughts of how little you're worth. Jesus loves <u>you</u> and gave Himself for <u>you</u> (Galatians 2:20). Fix that in your heart and mind. <u>Don't put it off! Do it now.</u> Be diligent to it.

Talk about it to yourself. Then reach out to someone. Do something to <u>BLESS someone.</u> <u>BLESS.</u> <u>Encourage.</u> <u>Build up.</u> Smile. Speak grace and faith. Things will begin coming into your hands with which to BLESS people. Out of that supply will begin flowing more than enough to swallow up your every need. I'm telling you, it's thrilling and overflowing with the joy of life!

Lay your hands on your seed this month and make the commitment to do these things. Ask the Lord to remind you daily to be diligent until your way of thinking has been renewed according to Romans 12:2:

2	And be not conformed to this world: but be ye transformed by the renewing of your mind, that ye may prove what is that good, and acceptable, and perfect, will of God.

It <u>all</u> starts and ends with "My Father loves me as much as He does Jesus." That love has been shed abroad in our hearts by the Holy Ghost (Romans 5:5). Stir it up. Release it. Shout, dance, rejoice until fear is completely gone. Love <u>never</u> fails!

Gloria and I just returned from London and a great weeklong meeting with Creflo Dollar. Packed out. Overflow. Shouting, faith-filled people. God is moving. THE BLESSING is the place to be.

Gloria and I love you and pray for you every day.

Love,

Ken

P.S. One of my Partners said to me today, "Yield to THE Plan, not to the pressure!"

November 2009

Flat as a Flitter but Never a Quitter

Dear Partner

Have you ever had your faith just go flat?

It's especially easy to notice when you've been in a high Word environment like a Believers' Convention or a series of meetings at your church. You release your faith on something, and you KNOW it's yours. It's done! No one can take it away from you. That knowing that you know that you just know drops down into your innermost being. Just the mention of it brings a smile to your face. It's so close you can taste it.

That goes on for a few days, but then you begin to detect a kind of emptiness. The thing that was so close is drifting away. I've had this happen to me. I go back to the same scripture verses and confess them over—even louder—but I can tell something has happened. My faith is not alive like it was. It's gone flat.

This is a very critical moment. It's no time to quit, which is what the devil will try to get you to do. "Well," he'll say, "it's because you were on an emotional high in that meeting." Then the old standby: "God probably didn't want you to have all that stuff." If you listen to his line of BULL, he'll steal the Word you received. Don't listen to him!!

There is a two-step procedure that will put you back on your faith and take you on to victory. In Jesus' foundational teaching on releasing faith and receiving the results in Mark 11:22-26, we first have to look at verses 25-26:

> 25 And when ye stand praying, forgive, if ye have aught against any: that your Father also which is in heaven may forgive you your trespasses.
> 26 But if ye do not forgive, neither will your Father which is in heaven forgive your trespasses.

FORGIVE. Faith works by love. God is Love. "Have faith in God." You forgive, God forgives—that's the connection to the life of your faith.

No forgiveness, no connection. It's obvious why faith will go flat under those conditions. Like a flat tire has lost its power and support—air—faith without Love cannot stand up under the load.

So then, step No. 1 is to check yourself on the commandment of Love. Repent and forgive. Repent by faith in Jesus' power to forgive and cleanse from <u>all</u> unrighteousness (1 John 1:9). Forgive by faith. Obey the command of Jesus and do it.

To do anything by faith, one must take control of the seeing, feeling, natural man of the flesh. We walk by faith, not by sight. This is especially true when it comes to forgiveness, guilt or anything else emotional.

That brings us to the second step: Take control of your mind, your will and your emotions. Let's look at what Jesus said in Luke 21:19:

> 19   In your patience possess ye your souls.

He said this right in the midst of describing an extremely high-pressure time. Possess, or take control of, your thoughts, your will, your actions based on what you think, and your emotions—your "feelings."

The key here is in patience. Patience is the force of the spirit in Galatians 5:22-23, along with faith, love, joy, peace, goodness, meekness and temperance. In the King James translation it's *longsuffering*. It means "constantly, consistently the same." It does not mean to just "put up with." It means to be like Jesus, the same yesterday, today and forever. How does He do that? <u>THE WORD!</u>

God and His Word never, ever change. Jesus thinks the Word, wills the Word, feels the Word. With Him it is settled forever. That's also the way we do it. He has given us His mind, the mind of Christ. We forsake our way of thinking by casting down imaginations and bringing every thought into captivity to obey His thoughts. We have <u>THE MIGHTY POWER</u> with which to do this, according to 2 Corinthians 10:3-5. So, we take control of our minds by taking His mind.

Now take control of your will. How? By taking the will of God.

Look at the contrast between these two responses. Jesus says: "When you stand praying, forgive."

The natural man's reaction is: Either I will (then do it) or I won't (maybe later, or I just can't, etc.). That's a mixture of will and emotions.

Take control of your hurts, feelings, weaknesses, etc. How? Take His joy. We saw in Galatians 5:22 that joy is a spiritual force. How did Jesus control His emotions in the face of shame, meanness and abuse like no one has ever endured, both on earth and in hell itself? Look at Hebrews 12:2-3:

> 2 Looking unto Jesus the author and finisher of our faith; who for the joy that was set before him endured the cross, despising the shame, and is set down at the right hand of the throne of God.
>
> 3 For consider him that endured such contradiction of sinners against himself, lest ye be wearied and faint in your minds.

Do you see that? For the joy that was set before Him. The joy of the Lord is our strength. It's the same joy He used to overcome all that, and He's made it available to us. Surely if it overcame all He endured, it will overwhelm <u>anything</u> you or I are facing.

Read the words of Jesus and shout John 15:10-11:

> 10 If ye keep my commandments, ye shall abide in my love; even as I have kept my Father's commandments, and abide in his love.
>
> 11 These things have I spoken unto you, that my joy might remain in you, and that your joy might be full.

Then in John 17:13 Jesus prayed:

> 13 And now come I to thee; and these things I

speak in the world, that they might have my joy fulfilled in themselves.

He said it! He prayed it! Now you receive it!

Take the time to pray, seek, praise and—above all—listen and let the Holy Spirit reveal and correct the things that need to be addressed. BE CORRECTABLE! Correction brings direction. Direction brings perfection. Perfection brings protection.

Rise up. Slam your pumped-up faith back into the mountain. Blow it into the sea and stand. Glory to God! Victory is so sweet. Now go forward. We walk by faith. We live by faith. We overcome by faith. THE BLESSING wall is back up. Protect it. Keep it strong by keeping the Word ever before your eyes and in your heart and in your mouth. Peter knew so well the agony of failure and the pure joy of victory. He said in 2 Peter 1:2-8:

> 2 Grace and peace be multiplied unto you through the knowledge of God, and of Jesus our Lord,
> 3 According as his divine power hath given unto us all things that pertain unto life and godliness, through the knowledge of him that hath called us to glory and virtue:
> 4 Whereby are given unto us exceeding great and precious promises: that by these ye might be partakers of the divine nature, having escaped the corruption that is in the world through lust.
> 5 And beside this, giving all diligence, add to your faith virtue; and to virtue knowledge;
> 6 And to knowledge temperance; and to temperance patience; and to patience godliness;
> 7 And to godliness brotherly kindness; and to brotherly kindness charity.
> 8 For if these things be in you, and abound, they make you that ye shall neither be barren

nor unfruitful in the knowledge of our Lord Jesus Christ.

As you sow your BLESSING seed this month, lay hands on it and obey Galatians 6:8. Paul had just taught on the forces of the reborn spirit, including patience, in chapter 5, and is concluding his teaching on how to release their power. Sow the seed and don't get weary. Don't stop. Don't ever quit! Patience <u>will</u> have her perfect work and you'll be entire, wanting nothing (James 1:4). Then verse 6, "Let him ask in faith—nothing wavering...." Well, here we go again.

God is so good. Gloria and I are doing these same things right now. We're pressing stronger and higher than ever before in our lives and ministry. Together we can and will get this job done. We love you and we pray for you every day.

Love,

Ken

December 2009

I Believe! I Will! I Take It!
I Have Faith! Thank You!

Dear Partner

Anyone who "lives by faith" never changes to fit the times. The "times" have to change to fit the Word of God and faith.

Romans 1:17, Galatians 3:11 and Hebrews 10:38 all say, "The just <u>shall</u> live by faith." That's our living.

Now let's get a "Word picture," or profile, of one who lives by faith, and one who puts his trust in something or someone else. The prophet Jeremiah lays it out in Jeremiah 17:5-8:

> 5   Thus saith the Lord; Cursed be the man that trusteth in man, and maketh flesh his arm, and whose heart departeth from the Lord.
> 6   For he shall be like the heath in the desert, and shall not see when good cometh; but shall inhabit the parched places in the wilderness, in a salt land and not inhabited.
> 7   Blessed is the man that trusteth in the Lord, and whose hope the Lord is.
> 8   For he shall be as a tree planted by the waters, and that spreadeth out her roots by the river, and shall not see when heat cometh, but her leaf shall be green; and shall not be careful in the year of drought, neither shall cease from yielding fruit.

In verse 5, the curse is active and in full control of this man's life. This is not referring to someone who doesn't know better. It's talking about a departed one. Someone who knows God but does not live by faith. Faith in God is not his source. Consequently, God is not his supply. He trusts or looks to people, including himself, and what he can earn or "make." When that fails along with his job or the stock market, he fails along with it.

The next step he takes is to look to the government and political parties, etc. When all that fails, what then? What is he going to do now?

I didn't say this person never prayed during all this. I didn't say that God wasn't any help at all. However, if all or most of his attention has been to learning, and developing his natural skills in the natural workplace, instead of his faith, he not only is unskillful in the Word of righteousness, but he does not know when good comes.

Notice the word *heath* in verse 6. That is a translation of a Hebrew word meaning "an isolated, naked, stunted thing growing in a salt flat or ground that won't produce anything edible." The hotter it gets, the more salty it gets. The more salty it is, the more the need for water. "Why doesn't someone help me?" They can't. They're too busy dealing with their own saltiness. "I pray and pray and nothing happens." Why? James 4:3: You ask and receive not because you ask amiss.

Now let's look at the man who lives by faith. The one who trusts God. When "the system" began to fail, this man didn't have to alter or change anything. His eyes, or hope, were on God and His Word, and they never change.

Jesus is our hope. He was yesterday. He is today. He will be tomorrow. We have been planted by the river of heaven's eternal flow—THE BLESSING. Our roots are strong and grounded in His great love for us. We don't see bad times when bad times come. We see a divine opportunity to produce more fruit in order to bless more people. Our leaves are always green. The word translated *green* means "continue flourishing."

The man who lives by faith is not anxious or nervous in drought. He never considers holding back his tithe or his giving just because things look bad. NEVER! Fear will cut off the roots that are tapped into his source of life. No, he increases everything. His time in the Word. His fellowshiping with the Lord Jesus. His giving and his faith are objects of his attention. More, not less.

Is there hope for the heath? Absolutely! How? Mark 11:22-26. "Aw, Brother Copeland, not that again."

No, not <u>again.</u> It was that all along. When Jesus answered Peter He could have said, "Now, boys, I don't want you trying to do this. Don't go around cursing trees. You'll fall flat on your face and give us all a bad name. After all, I'm the Son of God and I can do these things."

No! No! No! He expected them to do exactly the same as He did. Listen to what He said in Matthew 21:21:

> 21 Jesus answered and said unto them, Verily I say unto you, If ye have faith, and doubt not, <u>ye shall not only do this which is done to the fig tree,</u> but also if ye shall say unto this mountain, Be thou removed, and be thou cast into the sea; it shall be done.

How? <u>HAVE FAITH IN GOD!</u> Did He say, "Try to have faith in God"? No! HAVE FAITH IN GOD! Was that a suggestion? No! Was it a command? YES! <u>Absolutely.</u>

Gloria and I were preaching at Agape Church in Little Rock, Ark., last October. Early that Sunday morning the Lord woke me up and I saw Him in the Spirit standing in front of me, holding a huge tray filled with cookies. That tray was so big, His arms were stretched out from His sides as far as He could reach, holding the handles of the tray. You would think because He was holding a tray of cookies He would be smiling. He wasn't. He had a very stern look on His face and literally shouted at me, "<u>HAVE A COOKIE!</u>"

I suddenly realized that He wanted me to be like Abraham in Romans 4:19. Be not weak in faith. Stop staggering at the promises of God through unbelief. <u>Have FAITH in God,</u> giving glory to God. BE! <u>Fully</u> persuaded that what He has promised He is able, and He will perform it!

Then He sternly said, "Your response is, 'I <u>believe!</u> I <u>will!</u> I <u>take it!</u> I have a cookie! Thank You! I HAVE FAITH IN GOD!!'" I had to say it just as sternly and boldly as He said it to me. <u>I HAVE IT NOW!</u>

Now what? Mark 11:25:

> 25 And when ye stand praying, forgive, if ye have aught against any: that your Father also which is in heaven may forgive you your trespasses.

Just as boldly, shout, "I FORGIVE."

"Brother Copeland, I just haven't been able to forgive them...." HAVE FAITH IN GOD!

"But my finances...." HAVE FAITH IN GOD!

"But this pain...." HAVE FAITH IN GOD!

"My children...." HAVE FAITH IN GOD!

I HAVE FAITH IN GOD! I FORGIVE! THEY ARE FORGIVEN!

Now there's only one thing left. Son—Daughter, your faith HAS MADE YOU WHOLE! Glory to God! My faith has made me whole!

Every thought you think, good or bad, say out loud, "I have faith in God. I forgive." Someone says something about the economy, say it: "I have faith in God. I forgive."

You're not just forgiving someone, you know. You're releasing the grace of God—forgiveness—up and out of your spirit. That's not all. Your heavenly Father is doing the same to you. Look at verse 25 again. Do you really know just how important that is?

Look very carefully at Matthew 9:1-7:

> 1 And he entered into a ship, and passed over, and came into his own city.
> 2 And, behold, they brought to him a man sick of the palsy, lying on a bed: and Jesus seeing their faith said unto the sick of the palsy; Son, be of good cheer; thy sins be forgiven thee.
> 3 And, behold, certain of the scribes said within themselves, This man blasphemeth.

4	And Jesus knowing their thoughts said, Wherefore think ye evil in your hearts?
5	For whether is easier, to say, Thy sins be forgiven thee; or to say, Arise, and walk?
6	But that ye may know that the Son of man hath power on earth to forgive sins, (then saith he to the sick of the palsy,) Arise, take up thy bed, and go unto thine house.
7	And he arose, and departed to his house.

Do you see that?! The power of God to forgive and the power of God to heal are the SAME power! It's the Anointing. The Christ! The burden-removing, yoke-destroying power of God, in and on Jesus! We are the Body of that Power! <u>That's THE BLESSING in action. So put it in action. Now!</u>

"But, Brother Copeland...." No! Have FAITH IN GOD! FORGIVE! Your faith has made you whole!

Lay your hands on your Blessing seed this month. Of what? Of FAITH! Don't just mail it. BLESS it! If you have to, read this letter over. Read it until you rise up on the inside, standing tall like Abraham of old. Stand before Jesus, your Melchizedek, strong in faith with your hand lifted before Him in covenant with Him, boldly, sternly but filled with joy, shouting, "I HAVE FAITH IN GOD. I RELEASE GRACE TO FORGIVE! NOW I RECEIVE ALL GRACE ABOUNDING TOWARD ME. I receive it. I always have <u>ALL</u> sufficiency in all things. I abound today in this good work and every other good work Jesus calls me to enter into. I am the tree in Jeremiah 17:8. I am the BLESSED man in the 112th Psalm. I am the minister in 2 Corinthians 9:9-12. I abound in the GRACE in 2 Corinthians 8:9."

Now preach it to someone else. Tell them, "<u>HAVE FAITH IN GOD!</u>" Copy this letter and give it to them. Go into action. That's what Gloria and I and all of us here at KCM are doing. All our children and grandchildren are out there preaching it. Between Jesus, the Holy Ghost, your family and ours, we'll get this job done. We're a team, a "Holy Ghost Gang" growing to a million strong. We will do this thing commanded us. We will not come short! We will not fail! We will prosper and increase mightily. We will not lack! We will not want! We will not be diminished! We rest in Jesus and we rejoice in Him. He will do these things in the land of the living.

Gloria and I and all of our family love you and pray for you every day.

Love,

Ken

P.S. Merry Christmas! From all of us here at KCM. We love and pray for you every day! —Kenneth and Gloria

God gave us Jesus...His faith and love expressed in His Son.
We receive His faith—we receive His love!
We take it all and put it into action in this world!

January 2010

Whatever He Says to You, Do It!

Dear Partner,

There is a verse of Scripture in Romans 4 that's very familiar but oh, so very important. Before we look at it, stop for a moment and ask the Holy Spirit to open the eyes of your understanding and fill your spirit with light and understanding about what the Lord Jesus has for you through this word.

Romans 4:16—let's read it.

> 16 Therefore it is of faith, that it might be by grace; to the end the promise might be sure to all the seed; not to that only which is of the law, but to that also which is of the faith of Abraham; who is the father of us all.

Now Galatians 3:29:

> 29 And if ye be Christ's [in Christ], then are ye Abraham's seed, and heirs according to the promise.

The <u>seed</u> in Romans 4:16 is the seed to whom the promise is made SURE. That's YOU!

Romans 4:16 is why Jesus was and is so stern and firm about "HAVE FAITH IN GOD!" This is the reason for the word *impossible* in Hebrews 11:6. Without faith it is impossible to please God. Not because He's so mean and stubborn, but because He's so good and full of Love. He is Love. "HAVE FAITH IN GOD!" Why, Jesus? "SO THAT IT MIGHT BE BY GRACE!" Why, Sir? "So that the exceeding great and precious promises that were given to ME are just as strong and sure to you. Not what you deserve or are able to earn. No. No. What I so desire for you to have." What, Sir? "All Grace abounding toward you that YOU! Always! HAVING! <u>ALL</u> sufficiency in <u>ALL</u> things may abound to <u>every</u> good work!"

Grace abounds so you can abound. Abounding is not just barely getting by until the economy gets better. Abounding is not surviving until I can get another job. Abounding is not holding back and hoarding everything I can get my hands on, trying to hang on. There's NO FAITH in that. Only FEAR.

Fear never enters <u>into</u> Grace. It <u>always</u> stays on the outside looking in, saying, "That's just too much. I could never have that." Or, "I'm just so unworthy." SO? What else is new? It's not what you're WORTH or what you've done. No. A thousand times, no! It's what Jesus has done and what He's worth.

Remember, you and I are <u>in</u> Christ. And if we are in Him, we are Abraham's seed just as He is. Every promise of God in His Word is just as sure to come to pass and in just as much abundance as if Jesus were praying for Himself! What did He say about that? "Whatever you ask the Father in <u>MY</u> <u>NAME</u> HE WILL give it you" (John 16:23). God, our Father, looking through the eyes of Grace, sees no difference and hears no difference between you and Jesus.

"But Brother Copeland, He's so big and I'm so small. He's so good and I'm such a foul up. He's so smart and I don't know what I am."

All of that was true before you accepted Him as your Lord <u>and</u> Savior. Now you are in Him. He has given you <u>His</u> Name, His Spirit, His place or seat next to the Father. You are a joint heir—nothing less.

Faith in God's love to do this, and in His ability as <u>The</u> <u>Almighty</u> to re-create, or have you reborn, thrusts you into the arms of His Grace. The precious <u>BLOOD</u> of Jesus bought and paid for your life of Grace and abundance. It established an eternal covenant of promise, declaring you and me heirs of THE BLESSING of Abraham, the Eden Covenant of Isaiah 51:1-3:

> 1   Hearken to me, ye that follow after righteousness, ye that seek the Lord: look unto the rock whence ye are hewn, and to the hole of the pit whence ye are digged.
> 2   Look unto Abraham your father, and unto

Sarah that bare you: for I called him alone, and blessed him, and increased him.
3 For the Lord shall comfort Zion: he will comfort all her waste places; and he will make her wilderness like Eden, and her desert like the garden of the Lord; joy and gladness shall be found therein, thanksgiving, and the voice of melody.

Let's look now at GRACE and its abundance in action in John 2:1-11:

1 And the third day there was a marriage in Cana of Galilee; and the mother of Jesus was there:
2 And both Jesus was called, and his disciples, to the marriage.
3 And when they wanted wine, the mother of Jesus saith unto him, They have no wine.
4 Jesus saith unto her, Woman, what have I to do with thee? mine hour is not yet come.
5 His mother saith unto the servants, Whatsoever he saith unto you, do it.
6 And there were set there six waterpots of stone, after the manner of the purifying of the Jews, containing two or three firkins apiece.
7 Jesus saith unto them, Fill the waterpots with water. And they filled them up to the brim.
8 And he saith unto them, Draw out now, and bear unto the governor of the feast. And they bare it.
9 When the ruler of the feast had tasted the water that was made wine, and knew not whence it was: (but the servants which drew the water knew;) the governor of the feast called the bridegroom,
10 And saith unto him, Every man at the beginning doth set forth good wine; and when men have well drunk, then that which is worse: but thou hast kept the good wine until now.
11 This beginning of miracles did Jesus in Cana

of Galilee, and manifested forth his glory; and his disciples believed on him.

Burn and bury this as deep as you can into your mind and spirit. <u>Whatever</u> Jesus does is THE LOVE Himself in action. Whatever He does is by faith in God, and whatever He does is Life more abundant. GRACE! <u>Always</u> GRACE.

There was no great life-threatening emergency at this wedding. What was there? A bridegroom and his bride about to be embarrassed. Jesus' mother obviously cared for these people and didn't want that to happen. Jesus said to fill the waterpots. Not just one but all six pots. That was 180 gallons!! How big of a wedding was this? Did they really <u>need</u> 180 gallons of wine? More than likely one pot—30 <u>gallons</u>— would have been enough. But that's not the way of God's GRACE. Love overflowed the place with the best wine anyone had ever tasted. Not only was the bridegroom saved from embarrassment, he and his bride began their marriage lifted up and well thought of by everyone there and throughout the community. Not only that, but all that <u>fine</u> wine left over would have prospered them greatly should they have chosen to sell it.

That's just the way our heavenly Father is. All GRACE! ABOUNDING GRACE! Far more than just what you need. Enough to lift you up and set you in a place with Him far above all the curse and lack. Not just for you, but for everyone and every work you and I are called to. That's what THE BLESSING is and that's what it does. That's what Jesus is and that's what He does. Now here comes the shocker: That's what you and I are, and that's what we do! Whatever Jesus is, we are. Whatever He does, we do. We are in Him. We are <u>His</u> <u>Body.</u>

This is not just church talk. This is for real. It's heavenly reality. THE TRUTH! Ephesians 4:28-32 proves it:

> 28   Let him that stole steal no more: but rather let him labour, working with his hands the thing which is good, that he may have to give to him that needeth.
>
> 29   Let no corrupt communication proceed out of

	your mouth, but that which is good to the use of edifying, that it may minister grace unto the hearers.
30	And grieve not the holy Spirit of God, whereby ye are sealed unto the day of redemption.
31	Let all bitterness, and wrath, and anger, and clamor, and evil speaking, be put away from you, with all malice:
32	And be ye kind one to another, tenderhearted, forgiving one another, even as God for Christ's sake hath forgiven you.

The reason we do anything—work, talk, extend kindness, forgive—everything is to give and to minister GRACE. Therefore what He says to you, do it! He said HAVE FAITH IN GOD! Do it. When you stand praying, FORGIVE! Do it. HAVE FAITH IN THE NAME! Do it. LOVE ONE ANOTHER! Do it.

When? When do you need Grace to help in time of need? NOW! So do it now. Hebrews 4:14-16 says it all:

14	Seeing then that we have a great high priest, that is passed into the heavens, Jesus the Son of God, let us hold fast our profession.
15	For we have not an high priest which cannot be touched with the feeling of our infirmities; but was in all points tempted like as we are, yet without sin.
16	Let us therefore come boldly unto the throne of grace, that we may obtain mercy, and find grace to help in time of need.

He's without sin and we're in Him. Can you see it? Glory be to His Name! That's mercy and GRACE. That's why we can be so bold in His presence. It's the throne of GRACE. Not the throne of condemnation. Oh, aren't you glad? There is NOW no condemnation to those in Christ Jesus who walk after the Spirit (the promises) and not after the flesh (condemnation, feelings, etc.) (Romans 8:1). Your economy is based on faith so that it can be by GRACE. Your health care is by faith, mercy and Grace.

Your <u>everything</u> is by faith in GOD! His everything is by GRACE TO YOU! So that you can be a minister of seed to the sower, bread to the eater, a multiplier of the seed sown, and a minister of increase of the fruits of righteousness, causing great thanksgiving to God.

That's what you and I are doing together. That's our message. That's what we (you and I as Partners) do! That's who we are.

One final word. As you sow your financial seed—seed for all Grace, THE BLESSING—this month, do it on Philippians 2:5-6:

> 5 Let this mind be in you, which was also in Christ Jesus:
> 6 Who, being in the form of God, thought it not robbery to be equal with God.

That's GRACE! Let this mind, the mind of Grace, the MIND of Christ, work. See everything, especially yourself, through His eyes. His mind and thoughts of Grace. HE LOVES YOU! Sow this seed saying,

> I BELIEVE.
> I WILL.
> I TAKE IT.
> I have this mind working in me.
> I thank You, Jesus. Now whatever You say to me, I do it.
> I FORGIVE!

This, dear Partner, is a picture of 2010. Equal partners with Jesus, who is our Source.

Gloria and I, our family and our KCM family, pray for our Partner family every day. Not one day of 2010 will you be without prayer—and the Word. We love you very much.

Love,

Ken

February 2010

Well Done, Good and Faithful Servant!

Dear Partner,

I am writing this letter only a few days after the dynamic homegoing of my spiritual father, Oral Roberts. As you can imagine, memories and thoughts of my time with him are flowing from my spirit. When Jesus joined me to him 43 years ago, my life began to change drastically. I'll share some of those changes with you.

Let's look first at what Jesus said in Matthew 7:24-27:

24 Therefore whosoever heareth these sayings of mine, and doeth them, I will liken him unto a wise man, which built his house upon a rock:
25 And the rain descended, and the floods came, and the winds blew, and beat upon that house; and it fell not: for it was founded upon a rock.
26 And every one that heareth these sayings of mine, and doeth them not, shall be likened unto a foolish man, which built his house upon the sand:
27 And the rain descended, and the floods came, and the winds blew, and beat upon that house; and it fell: and great was the fall of it.

Notice in verse 24 Jesus said, "I will liken him unto a wise man." He didn't say he *was* a wise man. He said he was *like* a wise man. The wise man here is Jesus. It was His sayings the man heard and acted on. The man heard and did what a wise man did. Therefore he got a wise man's results. In verse 26, Jesus didn't call the man a fool. He said he was *like* a fool. He heard the Word of the Wise man, Jesus, but did not act on it. Therefore he got a fool's results.

Continuing to act on the Word and getting the Word's results is the way we receive the Wisdom of God. Faith comes by hearing and hearing by the Word of God. The Wisdom of God is received by faith (James 1:5-7).

Brother Roberts heard and acted on what Jesus taught him. He had received the results for 20 years before I got there. When I arrived at ORU I was desperate for Jesus' power in my life. What little I had learned up until that time was very precious to me, but until I obeyed God I was not where I was supposed to be. When I finally did obey, I realized it immediately. Suddenly, the Word began to explode in me, changing me, Gloria and our children, and the solid pillars of our future were being put into place. What a time it was—powerful soul-winning campaigns filled with the Word, and every kind of miracle one could ever hope to see.

The first thing that was driven home to me was John 10:10:

> 10   The thief cometh not, but for to steal, and to kill, and to destroy: I am come that they might have life, and that they might have it more abundantly.

God is a Good God! And the devil is a bad devil! I saw it!! I saw a line drawn right down the middle of that verse. Jesus <u>never</u> does bad things! The devil <u>never</u> does good things. Period! Jesus came to bring Life—God's Life, abundant Life. The devil is a thief, a killer and a destroyer.

In his sermon "The Fourth Man," I heard Brother Roberts say, "If you bow, you burn! If you don't bow, you can't burn! <u>Whatever you compromise to keep, you will eventually lose!</u>" That set the stage for the rest of our lives and ministry. We committed with all our hearts to never compromise God's Word, and to never bow the confession of our mouths to doubt, fear or unbelief.

One day, shortly after that, I heard this: "When the finances drop, there's a bottleneck somewhere. In every situation there is a <u>key issue</u> that can only be seen through faith. Deal with that issue and the rest will unravel."

In another meeting, actually one of the last tent meetings, I suddenly realized that Brother Roberts used his faith on purpose, instead of just "hoping and praying" that something might happen. It hit me: *He's using his faith the way a mechanic chooses and uses a specific tool—on purpose!* He said to me in the invalid tent, my first time to pray for seriously ill people, "Don't touch them until you're ready to release your faith." Wow! It worked. It still does 43 years later.

One thing I saw in him and in his ministry was uncompromised integrity. His word was good even if he had to swear to his own hurt to keep it. He said, "If your word is not good, God's Word will never be real in your life."

One of the things that has simplified my life and ministry decisions was this word of wisdom: "The first two questions that <u>must</u> be answered are: '<u>Will it meet the needs of the people?</u>' and, '<u>Will it win souls?</u>' Their needs come first. Not mine and not the ministry's."

My first contact with Brother Roberts was when he hired me as a crew member on the ministry's airplane. I was interested, of course, in how to effectively use an airplane in the work of the ministry. I had come out of business aviation and had some understanding of being able to do so much more with the tool of aircraft than with commercial airlines or any other means of transportation. Everything else was too slow and could only do about 35-50 percent of what Brother Roberts was doing. The airlines don't go everywhere. Even back then there were more than 13,000 all-weather airports. The airlines only served about 600 of those. It's even worse now. Out of more than 18,000 airports, the airlines serve approximately 400.

However, I was to learn something about Brother Roberts, his ministry and his way of thinking, to which I immediately committed to in mine: <u>Protect the Anointing</u>! When you're in a meeting or going to or from a service, keep your mouth shut. Surround yourself with the Word. Be still and hear from God. Pray in the spirit. Then preach the Word and meet the needs of the people.

Oh, there are so many things. Like driving to a service one day (I was driving him) when he suddenly said, "Kenneth!" I jumped. He then said, "People will always tell you it can't be done. Don't listen to that. Do these three things and <u>you will always succeed:</u> 1. Find out the will of God; 2. Don't confer with flesh and blood; 3. Get your job done at all costs."

That's still my process today. It has proven out over all these years to be true.

As I said, there are so many wonderful, powerful, life-changing truths I learned from the Word through him. But the truth of the <u>power of a faith-filled seed</u> totally revolutionized my existence, and is still a working, ongoing revelation in my life. Seedtime and harvest has changed the way untold millions of believers conduct their lives. "Don't ever try to accomplish <u>ANYTHING!</u> without first sowing the seed. It is impossible to reap a harvest without the seed of faith being sown." Oh how true it is! Nothing exists on this earth that didn't come from a seed.

Then there's, "Love Jesus first and more than anyone else. Then you'll be able to love others like He does."

"You cannot demand excellence from others and not demand excellence from yourself."

"There's nothing too big for God."

"Expect miracles. They come by faith, not by accident."

"Jesus is my Source. My only Source. He supplies our every need. <u>We ain't gonna be poor no more!!</u>"

"Something good is going to happen to you. Believe it. Expect it."

I could go on and on, but I must close with this: Brother Roberts taught me by word and example to love my Partners. "<u>They are family,</u>" he said to me so many times. He taught me how to release my faith into a letter and expect it to be as anointed as ministering face to face. That love seed toward you, that he planted in Gloria and me so many years ago, has continued to grow into what this ministry is today. Our lives and the lives of our children have been dedicated to meeting the needs of our Partner family. Bible partnership is not some cute way to raise money. I despise that whole idea. This relationship goes very deep with us. I only wish—no, I pray and believe that we can be here for you in many more ways than we have been in the past. I expect it!

As you sow your financial seed this month and believe for the greatest year we've ever had together, remember where that truth came from. Jesus gave it to a young, financially strapped preacher in Oklahoma more than 60 years ago. Then he handed it to you and me, and together we are taking it from the top of the world to the bottom and all the way around. Hold it! I've got to shout! Praise the Almighty God and His Son, Jesus!

Gloria and I love you very much and we pray for you every day.

Love,

Ken

Kenneth ministering alongside his spiritual father, Oral Roberts.

March 2010

Our Job Is Faith in God!

Dear Partner,

We just finished our annual Ministers' Conference and my, oh my, how the Lord Jesus met us there! It was the 20th year of this meeting, and it was truly glorious. A number of things were revealed about 2010, and the bottom line is still: Jesus came that we might have life and have it more abundantly, and the devil is doing everything he can to steal, kill and destroy.

It is abundantly clear that our job is faith—faith in God to <u>always</u> have <u>all</u> sufficiency in <u>all</u> <u>things.</u> Not just so we can get through all this death and destruction, but so we abound to <u>every</u> good work (2 Corinthians 9:8). It is good work to abound to people's aid when disaster strikes. But remember—a rescued sinner is still a sinner. Our sufficiency is to be able to get God's Word to disaster-struck people, as well as having the wherewithal to be there with food, clothing, shelter, etc.

No political mess can stop us. The government is not our source. God is our source! His Word is our source. His Love is our source. Because of His Love, He sent the Word. The Word became flesh and dwelt among us. His Name is Jesus. He belongs to us! He's responsible to the Father for our lives being in abundance, instead of being taken from us by financial storms or any other kind of murderous thing the devil and sin bring to us.

This is our time! 2010 will be the greatest year of divine release of miracles and supernatural manifestations of the Holy Spirit we've ever seen. Every realm—spirit, soul and natural—will be affected. More souls will be born into the kingdom in 2010 than any year before. Wayward children are coming home. Marriages are being healed. Churches that preach the word of faith and love will explode in ministry and in size. The Body of Christ will come together in the unity of faith as never before. It will become very obvious that THE BLESSING is the place to be.

Genesis 26:12-13 is a picture of you and me during the calamity and hard times coming on people—people who do not know how to trust God in 2010. Those hard times include the financial mess we've seen lately and the Haiti disaster—not only loss of life, but government boondoggles of every kind trying to manage such overwhelming need. People of faith in God know how to excel in darkness with the Light of THE BLESSING of THE LORD. Look at Genesis 26:12-13 with me:

> 12   Then Isaac sowed in that land [in famine], and received in the same year an hundredfold: and the Lord blessed him.
> 13   And the man waxed great, and went forward, and grew until he became very great.

Isaac knew his father's BLESSING was on him wherever he was, in any situation. He also knew how his father's, Abraham's, faith worked. Notice in verse 12, the Lord BLESSED him. Then in verse 13, he went forward in famine. Not backward! Faith people go forward, always looking at God's Word—not the famine. Jesus is not behind us. He is always leading. He's always what we keep our eyes on.

As long as Isaac went forward, he went from great to greater. Let's look at these verses from the *New Living Translation:*

> 12   When Isaac planted his crops that year, he harvested a hundred times more grain than he planted, for the Lord blessed him.
> 13   He became a very rich man, and his wealth continued to grow.

Now the *Complete Jewish Bible:*

> 12   Yitz'chak planted crops in that land and reaped that year a hundred times as much as he had sowed. Adonai had blessed him.
> 13   The man became rich and prospered more and more, until he had become very wealthy indeed.

Look at that! That's what they'll be saying about you and me come the end of this year.

Why did THE BLESSING kick in to super-high gear all of a sudden like that? Isaac was already doing well, as far as his personal life was concerned. But God needed him BLESSED in order to overcome that famine. Everyone else dug dry holes. Isaac hit water. He knew what to do. He knew where to dig.

Whose BLESSING was this? Abraham's. How? By faith. That BLESSING has never changed. Faith has never changed. It is doing the same thing now as it was then. Hebrews 11:9 makes everything very clear:

> 9 By faith he sojourned in the land of promise, as in a strange country, dwelling in tabernacles with Isaac and Jacob, the heirs with him of the same promise.

Isaac was heir with Abraham of the same promise BY FAITH!

Now Galatians 3:9:

> 9 So then they which be of faith are blessed with faithful Abraham.

Then 3:13:

> 13 Christ hath redeemed us from the curse of the law, being made a curse for us: for it is written, Cursed is every one that hangeth on a tree.

And verse 29:

> 29 And if ye be Christ's, then are ye Abraham's seed, and heirs according to the promise.

That's powerful, but we're not just heirs of Abraham. We are <u>joint heirs</u> with Jesus! Isaac was BLESSED on Abraham's level of faith. Jesus is the Author of our faith. We're BLESSED on His level! His Name is ours. His Spirit is ours. Everything the Father has is His and He has given it all to us! (See John 16:13-15.) He is the designer and Creator of the Garden of Eden, His perfect will for all men, for all time. Satan stole it. Jesus took it back. It belongs to Him. If it belongs to Him, it belongs to us. It was THE BLESSING that made it grow in the first place, and it's THE BLESSING that plants and makes it grow through and around you and me. NOW! HERE! That's who we are. That's what we are and that's why we are—carriers of THE BLESSING of Abraham.

Gloria and I and our family have never been so fired up in our lives to get this job done. New fire! The old eagle has been renewed, stronger and bolder than ever. Regardless of what the devil throws at the world in 2010, together we'll storm the famine and darkness with THE BLESSING of THE LORD. We are the victors! Not the victims. We have faith in God! <u>Shout</u> these things as you sow your faith BLESSING seed this month: "With this seed I go forward! Victory is mine. I shall not come short! I will not fail! I will not lack! I will not want! I will never, ever be diminished! My job is faith in God! I AM BLESSED!"

Gloria and I are holding you up in prayer and faith. So is our family and our staff. Hold us up. Together we will get this job done. We love you.

Love,

Ken

P.S. Big news! Two great-grandbabies are on the way. One in May. One in September. Mimi and I can't wait!!

April 2010

Haiti Shall Be Saved!

Dear Partner

A few days after our relief efforts began in Haiti, I heard a missionary say, "We have to raise all the money for our complete recovery now while it's on everyone's mind. After the photo ops are over and the governments pull out, it's all over."

That really hit me hard. Mainly for two very important reasons. The most important being the huge unbelief of a Christian missionary. Is God only able to supply as long as the "photo ops" exist, or while the news media is still interested?

The second is the vital importance of the word of faith being preached throughout that nation, not only to win every soul on that island, but to teach the people how to believe God for themselves. Of course, we're there responding to the ministries of our Partners and their needs first, and through them reaching out to the rest of Haiti.

It was while praying for them that the word of the Lord came to me saying, *I want you to stay in Haiti for the long haul. I am assigning that nation to you and to your ministry. If you will commit to this assignment, I will raise up 10 "Reinhard Bonnkes" who will preach the gospel of Jesus Christ with power. Haiti will be saved. The island, including the Dominican Republic, will be saved and become the Lighthouse of the Caribbean. Take My Word in Acts 26:18: "To open their eyes, and to turn them from darkness to light, and from the power of Satan unto God, that they may receive forgiveness of sins, and inheritance among them which are sanctified by faith that is in [Jesus Christ]." Stand on it. Believe it. Speak it over Haiti. Act on it and watch Me do this thing to the glory of God the Father.*

Oh, thank God! Did I take the assignment? Absolutely! We immediately doubled our efforts. Angel Flight's Super DC3 with which we partnered during Hurricane Katrina, was in for inspection, so we chartered a DC3 from Miami. At the same time we put extra people on Brother Glen Hyde's Super 3 at Angel Flight to get Angel 44 back in the air. We also have a great mission-flying husband-and-wife team who came on board with their Cessna 206 to haul medical supplies, and in some cases medical personnel, into small, unimproved airstrips and roads that are within a few minutes' flight from our Partners' orphanages, clinics, churches, compounds, etc., that are taking care of thousands of people. Not one of our orphans was killed. There were only a few minor injuries. Thank God for the Word of His power, and knowing how to use it.

We are building up our resources, such as the rest of our air fleet the Lord Jesus instructed us to build. This includes the final work to be done on the Super 3, the purchase of a Quest Kodiak, a special missionary-built medium-size cargo and people hauler, and additional operational gear. All this is not only for Haiti, but for future operations in the perilous times of these last days.

All of this is added to what we have been assigned to do. Not instead of. "That's a little much, isn't it, Brother Copeland?" I wouldn't have it any other way! <u>Big assignments bring big victories. Big victories bring great joy.</u> "Yeah, but don't they cause big fights?" Yes, they do. However, your and our answer is simple. Romans 8, the great victory chapter, states in verse 18:

> 18   For I reckon that the [battles] of this present time are not worthy to be compared with the glory which shall be revealed in us.

That verse sets us up to fulfill verse 19:

> 19   For the earnest expectation of the creation waiteth for the manifestation of the sons of God.

Let's read on here, because the following verses explain what's happening in places like Haiti. First, let's look at Genesis 1:28:

> 28   And God blessed them, and God said unto them, Be fruitful, and multiply, and replenish the earth, and subdue it: and have dominion over the fish of the sea, and over the fowl of

the air, and over every living thing that moveth upon the earth.

Notice there the word *replenish*. THE BLESSING itself, in and on Adam and his wife, was to replenish, or refill—replace worn parts—subdue and dominate the creation, and keep it the way God had created it. It was not created to house the curse, sin and destruction. Without the creative power of THE BLESSING, it has moaned and travailed. Under the load of sin, from time to time, it breaks. It's not caused by greenhouse gasses or any other man-made thing. It's THE CURSE!

Why is it crying out for the sons of God? Let's go back to Romans 8:19:

> 19 For the earnest expectation of the creation waiteth for the manifestation of the sons of God.

Read verse 22:

> 22 For we know that the whole creation groaneth and travaileth in pain together until now.

Again, why? Let's turn to Galatians 3:13-14:

> 13 Christ hath redeemed us from the curse of the law, being made a curse for us: for it is written, Cursed is every one that hangeth on a tree:
> 14 That the blessing of Abraham might come on the Gentiles through Jesus Christ; that we might receive the promise of the Spirit through faith.

Now verse 26:

> 26 For ye are all the children of God by faith in Christ Jesus.

Tie that in again with Romans 8:19:

> 19 For the earnest expectation of the creation

waiteth for the manifestation of the sons of God.

The creation is looking for THE BLESSING to subdue the travail, replenish or repair what sin has done through the curse, and dominate it with THE LOVE of the Creator. Now Galatians 3:29:

> 29 And if ye be Christ's, then are ye Abraham's seed, and heirs according to the promise.

We are carriers of THE BLESSING. Now cap this off with Isaiah 51:1-3. Remember now: You are the seed of Abraham, and in Jesus joint heirs to THE BLESSING:

> 1 Hearken to me, ye that follow after righteousness, ye that seek the Lord: look unto the rock whence ye are hewn, and to the hole of the pit whence ye are digged.
> 2 Look unto Abraham <u>your father,</u> and unto Sarah that bare you: for I called him alone, and <u>blessed him,</u> and increased him.
> 3 For the Lord shall comfort Zion: he will comfort all her waste places; and he will make her wilderness like Eden, and her desert like the garden of the Lord; joy and gladness shall be found therein, thanksgiving, and the voice of melody.

There it is. The power of God to relieve and <u>comfort</u> the travail of the waste places, and replenish it with the Garden of the Lord. Then comes the joy and gladness, thanksgiving and the voice of singing. This is being sown in Haiti right now as people hear the gospel. What gospel? The gospel of Jesus which is Galatians 3:8:

> 8 And the scripture, foreseeing that God would justify the heathen through faith, preached before the gospel unto Abraham, saying, In thee shall all nations be blessed.

Salvation—being born again, filled with <u>THE Comforter</u> Himself.

Healed and restored. Blessed coming in, and Blessed going out. Being taught the believer's authority over the devils that have crushed them in days gone by. NO MORE!! FREE! And BLESSED financially, so they know who they are and take THE BLESSING to their part of the world.

That's the way it works. That's our job. Take people from religion to reality. From the milk of The Word to the meat of The Word. From being a baby in Christ to becoming of full age by becoming skillful in The Word of righteousness. To walk by faith and not by sight. Not just in Haiti, but also the Dominican Republic and the rest of the world.

TOGETHER WE CAN DO IT!
TOGETHER WE ARE DOING IT!
TOGETHER WE WILL GET IT DONE!

As you sow your BLESSING seed this month, say this out loud, and say it strong: "I am a full partner in all of this. I am a manifestation of a son of God. I am in THE Son of God and HE, Jesus, is in me. THE BLESSING of Abraham is working in me NOW! All grace is abounding toward me so that I can abound to every good work."

Keep these words strong in your heart and strong in your mouth. Now shout with the song of thanksgiving and praise.

The Garden is growing!

Gloria and I and our whole family, along with our KCM family worldwide, love you and are praying for you every day. You'll never ever be a day without being prayed for again. Not one day!

Love,

Ken

May 2010

Always a Victor Never! a Victim

Dear Partner

Let's begin our letter this month by reading what Jesus said in Mark 4:14-20:

14 The sower soweth <u>the word.</u>
15 And these are they by the way side, where <u>the word</u> is sown; but when they have heard, Satan cometh immediately, and taketh away <u>the word</u> that was sown in their hearts.
16 And these are they likewise which are sown on stony ground; who, when they have heard <u>the word,</u> immediately receive it with gladness;
17 And have no root in themselves, and so endure but for a time: afterward, when affliction or persecution ariseth for <u>the word's</u> sake, immediately they are offended.
18 And these are they which are sown among thorns; such as hear <u>the word,</u>
19 And the cares of this world, and the deceitfulness of riches, and the lusts of other things entering in, choke <u>the word,</u> and it becometh unfruitful.
20 And these are they which are sown on good ground; such as hear <u>the word,</u> and receive it, and bring forth fruit, some thirtyfold, some sixty, and some an hundred.

Now go back and look at each verse. What is the one word or subject in every one? <u>THE WORD!</u> God's Word was available and heard gladly by each person. THE Word did its part. It went into the heart of every person who heard it. Then what happened? Well, look at the pattern: The people heard; satan attacked. He didn't come against people just to get at them. <u>He attacked The Word.</u> The Word is his problem in the earth. People who don't hear and act on The Word of God are no threat to anything he tries to do. However, when someone—anyone—becomes a doer of <u>The Word</u> and not just a hearer, <u>The Word</u> becomes the <u>perfect law</u> of <u>liberty.</u> How? Look at James 1:25:

> 25   But whoso looketh into the perfect law of liberty, and continueth therein, he being not a forgetful hearer, but a doer of the work, <u>this man shall be <u>blessed</u> in his deed.</u>

<u>The Word,</u> or in this case the perfect law of liberty, produces THE BLESSING in the life of a person who refuses to compromise with the cares of this world. As he or she continues to hold on to faith in God and <u>His Word,</u> THE BLESSING continues to grow—thirtyfold, sixtyfold, a hundredfold! <u>The Word won't quit if you don't quit.</u> That's the story of Job. THE BLESSING was the devil's problem. It was then the same as it is now. But THE BLESSING WALL was up and satan couldn't get through. In Mark 4:20 <u>The Word</u> produced THE BLESSING, and in those cases verse 22 becomes active:

> 22   For there is nothing hid, which shall not be manifested; neither was any thing kept secret, but that it should come abroad.

Now let's compare that with James 1:22:

> 22   But be ye doers of the word, and not hearers only, deceiving your own selves.

Now we know what happened to the 75 percent—the people who heard <u>The Word</u> and failed. They became deceived by getting their eyes off <u>The Word</u> and becoming caught up in affliction, persecution, offenses, the <u>cares</u> of this world and lusts of other things. These things entering in choke <u>The Word,</u> which stops THE BLESSING of Abraham, which is the answer to the afflictions, persecutions, offenses, <u>cares</u> of this world and lusts of other things.

The thing being pressed the hardest in the U.S. right now is the government takeover of health <u>care.</u> The government cannot ever eliminate the <u>cares</u> of this world. They can't do it. The more they try, the more <u>cares</u> they create. So what are we to do? <u>First, get your eyes off the world!</u> Take your stand of faith on Colossians 3:1-2:

> 1   If ye then be risen with Christ, seek those things which are above, where Christ sitteth on the right hand of God.
> 2   Set your affection on things above, not on things on the earth.

Then put Galatians 1:4 in your eyes and in your mouth:

> 4   Who gave himself for our sins, that he might <u>deliver us from this present evil world,</u> according to the will of God and our Father.

"I am delivered from the cares of this world! That's God's will and <u>His Word</u> for me!"

Now comes the fight of faith. Attack the devil with what he fears the most—<u>The Word!</u> Don't wait until he attacks you.

Our battle Word is 1 Peter 5:5-10:

> 5   Likewise, ye younger, submit yourselves unto the elder. Yea, all of you be subject one to another, and be clothed with humility: for God resisteth the proud, and giveth grace to the humble.
> 6   Humble yourselves therefore under the mighty hand of God, that <u>he may exalt you</u> in due time:
> 7   Casting all your <u>care</u> upon him; for he careth for you.
> 8   Be sober, be vigilant; because your adversary the devil, as a roaring lion, walketh about, seeking whom he may devour:
> 9   Whom resist stedfast in the faith, knowing that the same afflictions are accomplished in your brethren that are in the world.

> 10   But the <u>God of all grace,</u> who hath called us unto his eternal glory by Christ Jesus, after that ye have [resisted] a while, make you perfect, <u>stablish, strengthen, settle you.</u>

"Father, I humble myself under Your <u>mighty</u> hand. I cast the whole of my <u>cares</u> over on You. Jesus paid for my health <u>care,</u> not the government. All my financial <u>cares.</u> All my family <u>cares.</u> (Put your cares in here—whatever they are.) Now, satan, I command you to stop and desist in your attempt to steal <u>The Word</u> of God from me. I stand against you in the Mighty Name of Jesus! I resist you steadfast in faith! I don't touch any of these <u>cares</u> with my thought life now or ever! I have <u>The Mighty Power!</u> to control every thought (2 Corinthians 10:4-6) that tries to turn me away from <u>The Word</u>."

Now verse 10 of 1 Peter 5 is <u>your</u> promise:

> 10   But the God of all grace, who hath called us unto his eternal glory by Christ Jesus, after that ye have [resisted the devil] a while, make you perfect, stablish, strengthen, settle you.

Shout it—"<u>I believe, I will, I take</u> being exalted above all these cares; <u>I have it! I thank You,</u> Jesus, for Your mighty grace. I am perfected. I am established. I am strengthened, I am settled. <u>I don't have a care!</u> To God be the glory!"

Now keep your mind with these things. When <u>care</u> thoughts try to come in say it—don't just think it—"No you don't! That's not my <u>care</u> and not my thought." Read Psalm 112 to the devil and remind him, "That's me, devil! I'm BLESSED! <u>I don't have a care!</u> In fact I just can't tell you how much <u>I don't care!</u> Jesus is my Lord and He has taken <u>care</u> of it."

Praise God! I'm about to jump out of this chair just writing these things. In fact, I just did! We are the victors! Not the victims!

This is our message of God's Love and Grace for us. Together, you and Gloria and I will continue to preach it to all who have ears to hear. And now, as you have probably noticed, our children and our grandchildren are out there preaching it as well. Pray for us. It's a huge job, but that's not a care—it's a BLESSING.

Together we can and will get it done.

Gloria and I love you very much and we pray for you every day.

Love,

Ken

June 2010

Cheer Up! God Has a Plan!

Dear Partner,

Let's begin our letter this month by looking at Acts 27 and the violent storm the Apostle Paul was sailed into. Read verses 18-25:

18 And we being exceedingly tossed with a tempest, the next day they lightened the ship;
19 And the third day we cast out with our own hands the tackling of the ship.
20 And when neither sun nor stars in many days appeared, and no small tempest lay on us, all hope that we should be saved was then taken away.
21 But after long abstinence Paul stood forth in the midst of them, and said, Sirs, ye should have hearkened unto me, and not have loosed from Crete, and to have gained this harm and loss.
22 And now I exhort you to <u>be of good cheer:</u> for there shall be no loss of any man's life among you, but of the ship.
23 For there stood by me this night the angel of God, whose I am, and whom I serve,
24 Saying, Fear not, Paul; thou must be brought before Caesar: and, lo, God hath given thee all them that sail with thee.
25 Wherefore, sirs, <u>be of good cheer:</u> for I believe God, that it shall be even as it was told me.

Also look at verse 14:

14 But not long after there arose against it a tempestuous wind, called Euroclydon.

The dictionary calls a *hurricane,* "any violent tempest." That term is used to describe this storm in three separate verses. They sailed into a hurricane and couldn't break out of it.

Look again at verse 20. Days and days without sun nor stars. Then in verse 27, 14 days. Two weeks of this! All hope of being saved was lost. Can you imagine all the slamming around, with everyone sick, weak, weary, scared out of their minds, and now no hope? For 14 days and nights! So what does this preacher do in the midst of all this? He stands up and shouts, "<u>Cheer up!</u> Let's eat! I exhort you, be of <u>good</u> cheer!"

Suddenly, here is a man of hope standing where there was no hope. How could he do this? How could he <u>expect</u> anything good to come out of all this? He was reminded of God's plan for him to go before Caesar. It was not in the plan of God for him to sink and drown. He got his eyes off that storm, and renewed his mind with the plans Jesus had for his life and future. He believed it. When he believed it, it brought hope where there was no hope. Suddenly, <u>he could see beyond that storm all the way to Rome.</u> "<u>Cheer up!</u>" he shouted. "Be of <u>GOOD</u> cheer! Something GOOD is going to happen. We're not going under! We're not going to the bottom. We're going to Rome."

Do you see what faith and real Bible hope does? <u>Suddenly, you can see through and beyond the storm. The future turns from darkness to light.</u> All of a sudden, God's plan for success and life by the power of the Holy Ghost overthrows satan's plan for failure and death.

It's good to remember here that the Apostle Paul already knew he was supposed to go to Rome. He didn't learn that from the angel that appeared and spoke to him aboard that ship. The angel reminded him of it. <u>He also commanded him to stop the fear.</u> Paul did what he was told. Instead of, "How can I be of good cheer when I'm losing everything?" he said, "<u>I believe God.</u> It will be just like God said it would be."

"But, Brother Copeland, he had an angel appear and speak to him."

So what? You have the entire written Word of God speaking to you. He didn't have the New Testament to read and meditate on like you and I do. He heard an angel say fear not. We can hear it from Jesus Himself: "Fear not! Believe only! And she <u>shall</u> be made whole!" (Luke 8:50).

Well, <u>fear not.</u> Believe only and <u>you</u> will be made whole. Fear not. Believe only, and you <u>will</u> get through this storm! Fear not. Believe only.

God's not through with you. It's not in His plan for you to go down. You're supposed to be raised up. Cheer up! Be of GOOD cheer! You're supposed to be healed. You're supposed to prosper. You're supposed to triumph in Christ Jesus. You're supposed to overcome the world. This is the faith that overcomes the world, its economy, its doubt, its unbelief and all its storms. Look beyond the storm. We win! Look up, and cheer up!

We will close by believing Romans 15:13 together:

> 13   Now the God of hope fill you with all joy and peace in believing, that ye may abound in hope, through the power of the Holy Ghost.

Say it:

I believe.

I will.

I take it—all joy; all peace in believing.

I have it—NOW! I'm filled. I abound in hope through the power of the Holy Ghost.

I thank You, Jesus. Oh, thank God, I'm not going under. God is working His plan of grace. I HAVE FAITH IN GOD! I'm cheered up with GOOD cheer.

And now I forgive if I have aught against any. I'm filled with faith and hope, and now I'm filled with Love. These three are alive in me.

Go over and over these scriptures. Pray them. Confess them. Shout them until you're like the Apostle Paul and you begin to announce to anyone who will listen, "Cheer up! We're not going under. Jesus has a plan. A good plan. Good cheer."

As you sow your Blessing seed of faith this month, sow it in good cheer. Whether you feel cheerful or not. Cheer up because you believe it, not because you feel it. Feelings will get in line as faith, hope and Love rise up inside your spirit. These are not bad days if they're faith days.

Believe it with Gloria and me, our family and our KCM and EMIC family. Let's tell the world, "Cheer up! Jesus is alive. He has a plan for your life and it's GOOD!"

All of us love you very much, and we pray for you every day!

Love,

Ken

July 2010

Dear Partner,

It's almost like watching something in a cage trying desperately to escape. I'm talking about people trying to rebuild their houses after the sandy foundation has washed out from under them. Bring in more sand! Cry about it! Worry about it! Fight about it! Then cry about it some more. None of that does any good. In fact, it makes it worse. The more someone cries, "It's falling, it's failing—all is lost!" the more it caves in and falls around them. When people cry, "Lost! Lost! The loss of everything!" <u>the more they arm and authorize the thief to take everything.</u>

Oh, I'm not talking about sinners—people who don't know, or claim to know, Jesus as their Savior. I'm talking about Christians. <u>The very people who should be preaching and witnessing</u> to the ones who don't know we're supposed to be their source of supply. <u>We're the ones at peace in the middle of all this storm.</u>

<u>Jesus is our source</u>—not the government. Aren't you glad!? The government has failed. The Word is our strength and the unfailing seed of our future—not the banks. <u>The blood covenant of Jesus and our great Father God is the solid rock of our foundation.</u> We have no fear of collapse. We have no need of Wall Street, the stock market, or some secular job or company to provide our retirement. We don't work for a living. We live by faith. If we are employed by a secular company, it's because Jesus needs us there. <u>The truth is, they need us a whole lot more than we need them.</u> If they let you go, you didn't lose your job. You don't <u>WORK</u> for them. You work for Jesus, on assignment to that company. <u>Just inquire of Him about your new place.</u> Relax! He's responsible for supplying <u>all</u> your needs, your wants, your health care and your eternal future.

Have you caught on to what we're doing here? We're renewing our minds to solid, Bible truth instead of the phony picture the world has about their way of life. <u>The man and woman of faith in God never</u>

have to change their way of living because of the "times." The times and circumstances around them must change because of their faith. In order for that to happen, there must be mind renewing, from the mind of the world and the way it thinks, to the mind of Christ and the way He thinks. Not, I might add, the way people *think* He thinks, but according to the Word. According to FAITH, HOPE and LOVE! For instance, He said in Matthew 11:28-30:

> 28 Come unto me, all ye that labour and are heavy laden, and I will give you rest.
> 29 Take my yoke upon you, <u>and learn of me;</u> for I am meek and lowly in heart: and ye shall find rest unto your souls.
> 30 <u>For my yoke is easy, and my burden is light.</u>

Have you learned this of Him? If you haven't, you've been reading the wrong books instead of the Bible. He said to learn this about Him. He did not say, "Take My yoke and see if My yoke is easy and My burden is light." He said, "Learn from Me that My yoke <u>is</u> easy and My burden <u>is</u> light." If the yoke you're collared with is hard, it's not His yoke. If the burden you're under is heavy, it's not His burden. Break the yoke and dump the burden. NOW! How?

Read verse 28 again:

> 28 Come unto me, all ye that labour and are heavy laden, and I will give you rest.

Now read it out loud. <u>LOUDER!</u> Say, "That's no longer my burden. I've just heard THE TRUTH AND THE TRUTH HAS MADE ME FREE!"

Now listen to Isaiah 10:27:

> 27 And it shall come to pass in that day, that his burden shall be taken away from off thy shoulder, and his yoke from off thy neck, and the yoke shall be <u>DESTROYED</u> because of the anointing.

Notice, it said *destroyed*—not broken. Something broken can be repaired. *Destroyed* literally means no longer fit for use. Jesus' Anointing has rendered that yoke no longer fit for the devil's use to keep you bound.

Now read Matthew 11:28 again, saying, "Jesus said that! I am His disciple. He is my Lord. I continue in these words. They are TRUTH. The yoke is destroyed. I am FREE! I dump this burden of debt! I dump this burden of _____! It's heavy. It can't be from Jesus! I REFUSE TO TRY TO CARRY IT!"

"But Brother Copeland, what am I going to do about it?"

YOU JUST DID IT! Now, have faith IN GOD!

I believe.

I will.

I take it.

I have it.

"Oh, Jesus! I THANK YOU! I'M FREE! I forgive if I have aught against anyone—they ARE FREE!"

In closing let's read 2 Corinthians 10:3-6:

3	For though we walk in the flesh, we do not war after the flesh:
4	(For the weapons of our warfare are not carnal, but mighty through God to the pulling down of strong holds;)
5	Casting down imaginations, and every high thing that exalteth itself against the knowledge of God, and bringing into captivity every thought to the obedience of Christ;
6	And having in a readiness to revenge all disobedience, when your obedience is fulfilled.

You have the MIGHTY POWER to control your imagination. You

have the authority to sit in judgment over your every thought. Rise up, Mighty Judge, always in readiness to revenge <u>every</u> disobedient thought. "No! I refuse to think that thought from the days of burden and bondage. Thought! I judge you and I sentence you to life in prison. You'll never come to my mind again!"

Drop the gavel. Hammer down! You have the <u>MIGHTY</u> <u>POWER!</u> The <u>mind of CHRIST!</u> His words are His MIND! Think them. Speak them. Act as though they are true. They are. Think like Him. Talk like Him. Act like Him. <u>You <u>will</u> get His results.</u>

Now what? Go help those who are sinking under yokes and burdens. Minister the Word to them. Use Jesus' Anointing. He is Christ—Anointed. You are Christian—Anointed—<u>His Body.</u> Now Go, Mighty One! THE BLESSING IS YOURS!

"Those things, which ye have both learned...and seen in me, DO: and the God of peace—light burdens and easy yokes—shall be with you" (Philippians 4:9).

Gloria and I love you very much. We pray for you every day (the whole Copeland family including <u>Justus James Pearsons</u> born May 8, 2010—great-grandchild No. 1). Wow!

Love,

Ken

Haiti SHALL BE SAVED!

August, 2010

Hey! Trouble! My Name Is
Kenneth Copeland and I'm With God!

Dear Partner,

Is there anyone you know who's having a hard time? Would you say these are hard times?

Actually, when you think about it, there haven't been any good times since sin and death came into the world. So, does that mean we just have to put up with hard and troubled times until we die and go to heaven? No! Absolutely not. Jesus came that we have life—*ZOE*—the life of God, and have it <u>more</u> abundantly. Jesus said that <u>in the world</u> we would have tribulation, or hard times, BUT, "<u>be of good cheer (cheer up!); I have overcome the world.</u>" In that same verse, John 16:33, He gave us the key to abundant life right in the middle of all the trouble. Let's look at the entire verse:

> 33 These things I have spoken unto you, that in me ye might have peace. In the world ye shall have tribulation: but be of good cheer; I have overcome the world.

Do you see the dividing line? The trouble is <u>IN THE WORLD.</u> The peace is <u>IN HIM.</u> Oh, praise God! Wait a minute, though. That's not all He said. "These things have I <u>spoken</u> to you, that in me you might have peace." His Word is the big thing here. Trying to get through hard times without putting The Word first place and final authority is a losing battle.

"But Brother Copeland, you just don't know what an impossible place we are in."

That's the way things look through your eyes. If someone were to say to you, "You have $500,000 in my hand by one week from today, or it's all over for you!" would that look hard? Not if you're in Bill Gates' class, financially. However, if the price went up to $100 billion, it would look too hard for him.

Hard times, then, are based on whomever's eyes you're looking through. We are in Christ Jesus. So let's look through His eyes. Can we do that? Sure we can. Look at 1 John 4:9:

> 9 In this was manifested the love of God toward us, because that God sent his only begotten Son into the world, that we might live through him.

Jesus came so that we could live our lives <u>through</u> Him. We look through the eyes of faith. We are not alone in this world! We are in Him. So, looking through His eyes we see Jeremiah 32:17:

> 17 Ah Lord God! behold, thou hast made the heaven and the earth by thy great power and stretched out arm, <u>and there is nothing too hard for thee.</u>

Now let's go straight to the words of Jesus in Matthew 19:26:

> 26 But Jesus beheld them, and said unto them, With men this is impossible; but with God all things are possible.

Then in Mark 9:22-23, and again in Luke 18:27, He said:

> 27 The things which are impossible with men are possible with God.

Have you ever had anyone ask you whom you're with? When I was a young boy, I would hear my dad say, "My name is Copeland. I'm with_____," and he would boldly say the name of the company he was W-I-T-H!

HELLO, MY NAME IS KENNETH COPELAND, AND I'M WITH GOD! All things are possible <u>to</u> me because I'm a believer. That's Mark 9:23. Jesus said that, and I believe it. I'm with Him, so nothing is impossible or too hard. That's Luke 18:27. <u>I'm not with, or looking to, men. I'm with, and looking to, Jesus</u> for all the answers to all the hard questions.

In closing, let's go back to the core truth upon which every victory in life depends. Obey it, and you win. Violate it—you lose. There's no middle ground. Matthew 12:33-37 says, <u>by your words!</u>:

> 33   Either make the tree good, and his fruit good; or else make the tree corrupt, and his fruit corrupt: for the tree is known by his fruit.
> 34   O generation of vipers, how can ye, being evil, speak good things? for out of the abundance of the heart the mouth speaketh.
> 35   A good man out of the good treasure of the heart bringeth forth good things: and an evil man out of the evil treasure bringeth forth evil things.
> 36   But I say unto you, That every idle word that men shall speak, they shall give account thereof in the day of judgment.
> 37   For by thy words thou shalt be justified, and by thy words thou shalt be condemned.

Not what someone else said. Not what *they* did, or did not do, to you or for you. It's what *you* say about it that settles it in your life. Forget about who's to blame! Get your eyes off them and back on The Word of God. He loves you. He has a plan for you that does not call for your defeat. His Word is called the perfect <u>LAW</u> of liberty.

The faith process to follow is laid out in Proverbs 4:20-24:

> 20   My son, attend to my words; incline thine ear unto my sayings.
> 21   Let them not depart from thine eyes; keep them in the midst of thine heart.
> 22   For they are life unto those that find them, and health to all their flesh.
> 23   Keep thy heart with all diligence; for out of it are the issues of life.
> 24   Put away from thee a froward mouth, and perverse lips put far from thee.

Write it down step by step, and follow it faithfully every day—not just when you have time. Give yourself to <u>the Plan</u> completely. Do it now. Do it all, and do it right. The victory is here, and it's yours. It *has* been all the time. It may look really dark now, but look at the 18th verse of that same 4th chapter.

> 18   But the path of the just is as the shining light, that shineth more and more unto the perfect day.

The more you walk in The Word, the brighter things become. Where you once stumbled and fell, now you walk in faith. Where you walk now, you'll soon be running. Not in your strength. You're not in your strength anymore. You're <u>*with*</u> Jesus! He's your strength. And don't forget we're together in Him. You are being prayed for every day. You are going to make it! Together we can and we will get this job done. PREACH THE WORD!

Shout over your BLESSING seed, "Hey! (whatever the hard thing is) MY NAME IS _____ AND I'M WITH GOD! Nothing is too hard or impossible to me. I have faith in God, and I'm born of God. Whatsoever is born of God overcomes the world, and I am an overcomer. This is the seed to the Lord of the harvest of my victory: Jesus."

Thank you from the bottom of our hearts for being our Partner and being so faithful to pray and believe with us. We love you dearly, and we pray for you every day.

Love,

Ken

September 2010

Why Do I Do What I Do?

Dear Partner,

Let's begin this letter by going to the words of Jesus in John 15:5-7:

> 5   I am the vine, ye are the branches: He that abideth in me, and I in him, the same bringeth forth much fruit: for without me ye can do nothing.
> 6   If a man abide not in me, he is cast forth as a branch, and is withered; and men gather them, and cast them into the fire, and they are burned.
> 7   If ye abide in me, and my words abide in you, ye shall ask what ye will, and it shall be done unto you.

Take another long look at verse 5: "<u>For without me ye can do nothing</u>"! There has never, ever been a time when we need Jesus more than now. Men, trying to do things without Him, have created this monster of a mess all around us. It's not just the mess that's been made of the economy—that's bad enough. But all the stealing, killing and destroying everywhere you look is heaping heartache on top of heartache for so many people, especially for those who don't know Him as Lord and Savior.

Trying to meet your own needs without God is hopeless, and makes bad things worse. What's even more tragic is to see people who know Jesus is their Savior getting caught up in the same wave of failure and loss as those who don't. What's the answer? How can we not only escape and avoid all this, but actually help those who are hurting?

Let's go back to the words of Jesus. That's always the place to go. When Jesus said, "Without me ye can do nothing" (verse 5), notice He was talking about our bearing much fruit. I don't care what's going on in the world—good times or bad—without Jesus, things get bad, and then worse. However, when He's involved and His plan is being carried out in our lives, THE BLESSING takes over. Not only does the curse lose its power to wreck our lives, but you and I become Jesus' hand of help and deliverance to those around us.

Ask yourself, "Where do I live and why do I do what I do?" Jesus said, "Abide, or live, in Me." That's not just going to church. That's hanging on every word that comes from the mouth of God. Every word, all the time, first place, every day. Living in the secret place, abiding in His love and grace. Resting, not panicking. Faith rests. Fear panics. Panic always makes things worse and never brings glory to God. It magnifies the works of darkness and makes the devil look big and powerful, which he is NOT! The seventh verse is the key!

> 7   If ye abide in me, and my words abide in you, ye shall ask what ye will, and it shall be done unto you.

The Word!

Now, why do you do what you do? Why do you get up Monday morning?

"Because I have to go to work."

Why?

"Because I have bills to pay."

Why else?

"Because things are bad enough *with* a job. I couldn't make if I were to lose my job."

Why?

We could go on with the whys, but it's plain to see why this person is doing what he does. He's meeting his own needs. That's the purpose of his life. Jesus said to stop doing that. Stop thinking about food and clothes. That's <u>NOT</u> the goal of life in Him. You know what He said: "Seek ye first the kingdom of God and His righteousness, and <u>all these</u>

THINGS shall be ADDED unto you"! Seek ye first. Abide in the Word. What am I looking for, Brother Copeland? You are looking for, studying, praying, believing and seeking Jesus' words and thoughts on everything, and His way of doing things. That's what "His righteousness" means. He is always right! His way works. Look at Matthew 6:25-34:

> 25 Therefore I say unto you, Take no thought for your life, what ye shall eat, or what ye shall drink; nor yet for your body, what ye shall put on. Is not the life more than meat, and the body than raiment?
> 26 Behold the fowls of the air: for they sow not, neither do they reap, nor gather into barns; yet your heavenly Father feedeth them. Are ye not much better than they?
> 27 Which of you by taking thought can add one cubit unto his stature?
> 28 And why take ye thought for raiment? Consider the lilies of the field, how they grow; they toil not, neither do they spin:
> 29 And yet I say unto you, That even Solomon in all his glory was not arrayed like one of these.
> 30 Wherefore, if God so clothe the grass of the field, which to day is, and to morrow is cast into the oven, shall he not much more clothe you, O ye of little faith?
> 31 Therefore take no thought, saying, What shall we eat? or, What shall we drink? or, Wherewithal shall we be clothed?
> 32 (For after all these things do the Gentiles seek:) for your heavenly Father knoweth that ye have need of all these things.
> 33 But seek ye first the kingdom of God, and his righteousness; and all these things shall be added unto you.
> 34 Take therefore no thought for the morrow: for the morrow shall take thought for the things of itself. Sufficient unto the day is the evil thereof.

If that's not a picture of today! Get your eyes off the mess! Stop working for yourself. Quit thinking about food, clothes and survival. Say: "Today I'm working for THE KINGDOM OF GOD. Today, <u>Lord</u> Jesus, I am Yours to command. I am Your hand extended. I am <u>dumping</u> all the cares of this world on You. You said my heavenly Father knows I have need of things—food, clothes and all things. Today, I abide in You. Those words in Matthew 6 and John 15 are alive in me. I HAVE FAITH IN GOD! NOW! You said it, Jesus (Mark 11:22). So I believe. I will. I take it. I have it. I thank You. I'm so grateful to You for making faith available to me. I forgive! If I have anything against anyone, I forgive them now. Judge my heart, Lord Jesus, and forgive and cleanse me. Without You, I can do nothing. Without faith, I can do nothing. BUT, THANKS TO YOU, I AM NOT WITHOUT YOU, AND MY FAITH IS BIG. It's strong. Now, how can I be of service to You today?"

Now, get up and go to work! Everything's different. Jesus is in charge. Enjoy the day in His presence. Think about Him, not the world around you. I know it's not easy, but I've done it and still do it every day. You can, too.

Don't *try* to do it. Do it!

Whose words did you put in your mouth? JESUS'.

Who has to back those words? JESUS.

In whose Name does that mountain have to bow its knee? JESUS'.

Under whose law do you live—Moses' or Jesus'? JESUS'.

What is that law? The law of Love.

Whose Love? JESUS'.

Who is the author of your faith? JESUS.

Who said, "Have faith in God"? JESUS.

Who said speak to the mountain? JESUS.

Who said, "Believe you receive"? JESUS.

Who gave Himself for you? JESUS.

Who receives and blesses your tithe? JESUS.

Who is faithful and just to forgive and cleanse you from sin? JESUS.

Who cleanses you from unrighteousness? JESUS.

In whose light do you walk, as He is in the light? JESUS'.

Whose blood cleanses you from ALL sin? JESUS'.

Who gave the commandment: "Love the Lord thy God"? JESUS.

Who commanded, "Love one another as I have loved you"? JESUS.

Who said, "WHEN YOU STAND PRAYING, FORGIVE"? JESUS.

THEN DO IT! NOW!

He loves you. No, I really mean He really loves you. You're on His mind. You're on His heart.

Now you know why you were born: because He loves you. You know who you are: You're His love child. You know your job: Seek Him. Seek His kingdom. Learn His way of doing things. His burden is light. His yoke is easy.

Now, let's tell the rest of the world about it. Together, we can.

Together, we will.

Go back over this letter slowly and deliberately. Pray it over your financial seed. Sow it strong in faith. Your time has come to know greater than ever before: Greater is He that is in me than he that is in the world, and that Jesus loves me. He's my life, forever.

Also know this: Gloria and I and our family love you. We're praying for you and standing with you every day. The KCM staff is working to see to it you are BLESSED every way we can. We are here for <u>you</u>!

Love,

Ken

October 2010

Thank God, I'm the Head and Not the Tail!

Dear Partner,

A few days ago, the word of the Lord came to me saying, "We have wallowed in and squandered the precious freedom we have so long enjoyed." It is time to restudy, rethink and recommit ourselves to THE God who paid the price to make this freedom available to all men. It is not His will for any man to live in hell—not here on earth, and not in the hereafter.

It truly amazes me that the tyrants who bring such suffering to people, such oppression, death and pain to so many, have to live in the hell on earth they have created. And because of their blasphemous grudge against their Creator, they have created their place in hell in the hereafter.

Restudy. Rethink. Recommit: to the Love Jesus gave us, to the laws (the constitution) Moses provided us, and, to the restoration of freedom's "Beacon on a Hill," a shining light for all peoples to see clearly—the United States of America! And, once again, to IN GOD WE TRUST.

What opens the door to the curse that's in the earth, whether it's an individual, a family, a business or a nation? To answer this question, let's go to the curse itself spelled out very plainly in Deuteronomy 28:15-68. Let's look at verses 43-48:

43 The stranger that is within thee shall get up above thee <u>very high;</u> and thou shalt come down <u>very low.</u>
44 <u>He shall lend to thee,</u> and thou shalt not lend to him: <u>he shall be the head,</u> and thou shalt be the tail.
45 Moreover <u>all these curses</u> shall come upon thee, and shall pursue thee, and overtake thee, till thou be destroyed; because thou hearkenedst not unto the voice of the Lord thy God, to keep his commandments and his

	statutes which he commanded thee:
46	And they shall be upon thee for a sign and for a wonder, and upon thy seed for ever.
47	<u>Because thou servedst not the Lord thy God with joyfulness, and with gladness of heart, for the abundance of all things;</u>
48	<u>Therefore shalt thou serve thine enemies</u> [that] shall [come] against thee, in hunger, and in thirst, and in nakedness, and in want of all things: and he [your enemy] shall put a yoke of iron upon thy neck, until he have destroyed thee.

There it is! All these curses, including every sickness and every disease (verse 61), shall come on you because YOU DID NOT SERVE GOD WITH JOYFULNESS AND GLADNESS OF HEART FOR THE ABUNDANCE OF ALL THINGS! <u>Wallowing in the abundance and giving THE GOD OF FREEDOM no praise.</u> I'm talking about in church! The Body of Christ even preaching poverty as a blessing instead of the curse it is. Jesus came to give abundant life, and Christians squandered it, abused it and gave the credit for it to education, the world's system and, of course, <u>LUCK.</u> That's blasphemous!

What do we do now? <u>HAVE FAITH IN GOD!</u> I believe. I will. I take it! I have it! I am so grateful for it. I forgive if I have aught against any! <u>Thank God, I'm not under the curse. THE BLESSING of ABRAHAM is mine! NOW!</u>

Remember when Deuteronomy 28:47-48 was talking about the abundance of all things? It was referring to verses 1-14, THE BLESSING of Abraham.

Now, put your eyes on Galatians 3:13-14:

13	Christ hath redeemed us from the curse of the law, being made a curse for us: for it is written, Cursed is every one that hangeth on a tree:
14	That the blessing of Abraham might come on the Gentiles through Jesus Christ; that

we might receive the promise of the Spirit through faith.

Put your eyes on those verses a lot. Every day! Put them in your mouth of praise. THE BLESSING does not depend on any economy, anywhere! It depends on the kingdom of God. It has its own resources. Its assets are eternal. It does, however, depend on faith which works by Love. Galatians 3:9 says:

> 9 So then they which be of faith are blessed with faithful Abraham.

Why is this so important? Look at Romans 4:6:

> 6 Even as David also describeth the blessedness of the man, unto whom God imputeth righteousness without works,

And 2 Corinthians 9:8:

> 8 And God is able to make all grace abound toward you; that ye, always having all sufficiency in all things, may abound to every good work.

Grace abounds so you can abound. Grace is far more powerful to cause you to abound than the curse (sin) is able to cause you to lack. Where sin abounds, GRACE much more abounds. Believing that, releases the grace that activates THE BLESSING.

Notice, "abound to every good work." What are those good works? Whatever Jesus needs you and me to do to preach, teach and heal by preaching the gospel of THE KINGDOM (Galatians 3:8; Luke 4:18) to those caught up in the crashing, failing, Babylonian, socialistic stytems of government which, simply put, is man (government) trying to meet his own needs without God.

Let's look again at John 15:5:

> 5 I am the vine, ye are the branches: He that abideth in me, and I in him, the same bringeth forth much fruit: for without me ye can do nothing.

Without Jesus—without THE BLESSING—people are confused, helpless, sick and hopeless. Remember, now, Jesus said "without me ye can do nothing."

Ephesians 2:12 spells it out:

> 12 That at that time ye were without Christ, being aliens from the commonwealth of Israel, and strangers from the covenants of promise, having no hope, and without God in the world.

With Christ, or without Him and His Anointing. Remember the yoke of iron in Deuteronomy 28:48? It's the anointing that <u>destroys</u> the yoke. Being aliens from the common—<u>wealth,</u> wealth that belongs to all those who are the seed of Abraham and strangers from the covenants (plural) of promise—the promise to Abraham. Without Jesus—no hope—no future—doomed, bound. Why? Without God. No covenant to stand on. No Name filled with power. That's a terrible, miserable way to live. That's what happens to governments as well as people. But, now! In Christ Jesus, our future is brighter than ever before.

Use your faith. Stand on The Word. Shake off every debt. Roll every care in your life over on Jesus. He cares for you. He will exalt you from being beneath to being above only—the head and never again the tail. He will make you perfect, establish and make you strong. He will settle you with His peace (1 Peter 5:6-10).

To Him be the Glory!

<u>Lay your hands on your seed this month,</u> and <u>BOLDLY</u> declare: "I am FREE! Debt FREE! Sickness FREE! I AM FREE FROM THE CURSE! I SERVE MY GOD WITH JOYFULNESS AND GLADNESS FOR THE ABUNDANCE OF ALL THINGS. I SOW THE SEED OF ABUNDANCE. JESUS, I SIT WITH YOU ON THE THRONE OF <u>GRACE.</u> I'LL NEVER

BE BENEATH AGAIN. WITH YOU, I AM THE HEAD, AND NEVER THE TAIL. I'M STRONG. I'M ESTABLISHED IN THE BLESSING—I AM THE SEED OF ABRAHAM. I'M SETTLED, AND IN YOU, I'M PERFECT. I RECEIVE HOPE AND GREAT PEACE. FOR THIS, I AM ETERNALLY GRATEFUL."

Oh, praise God forever! We win!

Just writing this letter has opened a floodgate of anointing and praise in me. Jesus is Lord—my Lord, and He is the mighty Lord of the harvest.

Gloria and I, and our whole family, including all here at KCM, love you and pray for you every day.

Love,

Ken

November 2010

Get Yourself Off Your Mind!

Dear Partner

What do we do now? <u>The same as we always do:</u> HAVE FAITH IN GOD! This is no time to start looking somewhere else for answers. Jesus is still THE answer. He hasn't changed. He hasn't left. He hasn't quit, and He never will. His love works. His Word works. Faith works when they are put to work.

Let's look at Jeremiah 17:5 from *The Amplified Bible:*

> 5   Thus says the Lord: Cursed [with great evil] is the strong man who trusts in and relies on frail man, making weak [human] flesh his arm, and whose mind and heart turn aside from the Lord.

The first thing we need to get hold of in this verse is the fact that this person is not some heathen who has never known God. This is a man who has allowed his mind to be drawn away from The Word and its promises, and become overrun by bad news of bad times, and what Jesus called in Mark 4, "the cares of this world." He said those cares and anxieties would enter in and choke The Word, and it would become unfruitful.

<u>It's very dangerous</u> when The Word of God is choked off in a person's life. All it takes to let that happen is to stop seeking the kingdom of God first, and little by little, allow the TV news and bad news from friends and family creep in and take over. The problem this creates is Jeremiah 17:6:

> 6   For he shall be like a shrub or a person naked and destitute in the desert; and he shall not see any good come, but shall dwell in the parched places in the wilderness, in an uninhabited salt land *(AMP).*

Our Father never stops reaching out to deliver us—especially when things are going bad. The problem is, if you're empty and The Word is choked, you can't see any of the good, only the bad. So, what to do? Get hold of your mind! Get hold of your eyes. Plant your feet and shout, "<u>Enough</u>! Stop!"

<u>Have faith in God</u>! Read Mark 11:22 over and over. Jesus is offering you His faith. Take it. NOW. Use the six I's of faith: I believe! I will! I take it! I have it! I thank You, Jesus! I forgive if I have aught against any! Read it and say it again and again, until it takes hold in your heart and in your mind. Don't quit.

Now, fix your whole attention back on Jeremiah 17:7-8:

> 7 [Most] <u>blessed</u> is the man who believes in, trusts in, and relies on the Lord, and whose hope and confidence the Lord is.
> 8 For he shall be like a tree planted by the waters that spreads out its roots by the river; and it shall not see and fear when heat comes; but its leaf shall be green. It shall not be anxious and full of care in the year of drought, nor shall it cease yielding fruit *(AMP)*.

Jesus is your hope—your future. He is <u>THE</u> source. Your source. Your <u>ONLY</u> source. Settle that now and forever. Sit down and take Holy Communion, and realize His BLOOD and broken body are His covenant to you to never leave nor forsake you. Nothing in this world order can overcome that. Feast your spirit being on 1 John 5:4-5:

> 4 For whatsoever is born of God overcometh the world: and this is the victory that overcometh the world, even our faith.
> 5 Who is he that overcometh the world, but he that believeth that Jesus is the Son of God?

Turn the world's news off. Get back on the Word of faith. Keep it coming into your ears, your eyes, and fill your mouth with it. Fall in love with the gospel of THE BLESSING. <u>Surround yourself with its power.</u>

It will transform, heal, bless, prosper and fill you with the joy of THE LORD. It will change you from the inside out. Ten days from now, you won't even recognize yourself. That's because yourself is becoming more like Jesus. That changes everything!

Now, start sowing toward it. SOW your time into someone else. HELP people. BLESS people. LOVE people. Get yourself off your mind and out of your way. Now, you don't see when the bad comes. God makes opportunities, and you see and lay hold of them. You're no longer the little, dried-up, stunted bush in the desert. You're the big, green, fruit-filled tree planted by the water, deeply rooted in The Word of love and faith.

As you sow your financial seed this month, sow toward the strength to take your stand. Stand strong! We're standing, praying and believing with you, with all our might. Pray and stand with us. Together, we will get this job done!

Gloria and I and our family, and all the KCM staff, love you and pray for you every day.

Love,

Ken

P.S. Our second great-grandchild, Eiley Oaks, was born Sept. 16. She is just wonderful!

December 2010

Come to Me—I Will! Give You Rest!

Dear Partner,

The panic button is being pushed everywhere you look.... Fear of what's coming.

What's happening? What's going to happen to me, my job, my business, my family? What am I going to do? HAVE FAITH IN GOD! Jesus did not say, "Try to have faith in God." He said, "HAVE FAITH IN GOD"!

"How do I do that, Brother Copeland, in the midst of all this turmoil?"

By entering into HIS rest. And that's done by mixing THE WORD with faith. Let's look at Matthew 11:28-29:

28   Come unto me, all ye that labour and are heavy laden, and I will give you rest.
29   Take my yoke upon you, and learn of me; for I am meek and lowly in heart: and ye shall find rest unto your souls.

Jesus is offering rest. He is offering it to all who labor and are heavy laden, or under a load. Does that sound like debt? Yes it does—it is. Notice, He said, "I will give." "I will" is as strong as a promise can be stated. There's no question whether or not He's willing, and faith begins where the will of God is known.

"Yeah, Brother Copeland, but I just don't see how anyone could fix this mess I'm in."

It's not your job to figure it all out. It's your job to mix faith with the words of Jesus. Let's go to Hebrews 4:1-3:

1   Let us therefore fear, lest, a promise being left us of entering into his rest, any of you should seem to come short of it.

> 2   For unto us was the gospel preached, as well as unto them: but the word preached did not profit them, <u>not being mixed with faith</u> in them that heard it.
>
> 3   For we which have believed do enter into rest, as he said, As I have sworn in my wrath, if they shall enter into my rest: although the works were finished from the foundation of the world.

Look again at that third verse: "We which <u>have believed</u> do enter...." Another thing is, your deliverance has been finished, or "worked out," or your mess was fixed, from the foundation of the world. <u>Take</u> your rest. Make your choice. Look at Matthew 11:28 again, and read it aloud—SLOWLY. You have a choice. You have, placed before you, rest from Jesus, or trouble from the world. BLESSING or curse. Life or death. Remember Deuteronomy 30:19?

> 19   I call heaven and earth to record this day against you, that I have set before you life and death, blessing and cursing: therefore choose life, that both thou and thy seed may live.

That's a no-brainer. Choose life. Choose Jesus. Choose THE WORD. Now, mix the promise with faith. How? The six I's of faith:

I BELIEVE.
I WILL.
I TAKE MY REST.
I HAVE IT.
I THANK YOU FOR IT, JESUS.
I FORGIVE IF I HAVE AUGHT AGAINST ANYONE.

Now, comes the <u>good</u> fight of faith: "I'm not moved out of my rest by what I see. I'm not moved out of my rest by what I feel. I am resting on the <u>integrity</u> and <u>strength</u> of the <u>Words of Jesus!</u>" Our Father never stops reaching out to deliver us—especially when things are going bad.

Now, let's look at Hebrews 4:11:

11 Let us <u>labour</u> therefore to enter into that rest, lest any man fall after the same example of unbelief.

Jesus said "all ye that labour" (Matthew 11:28). Were you laboring to get out from under all that pressure? Sure you were. Not only at whatever job you have, or had, but <u>thinking about it night and day</u> is the biggest job of labor and heavy burden there is. What if you obey verse 11 and labor as faithfully to rest in Jesus on His Word as you did when you were "working on the trouble" all the time—<u>eight hours a day seeking first THE KINGDOM OF GOD,</u> instead of the kingdom of trouble? Doing Psalm 127:2 at night instead of, "What are we going to do?" all night long?

2 It is vain for you to rise up early, to sit up late, to eat the bread of sorrows: for so he giveth his beloved sleep.

Read Matthew 11:28 three to five times every hour of every day instead of the newspaper and all its trouble. How about placing your Bible next to your bed and setting yourself to wake up every two hours, reading the promises of Jesus and saying, "Thank You, Jesus, for loving me so! <u>I have no fear of tomorrow. I am my Father's beloved,</u>" and then roll over and go back to sleep with a smile on your face. None of the devil's plans can stand up to that. Now, your angels have faith to work with, and they never sleep. God's plan for your long, satisfied life in Psalm 91:12-16 is no longer hindered by unbelief and fear.

<u>EVERYTHING IS GOING TO BE ALL-RIGHT!</u> In fact, that's what the Lord of the Harvest, Jesus, is saying about 2011: "HAVE FAITH IN GOD and every-thing is going to be ALL-Right."

Talk about it. Think about it. Act on it all year long. When other people bring up trouble, just smile and say, "My God has made a way for me. He has a plan, and every-<u>thing</u> is going to be ALL-Right. <u>ALL is right in the kingdom of God, and that's where I live.</u> I'm in that secret place with Jesus, and with Him, all <u>things</u> are possible!"

Every seed you sow all year long, sow it with thanksgiving that every-thing is going to be ALL-Right. When 2012 rolls around, we'll be laughing and shouting, "Every-thing is ALL-Right! Jesus said it would be, and it is. This is the victory that overcomes the world and all its trouble—even our faith. I HAVE FAITH IN GOD!"

Gloria and I love you and pray for you every day.

Love,

Ken

P.S. Have a Joy-filled, Love-overflow Christmas, and SHOUT with us, "Happy Birthday, Jesus!"

Kenneth Copeland has been ministering the uncompromised Word of God for more than 40 years, sharing the message that God's Word works to turn every area of life from failure to victory. This couldn't be done without the faithfulness of his Partners!

Prayer for Salvation and Baptism in the Holy Spirit

Heavenly Father, I come to You in the Name of Jesus. Your Word says, "Whosoever shall call on the name of the Lord shall be saved" (Acts 2:21). I am calling on You. I pray and ask Jesus to come into my heart and be Lord over my life according to Romans 10:9-10: "If thou shalt confess with thy mouth the Lord Jesus, and shalt believe in thine heart that God hath raised him from the dead, thou shalt be saved. For with the heart man believeth unto righteousness; and with the mouth confession is made unto salvation." I do that now. I confess that Jesus is Lord, and I believe in my heart that God raised Him from the dead.

I am now reborn! I am a Christian—a child of Almighty God! I am saved! You also said in Your Word, "If ye then, being evil, know how to give good gifts unto your children: HOW MUCH MORE shall your heavenly Father give the Holy Spirit to them that ask him?" (Luke 11:13). I'm also asking You to fill me with the Holy Spirit. Holy Spirit, rise up within me as I praise God. I fully expect to speak with other tongues as You give me the utterance (Acts 2:4). In Jesus' Name. Amen!

Begin to praise God for filling you with the Holy Spirit. Speak those words and syllables you receive—not in your own language, but the language given to you by the Holy Spirit. You have to use your own voice. God will not force you to speak. Don't be concerned with how it sounds. It is a heavenly language!

Continue with the blessing God has given you and pray in the spirit every day.

You are a born-again, Spirit-filled believer. You'll never be the same!

Find a good church that boldly preaches God's Word and obeys it. Become part of a church family who will love and care for you as you love and care for them.

We need to be connected to each other. It increases our strength in God. It's God's plan for us.

Make it a habit to watch the *Believer's Voice of Victory* television broadcast and become a doer of the Word, who is blessed in his doing (James 1:22-25).

About the Author

Kenneth Copeland is co-founder and president of Kenneth Copeland Ministries in Fort Worth, Texas, and best-selling author of books that include *How to Discipline Your Flesh* and *Honor—Walking in Honesty, Truth and Integrity*.

Now in his 43rd year as a minister of the gospel of Christ and teacher of God's Word, Kenneth is the recording artist of such award-winning albums as his Grammy-nominated *Only the Redeemed*, *In His Presence*, *He Is Jehovah*, *Just a Closer Walk* and his most recently released *Big Band Gospel* album. He also co-stars as the character Wichita Slim in the children's adventure videos *The Gunslinger*, *Covenant Rider* and the movie *The Treasure of Eagle Mountain*, and as Daniel Lyon in the *Commander Kellie and the Superkids*$_{TM}$ videos *Armor of Light* and *Judgment: The Trial of Commander Kellie*.

With the help of offices and staff in the United States, Canada, England, Australia, South Africa and Ukraine, Kenneth is fulfilling his vision to boldly preach the uncompromised Word of God from the top of this world, to the bottom, and all the way around. His ministry reaches millions of people worldwide through daily and Sunday TV broadcasts, magazines, teaching audios and videos, conventions and campaigns, and the World Wide Web.

Learn more about Kenneth Copeland Ministries
by visiting our website at **www.kcm.org**

World Offices
Kenneth Copeland Ministries

For more information about KCM and our products,
please write to the office nearest you:

Kenneth Copeland Ministries
Fort Worth, TX 76192-0001

Kenneth Copeland
Locked Bag 2600
Mansfield Delivery Centre
QUEENSLAND 4122
AUSTRALIA

Kenneth Copeland
Post Office Box 15
BATH
BA1 3XN
U.K.

Kenneth Copeland
Private Bag X 909
FONTAINEBLEAU
2032
REPUBLIC OF
SOUTH AFRICA

Kenneth Copeland
PO Box 3111 STN LCD 1
Langley BC V3A 4R3
CANADA

Kenneth Copeland Ministries
Post Office Box 84
L'VIV 79000
UKRAINE

We're Here for You!

Join Kenneth and Gloria Copeland and the *Believer's Voice of Victory* broadcasts Monday through Friday and on Sunday each week, and learn how faith in God's Word can take your life from ordinary to extraordinary.

You can catch the *Believer's Voice of Victory* broadcast on your local, cable or satellite channels.* And it's also available 24 hours a day by webcast at BVOV.TV.

Enjoy inspired teaching and encouragement from Kenneth and Gloria Copeland and guest ministers each month in the *Believer's Voice of Victory* magazine. Also included are real-life testimonies of God's miraculous power and divine intervention in the lives of people just like you!

To receive a FREE subscription to
Believer's Voice of Victory, write to:
Kenneth Copeland Ministries
Fort Worth, TX 76192-0001
Or call: 800-600-7395
Or visit: **www.kcm.org**

If you are writing from outside the U.S., please contact the KCM office nearest you. Addresses for all Kenneth Copeland Ministries offices are listed on the previous page.

* Check your local listings for times and stations in your area.